ALAN ASTRO

Editor's Preface: Jewish Discretion in French Literature

This issue of *Yale French Studies*, on Jewish identity in twentieth-century France, presents writings divided into two categories: literary texts and cultural contexts.

The authors of these literary texts, like most Jews in France, are very assimilated into French society and culture. However, like writers the world over, they are not entirely representative of the group from which they stem. French Jews tend to express whatever particularities they have as Jews with great reserve, a trait the philosopher Elisabeth de Fontenay has seen as deeply rooted in their Frenchness.[1] But if our writers remained discreet about their Jewish identity, could we still consider them Jewish writers?

Of course, it is one thing to portray discretion, and another to embody it. Thus in *Le Chant des êtres*, Gil Ben Aych depicts quite directly the reserve existing even among observant Jews in France. In that novel, we meet an Algerian-born Bar Mitzvah boy who is unimpressed by the synagogue in Paris, where his family has recently settled:

> In comparison to the grandiose synagogue Simon had known in Tlemcen, the one here seemed laughable and almost shabby. It made you feel as though Jews had no place in France and hid in order not to call attention to their activities. . . . Back there, in Tlemcen, in Algeria, the synagogue took up almost an entire block; here, you went in through the door of a house like all others.[2]

1. Elisabeth de Fontenay, "On the *Quant-à-soi*," article translated in this issue of *Yale French Studies*.
2. Gil Ben Aych, *Le Chant des êtres* (Paris: Gillimard, 1988), 39. An excerpt from

YFS 85, *Discourses of Jewish Identity in Twentieth-Century France*, ed. Alan Astro, © 1994 by Yale University.

The arrival of North African Jews following decolonization in the 1960s has made for a more exuberant expression of Judaism in France, now home to the fourth-largest Jewish community in the world. Yet even today, American Jews may feel as Simon did, when they are confronted with the reserve of French Jews.

Frankraykh frest yidn, goes a Yiddish saying: "France devours Jews," makes them assimilate into Frenchdom. French Jewry illustrates best of any Jewish population the verse that states the obligation placed on Westernized Jews ever since the Enlightenment: "Be a man in the street and a Jew at home."[3] Or consider these words—"Jews should be denied everything as a nation, but granted everything as individuals"—by the French revolutionary Count Stanislas de Clermont-Tonnerre, a defender of equal rights for the Jews, though obviously not of their identity as a people.[4]

The progress of the nationalist, secularist and anticlerical ideology of the French republics has meant for the Jews a weakening of their ties to the Jewish people and religion. However, those ties have not been completely cut, as is shown by the writers in this issue of *Yale French Studies*. As a rule, I have chosen authors little known in the English-speaking world, which explains the absence of some names—Elie Wiesel, André Schwarz-Bart, Albert Memmi, Albert Cohen—that the reader may have expected to see. Instead, most of the literary texts here date from the period starting in the 1970s that has seen greater expressiveness in France among diverse ethnic groups—if one may use this American term to speak of populations as different from each other as regional minorities (Bretons, Occitans, Alsatians, Flemings), Moslem immigrants from North Africa, black Africans, Jews.

The texts here from the 1970s to today bear witness to the diversity of French Jewry. The lives of Algerian Jews in Paris are recounted by Gil Ben Aych; Paula Jacques recreates the Jewish community transplanted from Egypt to France; Cyrille Fleischman, Rysia Poloniecka and Henri Raczymow tell us of Eastern European Jews and their descendants in the French capital; Bernard Frank speaks as the scion of Alsatian Jews,

---

this novel, under the title "The Chant of Being," appears in this issue. (All translations in this preface are mine, unless otherwise noted.)

3. This verse from Judah Leib Gordon's Hebrew poem, *Hakitzah ami*, is translated in Hannah Arendt, *The Origins of Totalitarianism*, new ed. (New York: Harcourt Brace Jovanovich, 1979), 65.

4. Quoted in *Encyclopaedia Judaica* (Jerusalem/New York: Keter/Macmillan, 1971), 5: 606.

who have been French citizens since the Revolution; Salim Jay, born of
a Jewish mother and a Moslem father, resembles many marginally
Jewish French, when he recounts his only real connection to Jewish
identity: an obsession with the fate of Jews in occupied France.

Some of our authors predate by far the intensification of minority
discourses during the 1970s. In a novel from 1926 excerpted here,
Nicolo-Peccavi ou l'Affaire Dreyfus à Carpentras, Armand Lunel depicted one of the most ancient Jewish settlements in France. Around
the same time, Sarah Lévy recounted the satisfactions and tribulations
of mixed marriage in novels translated into English and German.[5]
Gustave Kahn, best known for his innovation in the realm of free verse,
redirected his interest to the Jewish world as a result of the Dreyfus
case; his *Contes juifs*, one of which is included here, are among his last
writings. In addition, Paris had drawn a great number of Yiddish
writers from Eastern Europe, two of whom are featured in this issue:
Oser Warszawski and Wolf Wieviorka.

However, we would misrepresent Jews in France if we did not foreground some examples of discretion regarding Jewish identity in their
literature, even though the very purpose of discretion is to allow those
who exercise it to avoid being pointed out. Thus we shall consider at
length two authors not discussed elsewhere in this volume: Marcel
Proust and Georges Perec.

Ought we even consider Proust a Jewish writer? In a letter dated 19 May
1896 to his friend Robert de Montesquiou, who had launched into an
anti-Semitic tirade, Proust said that he, his father and brother were
Catholic, even though his mother was Jewish. Yet her ancestry had
serious consequences, for he found himself unable to share his friend's
opinions or even discuss them. He wrote, in a rather uneasy formulation: "Je n'ai pas indépendance pour avoir là-dessus celles [les idées]
que j'aurais peut-être" [I am not free to have on that topic the ideas I
might perhaps have].[6] Proust may not have identified himself as a Jew,
but he certainly identified with Jews and not entirely from the outside.

5. The English version of Sarah Lévy's *O mon goye!* (Paris: Flammarion, 1929) was
published in one of the first American paperback collections, "The Inner Sanctum
Novels": *Beloved! O mon goye!*, trans. William A. Drake (New York: Simon and Schuster, 1930). The selection featured in this issue is from the sequel to that work.
6. Marcel Proust, *Correspondance*, ed. Philip Kolb (Paris: Plon, 1976), 2: 66. For
studies of Jewish identity in Proust, see Henri Raczymow, *Le Cygne de Proust* (Paris:
Gallimard, 1989); and Jean Recanati, *Profils juifs de Marcel Proust* (Paris:
Buchet/Chastel, 1979).

The first-person narrator of *A la recherche du temps perdu*, often identified with Proust himself, is not a Jew. He speaks a great deal about Jews, about their attempts to conceal their Jewishness, about the Dreyfus case, but little of it seems Jewish in any specific sense. Even the Biblical references, while they usually come from the Old Testament, are nothing that would not be gleaned from a Christian reading of the Bible. However, there is one exception: the question of names, which haunts the narrator and relates to an important problematic within the Jewish exegetical tradition. At least one passage suggests that this connection is not just the product of critical fancy. It occurs in the first lengthy discussion of Jewish identity in the *Recherche*, when we meet the narrator's Jewish friend, Bloch, in *Du côté de chez Swann*.[7]

The first thing we learn about Bloch is that he considers a verse from Racine's *Phèdre*—"La fille de Minos et de Pasiphaé"—to be beautiful precisely because it means nothing. This surprising assessment is drawn in part from symbolist reflection on poetry; consider Mallarmé's call for "the disappearance of the poet as speaker, yielding his initiative to words."[8] However, Bloch's preference for senseless verse may also be traceable to the importance of the letter in the Jewish tradition. Gershom Scholem writes that for the Kabbalah, divine revelation is characterized by "absolute 'meaninglessness'"; the Torah is ultimately a *textus* or *textile*, an endless reweaving of the name of God.[9] This idea was known to thinkers outside Judaism. Mallarmé gave it the following form: "The poet's name mysteriously recomposes itself with the entire text."[10] In Proust, we may find an allusion to the name of God, of the creator, of the author, when Bloch speaks of "le nommé Racine." Indeed, it is a question of *nommer*-ing *racines*, of identifying roots, Jewish roots.

Bloch's own name suggests a block of sound without meaning, as any name must be in order to function as a name. In the passage we are

7. Proust, *Du côté de chez Swann*, in *A la recherche du temps perdu*, ed. Jean-Yves Tadié et al. (Paris: Gallimard, Bibliothèque de la Pléiade, 1987), 1: 89–91; *Swann's Way* in *Remembrance of Things Past*, trans. C. K. Scott Moncrieff and Terence Kilmartin (New York: Random House, 1981), 1: 97–99.

8. Stéphane Mallarmé, *Selected Poetry and Prose*, ed. Mary Ann Caws (New York: New Directions, 1982), 75.

9. Gershom Scholem, *On the Kabbalah and its Symbolism*, trans. Ralph Manheim (New York: Schocken, 1965), 42–43.

10. Mallarmé, *Oeuvres complètes*, ed. Henri Mondor and G. Jean-Aubry (Paris: Gallimard, Bibliothèque de la Pléiade, 1945), 529.

considering, the narrator speaks explicitly of Jewish names, of his grandfather's ability to ferret them out in the unlikeliest places. For example, when Marcel brings home a new friend named Dumont, Grandfather suspects the visitor is a Jew. He cries out: "Dumont! Oh, I don't like the sound of that," and "On guard! On guard!" A Jew might be hidden under Dumont, the Frenchest of names, which suggests that a Jewish allusion might turn up in the Proustian text when we least expect it. Indeed, this grandfather is Marcel's mother's father, and if the narrator is a veiled figure for the author, then this old man could be a crypto-Jew himself.

When Grandfather believes he has discovered a Jew, he signals this to his family by singing some line from one of various operas with Jewish themes. Some of these verses have a biblical, liturgical flavor: "O Dieu de nos Pères," "Israël, romps ta chaîne," "Champs paternels, Hébron, douce vallée," "Oui je suis de la race élue." Grandfather takes care to replace the words with nonsensical syllables, which recall Bloch's predilection for meaningless verse. Instead of the lyrics Grandfather sings: "Ti la lam ta lam, talim,"[11] and the narrator is afraid lest his guest decipher the imputation of Jewishness. But perhaps what is making the narrator uneasy is the return of the repressed, the return of his family's own hidden Jewishness. It is as though Grandfather were sending a message from one crypto-Jew to another, through the medium of a disguised common prayer.

The encoding of the mock-liturgical, operatic refrains into the syllables "Ti la lam ta lam, talim" is quite interesting. There is a Hasidic tradition of songs without words, called *nigunim*, melodies accompanied only by syllables such as "Bim bom." Could Proust ever have heard such songs? Might his mother have sung some lullaby based on them? Given her tendency to conceal her Jewishness, this seems rather unlikely.[12] It is doubtless more convincing to find a Jewish reminiscence in the syllables "talim," with the Hebrew plural suffix -*im* that Proust no doubt knew from the word *goïm* or *goyim*, familiar to even the most de-Judaized Jews as well as many non-Jews.[13] "Talim" also sounds like *taleth* or *talit*, one of the few Hebrew words incorporated

11. Translated in the English version as "um-ti-tum-ti-tum, tra-la."

12. See Armand Lunel, "Marcel Proust, sa mère et les Juifs," *Europe* 502–03 (1971): 64–67; reprinted in Lunel, *Les Chemins de mon judaïsme et divers inédits*, ed. Georges Jessula (Paris: L'Harmattan, 1993), 135–39.

13. The term is attested in 1878 by a *Dictionnaire du jargon parisien*, according to the *Trésor de la langue française* (Paris: Centre National de la Recherche Scientifique, 1981), 9: 381.

into French, which designates the prayer shawl (remember I have suggested that Grandfather is reciting a kind of liturgy). Moreover, there is something palindromic about the sequence "ta lam, talim," which is not very different from "talim, ta lam." The Jewish relevance is that a palindrome can be read both from left to right and right to left, like a sentence simultaneously in French and in Hebrew.

This interpretation of a palindrome was made by critic Bernard Magné, not with respect to Marcel Proust but to Georges Perec, a French novelist who was the author of the longest palindrome in the French language.[14] Perec was born in 1936 to Polish Jewish immigrants in Paris. The death of his parents at the hands of the Germans while he was still a child, his need to be hidden among Catholics during the Occupation, his adoption by an assimilationist branch of his family after the war— all this distanced Perec from Jewish culture. Perec himself died an early death of lung cancer in 1982.

In Perec's work, allusions to Jewish identity are at times explicit but usually indirect, often no more than dimly glimpsed by the author himself. Yet even his least Jewish writings can appear to allude to his Jewishness.[15] This has led his friend and fellow writer Marcel Bénabou to suggest an analogy with Kafka, whose fiction, often interpreted as a parable of the Jewish condition, never once contains the German words for "Jew" or "Jewish."[16]

Let us consider a short text by Perec, *Parenthèse en forme d'anecdote*, which on the surface has no Jewish content. Rather, it recounts Perec's having eaten, within three months, in Chinese restaurants in cities in four different countries: Paris, France; Sarrebrück, Germany; Coventry, England; and New York, U.S.A.:

> The décor of the restaurants was more or less the same and
> Chineseness [*sinoïté*] was indicated in each case by nearly identical
> signifiers (dragons, Chinese characters, lamps, lacquered pictures, red
> hangings, etc.). Concerning the food itself, things were not so clear:
> in the absence of any other point of reference, I had always naïvely

14. Bernard Magné, "Bout à bout tabou: About 'Still Life/Style Leaf'" in Mireille Ribière, ed., *Parcours Perec* (Lyons: Presses Universitaires de Lyon, 1990), 103; "Palindrome" in Georges Perec, *La Clôture et autres poèmes* (Paris: Hachette/P.O.L., 1980), 43–53.

15. See my articles: "Parenthèse sur la judéité chez Georges Perec," *Pardès* 15 (1992): 113–36; and "Allegory in Georges Perec's *W ou le souvenir d'enfance*," *MLN* 102 (1987): 867–876.

16. Marcel Bénabou, "Perec et la judéité," *Cahiers Georges Perec* 1 (1985): 15–30.

assumed that (French) Chinese food was Chinese food; but (German) Chinese food resembled German food, (English) Chinese food was like English food (the green of the peas . . .), and (American) Chinese food was quite unlike anything Chinese but seemed truly American.[17]

Perec concludes by saying, "This anecdote seems significant to me, but I am not exactly sure of what." I would suggest that this is an allegory of Jewish identity, that the Chinese diaspora is a stand-in for the Jewish one (after all, *sinoïté* sounds a lot like *Sion* and *Sinaï*[18]), that despite whatever signifiers of Jewishness they display (Hebrew characters instead of Chinese ones, gefilte fish or *poisson farci* instead of egg rolls or *rouleaux de printemps,* mezuzahs instead of wall hangings), French Jews resemble Frenchmen more than they do American Jews, American Jews are more like other Americans than they are like English Jews, etc.

This interpretation may convince us, but Perec's ironic comment that he is unsure of what the anecdote means should make us wary of interpreting all in Perec as a function of his Jewishness. After all, allegorical reading is infinitely extendible; with a certain critical flair, one can read anything as an allegory of anything else. Yet Perec himself made us clearly see allusions to Jewishness in a text apparently devoid of Jewish themes. One part of his *W ou le souvenir d'enfance,* a tale of adventure on the seas, without any Jewish content, turns out to be the allegorical version of another account in the same book, which tells of Perec's childhood during the Occupation.[19] Nonetheless, Perec gives us the key to the adventure story in *W,* whereas at the end of *Parenthèse en forme d'anecdote* he claims total ignorance as to what his text means. Yet we can see this peremptory dismissal of the meaning of his own text as an example of Perec's downplaying Jewish relevance in his life.

This minimization of Jewishness is evident in an oft-quoted statement by Perec. For him, being Jewish was defined mostly as what it was not:

17. *Parenthèse en forme d'anecdote* in Perec, *Penser/Classer* (Paris: Hachette, Collection Textes du vingtième siècle, 1985), 47 (ellipsis in the original). In this translation and elsewhere, I have scrupulously respected the use of parentheses in the original texts.
18. These associations are all the more called for, as the mistaken term Perec uses demands interpretation. The proper French word for "Chineseness" is not *sinoïté,* but *sinité.*
19. Perec, *W ou le souvenir d'enfance* (Paris: Denoël, 1975).

It didn't connect me to a religion, a people, a history, a language; it hardly involved me in a culture; it played no role in my daily life; it was inscribed in neither my first nor last name.[20]

Thus Perec denies the Jewishness of his surname, reminiscent of such Breton names as Gwerec'h or Klec'h, in which the ending -ec'h is pronounced like -ec. Yet if in Proust's text the name Dumont can hide a Jew, so Perec turns out to be *perets* (*c* in Polish is pronounced *ts*), a Hebrew word meaning "breach" or "split" that occurs in the Bible. *Perets* is the same as the Spanish name Pérez, often borne by Marranos, and was the signature of the classic Polish Yiddish writer Yitskhok Leybush Peretz (1852–1915), who was Perec's great-great-uncle (as we learn in *W*, 52).

Elsewhere I have proposed an interpretation for Perec's novel *La Disparition*, a *tour de force* that does not once contain the letter *e*, the most frequent vowel in the French language.[21] This book goes beyond a kabbalistic insistence on the letter generally. Rather, it constitutes an endlessly rewoven cryptic signature, reflecting the way Y. L. Peretz's name is usually spelled: with the three Hebrew consonants *pe, resh, tsadik (p, r, ts)*, but without the optional diacritics that are the only vowels in Hebrew. The signature *PRTs* can also be read as disseminated in the titles *La Disparition* (*disPaRiTion*, where the suffix -*tion* begins with a *t* graphically and an *s* phonetically) and *Parenthèse en forme d'anecdote* (*PaRenThèSe*, where the *n* does not have consonantal value but serves to nasalize the preceding vowel, and the *h* is silent).

An emblem for Perec's concealment of Jewish identity appears in *Un homme qui dort*, the title of which is taken from the first pages of Proust's work: "A man asleep [*un homme qui dort*] has in a circle around him the chain of the hours, the sequence of the years, the order of the worlds."[22] (Given these Proustian echoes, I wonder if we may attach any importance to the similarity between Perec's cryptic signature *PRTs*, and the consonants *PRST* in Proust's name.) As the sleeper in Perec's work awakens, he becomes aware of those who have "traveled the same roads" as he: they are "the banished, the pariahs, the

20. "Entretien: Perec/Jean-Marie Le Sidaner," *L'Arc* 76 (1979): 9.
21. Perec, *La Disparition* (Paris: Denoël, 1969); "Allegory in Georges Perec's *W ou le souvenir d'enfance*," 873.
22. Perec, *Un homme qui dort* (Paris: Denoël, 1967); Proust, *Swann's Way*, 5 (trans. modified).

excluded ones, the wearers of invisible stars"—a reference to the yellow insignia the Nazis made the Jews display on their clothing (129).
The invisible star, the unseen Jewish distinguishing mark, shows how
Jewishness is inscribed in Perec's work. It is there, but it is not always
evident. Playing on the title of *Parenthèse en forme d'anecdote*, we
may say Jewish identity is there, but between parentheses. Thus Perec
ends up depicting the obligation to "be a man in the street and a Jew at
home."

We find a disturbing association of a parenthesis with Jewish identity in a text almost as apparently lighthearted as *Parenthèse en forme
d'anecdote*. It occurs in *Considérations sur les lunettes*, a pastiche of
eighteenth-century encyclopedic discourse, where Perec farcically describes the history of eyeglasses and presents anecdotes on eyeglasses.
Now Perec did not wear glasses, but we discover the relevance they had
for him in this passage:

> Likewise, I remember a poster showing the face of a woman wearing
> an impressive helmet-like contraption whose function it was to
> examine her eyes (and also—sinister remembrance—the slogan of a
> famous optician, pointing out at the height of the Occupation that
> despite the sound of his name, he most definitely was not Jewish).[23]

The memory of the optician who advertised he was not a Jew is brack-
eted off, yet it is quite near the end of *Considérations sur les lunettes;*
it is obviously the reason for the text. In a most obsessive *mise en
abyme* (the title *Considérations sur les lunettes* is already a *mise en
abyme*), we can imagine Jews and tolerant Frenchmen not believing
their eyes when they came across the optician's advertisement. The
glasses one imagines one needs when one has seen such a sign could
well be portrayed by the parentheses here, each presenting concave and
convex sides, like two lenses. Let us point out that a parenthesis is the
palindromic figure par excellence and that the association of the hel-
met with this memory may be traceable to the anthropometric devices
used by the Nazis.

Writer Henri Raczymow makes the parenthesis into a specific image of
the disruption in Jewish history brought about by the Holocaust:

> After writing the slender volume in which I tried to re-create a
> Jewish Poland, I realized that my book formed a kind of parenthesis.

23. *Considérations sur les lunettes* in Perec, *Penser/Classer*, 148.

I opened the parenthesis on a Poland I knew led directly to
Auschwitz or Treblinka, and I closed it on a portrayal of the place of
immigration, the Parisian Jewish quarter of Belleville in the 1950s. In
the center of this parenthesis stood a blank.[24]

And Perec's friend mentioned earlier, writer Marcel Bénabou, rele-
gates the first explicit mention of his own Jewishness to a parenthesis,
as he evokes his early years in Morocco before settling in France:

I dreamt . . . of a kind of literature that could restore to me, in its
entirety, the feeling of harmony with the world that overcame me at
certain moments of my childhood (the always sunny Saturday
mornings on the familiar road to the synagogue, or the eves of the
major holidays, when I would sing the prayers as I stood to the right
of my father).[25]

Bénabou's book *Pourquoi je n'ai écrit aucun de mes livres* combines the preoccupations of Raymond Roussel (author of *Comment
j'ai écrit certains de mes livres*[26]) with those of Marcel Proust (whose
work, like Bénabou's, presents a narrator unable to write the very book
we are reading). Marcel Bénabou shares his first name, and a significant
vowel in his last, with Marcel Proust. If these associations seem kabbalistic, they are in consonance with Bénabou's assertion that he is
descended from kabbalists (84). In the kind of wordplay that occurs
throughout his text, Bénabou sees his name as being "as difficult to
bear as a bin held at arm's length" [*une* benne à bout *de bras*] (111,
emphasis added). It is not surprising that this name is difficult to bear,
when we consider that Bénabou means, in Hebrew and Arabic, "the
son of his father." This name suggests an imprisonment in an Oedipal
conflict that would make the realization of any desire nearly impossible. Thus *Pourquoi je n'ai écrit aucun de mes livres* recounts Bénabou's attempts to free himself from the anxiety of influence, from
the crushing example of his literary forbears, in order to write himself.

The excellence of Bénabou's predecessors is not the only element
that makes writing difficult. Bénabou also mentions that literary cul-

24. Henri Raczymow, "La Mémoire trouée," *Pardès* 3 (1986): 179. A full translation
of this text, under the title "Memory Shot Through With Holes," appears in this issue of
Yale French Studies.
25. Bénabou, *Pourquoi je n'ai écrit aucun de mes livres* (Paris: Hachette, 1986), 31–
32. For an analysis of this text, see my "Bénabou bien abouti," *Pardès* 14 (1991): 252–59.
26. Raymond Roussel, *Comment j'ai écrit certains de mes livres*, rev. ed. (Paris:
Pauvert, 1979).

ture came to take on "some of the prestige that the traditional religion was beginning to lose" (86). Otherwise put, to write is to leave Jewish culture.

It may seem paradoxical to claim that writing should be antithetical to the people of the book, but we must distinguish between a scriptural, exegetical tradition, and a literary one based in Christianity. The Torah is held to be divinely revealed, whereas the Gospels, though divinely inspired, were written by men. Moreover, Jesus said, "Render unto Caesar what is Caesar's, and render unto God what is God's" (Matthew 22:21), thereby allowing a division between a secular and a religious sphere. No such distinction obtains for the "holy people" that Jews are held to be (Deuteronomy 7:6). Thus the founders of modern Hebrew and Yiddish literature—adherents of the Jewish enlightenment movement known as the *Haskalah*—were acutely aware of their distance from traditional Jewish thought. In our time, the Alsatian Jewish writer Claude Vigée has made the contradiction in terms contained in the words of *roman juif* ["Jewish novel"] perfectly clear. Playing on etymology, he proposed the generic label *judan* in opposition to *roman*.[27]

The contradictory nature of something, however, does not prevent it from existing. We may wonder whether, common to authors discreet and outspoken on Jewish identity, there exists a French Jewish literature. This question enjoyed some press in the 1970s and '80s as part of the flourishing of minority discourses in France remarked upon earlier, but Armand Lunel had seen a French Jewish (or "Judeo-French") literature already forming in the 1920s and '30s, among such novelists as Irène Nemirovsky, Albert Cohen, and himself (*Chemins de mon judaïsme*, 95–107).

Can Jewish literature exist in non-Jewish languages like French or English, in tongues other than Hebrew, Yiddish, Judezmo (i.e., Judeo-Spanish, also called Ladino)? Writing in 1981, Rachel Ertel, a scholar of Yiddish and American studies, suggested this response:

If the Jewish people—geographically and linguistically dispersed, partaking of various national, social and cultural groupings—exists, so does its literature exist. It is created in the image of the Jewish people: it is diverse.[28]

27. Quoted in Shmuel Trigano, "De la nécessité de la lutte avec l'ange," *Traces* 3 (1981): 95.

28. Rachel Ertel, "Une littérature minoritaire," *Traces* 3 (1981): 91. A full transla-

These words have lost none of their relevance with the growing number of texts of all kinds that have appeared by and about Jews in France.

In preparing the section of the volume devoted to cultural contexts, we have taken the interdisciplinary title *Yale French Studies* very seriously. Some articles here are of a kind often found in this review, like the commentaries on literature by Ora Avni and David J. Jacobson; the philosophical considerations by Elisabeth de Fontenay and Seth Wolitz; and the psychoanalytic reflections by Gérard Haddad. Wishing to present French Jewry in a general way, we have included a sociological study, by Michel Abitbol, of the most dynamic element among them: the Jews of North African origin. Since many readers of *Yale French Studies* are acquainted with the Talmudic readings of Emmanuel Lévinas, it seemed useful to present remarks by a more official representative of observant Judaism in France. Hence the translation of a 1948 piece by the Chief Rabbi of Paris, Meyer Jaïs, which appeared near the time Lévinas began publishing some of the essays included in *Difficile Liberté.*[29]

To appreciate Rabbi Jaïs's vigorous defense of Judaism, we must recall its context. In addition to the explicitly racial anti-Semitism of the Nazis and their collaborators, there raged during the war, and even after, a vehement rejection of the Jewish religion—and not just in the name of French secularism. Thus George Steiner aptly quotes from philosopher Simone Weil, who was born Jewish: "At a time when her own people were being harried to bestial extinction, [she] refused baptism into the Catholic Church because 'Roman Catholicism was still too Jewish.'"[30]

Hardly more appealing than Weil's Jewish anti-Semitism was François Mauriac's Catholic philo-Semitism. In his preface to Wiesel's *La Nuit*, which first appeared in 1958, Mauriac suggests the faith of Christians is more resilient than that of the Jews after the Holocaust. He recounts what he might have said when he met Wiesel, who had come from Israel:

---

tion of this article, under the title "A Minority Literature," appears in this issue of *Yale French Studies.*

29. Emmanuel Lévinas, *Difficile Liberté: Essais sur le judaïsme*, 3rd rev. ed. (Paris: Albin Michel, 1976); trans. Seán Hand, *Difficult Freedom: Essays on Judaism* (Baltimore: Johns Hopkins University, 1990).

30. George Steiner, "Sainte Simone," *Times Literary Supplement* 4705 (4 June 1993): 3.

Did I speak of that other Israeli, his brother, who may have resembled him—the Crucified, whose Cross has conquered the world? Did I affirm that the stumbling block to his faith was the cornerstone of mine, and that the conformity between the Cross and the suffering of men was in my eyes the key to that impenetrable mystery whereon the faith of his childhood had perished?[31]

Remarks no less startling by Mauriac had already appeared in the foreword he wrote in 1951 for one of the first book-length studies of the Holocaust, *Le Bréviaire de la haine* by Léon Poliakov.[32]

The "Christianization" of the Holocaust—the promotion of an analogy between the passion of Jesus and the Nazi persecution of the Jews, to the detriment of any specifically Jewish understanding of the ₜtragedy—has not been halted by Vatican II, and may have even been abetted by it. The articles here by Armand Vulliet and Bernard Suchecky deal with two recent, and very distinct, examples of that tendency: an entry in a French encyclopedia; and the results of the negotiations during which Catholic and Jewish representatives, many from France, attempted to solve the dilemma posed by the Carmelite convent at Auschwitz. If the Christianization of the Holocaust has elicited greater concern in France than in the United States, this is doubtless an effect of the stronger secularism and anticlericalism in French society. (Incidentally, though his piece appeared originally in a French periodical, Bernard Suchecky is Belgian.)

Christianization is just one of the strange uses to which the Holocaust has been put. No doubt the most disturbing, called "revisionism" or more precisely "negationism"—the simple denial of the Holocaust—has received much media attention in France and the United States. It seemed to the author of these lines counterproductive to publicize this aberration further by yet another article analyzing it.[33] In any event, anti-Semitism per se is not the subject of this issue, but rather the discourses of Jews about their identity. Thus we feature

31. François Mauriac, "Foreword" in Elie Wiesel, *Night*, trans. Stella Rodway (New York: Discus/Avon, 1969), 10.

32. Mauriac, "Préface" in Léon Poliakov, *Le Bréviaire de la haine: le Troisième Reich et les Juifs* (Paris: Calmann-Lévy, 1951). This forward is replaced by one by the Protestant theologian Reinhold Niebuhr in the English translation: *Harvest of Hate: The Nazi Program for the Destruction of the Jews of Europe*, ed. Martin Greenberg (Syracuse/New York: Syracuse University Press/American Jewish Committee, 1954).

33. See Pierre Vidal-Naquet, *Assassins of Memory: Essays on the Denial of the Holocaust*, trans. Jeffrey Mehlman (New York: Columbia University Press, 1992); and Nadine Fresco, "The Denial of the Dead: On the Faurisson Affair," *Dissent* 28 (1981): 467–83.

an article on Maurice Sachs's Jewish self-hatred or ambivalence, but not one on Céline's hatred of the Jews. One exception: the piece by Armand Vulliet, who has asked it be mentioned he is not a Jew—though he is "delighted" and "very moved" that his piece has "touched the Jewish community."[34]

From the end of the war through the 1960s, one of the discourses that denatured the Holocaust downplayed the specificity of the anti-Semitic persecutions under the Occupation. Wishing to stress the unity of France, many French considered Jews to be no different from other victims of Nazism, despite the significantly greater percentage of fatalities among Jews arrested than among non-Jewish resistants in the same situation. On occasion, French Jews themselves propagated this view, as is shown in the article by historian Annette Wieviorka.

She is, by the way, the granddaughter of one of the Yiddish writers translated here, Wolf Wieviorka, who perished in the Holocaust. May this filiation, now inscribed on the pages of *Yale French Studies*, bear witness to the continuation, through various avatars, of a specifically Jewish intellectual life in France, despite the attempt to eradicate Jews and their culture.

Thanks are due to many for this issue of *Yale French Studies*, most of all to the authors of the articles as well as three people at Yale University: Professor Charles Porter, for his support of the initial project; Liliane Greene, the retiring managing editor of *Yale French Studies*, for her constant encouragement; and Alyson Waters, the new managing editor, for her great help in the final months.

34. Letter from Armand Vulliet, 16 August 1993.

I. *Literary Texts*

GIL BEN AYCH

The Chant of Being*
(Excerpts)

These passages from the novel show a Jewish family in Paris in the 1960s preparing and celebrating a bar mitzvah. Though quite observant, they call the ceremony a "communion"—a holdover from their days in Algeria, where Jews melded their French identity and ethnic traditions in a unique way.

They entered the active phase of preparation. There was intense busyness, a little like the days when the seamstress came to the house in Tlemcen, Algeria. Jeannette, Simon's mother, was running all about. She had to see to the reception at home. Joseph, Simon's father, was overcome. He was in charge of coordination with the synagogue and the rabbi, and had to invite the guests.

Gilberte, a cousin from Versailles, came to help out. Aunt Rosette, too. She lived in Créteil and often aided her younger sister following the birth of a child or at other exceptional moments. She would stay on rue Truffaut, in Paris, at Jeannette's and Joseph's place, as she did now. The trip seemed very long to her, and she would repeat that "back in Tlemcen, the distances weren't the same, here we're really far apart, do you realize how long it took me to get from Créteil to the 17th arrondissement, here. . . !"

Jeannette and Rosette had prepared a considerable number of main dishes and cakes, little omelettes and *méguinas*: patties made of egg and potato, stuffed with fresh vegetables, topped with lamb brains cooked in parsley.

Gilberte asked Simon if he believed. If he had faith. He answered no. Just like that. He added that it was to please his grandparents and receive gifts that he had agreed to the bar mitzvah. Or the communion, as they called it at Simon's house. But he had learned otherwise from

*Gil Ben Aych, *Le Chant des êtres* (Paris: Gallimard, 1988), pp. 21–22, 37–45, 56–57.

YFS 85, *Discourses of Jewish Identity in Twentieth-Century France*, ed. Alan Astro, © 1994 by Yale University.

the Hebrew school he attended last term with his brother Abram; and from a neighbor, a European Jewish woman; and from certain family acquaintances who were studying Hebrew. They taught him that a Jew did not take "communion," he had a "bar mitzvah" to mark his accession to religious adulthood. The nuance seemed decisive and distinctive. Nonetheless, the words "bar mitzvah" had a biblical or theological connotation that his parents did not attach to "communion." "Communion" was a more fitting word for a specific act in time, a good excuse for a festive family gathering.

In the afternoons, they sent out the last invitations, to people whose addresses they had only just gotten. They sat around the table, putting stamps on envelopes. The sun's rays flooded the old wooden floor, and their faces shone. The women ate dates to pass the time.

. . . .

They got up early. Joseph went quickly downstairs to warm up the car. He waited, honking the horn from time to time, to hurry them up. Jeannette reacted by asking: "What's wrong with Joseph? Why is he getting so worked up, today of all days?" The day of his bar mitzvah. The day. This day. Today is the bar mitzvah.

They washed up. They had installed a little shower in the kitchen. They did not have one before. Simon and Abram put on their "nice suits," with white socks and new black loafers. Jeannette kept saying: "Don't press down the back of your shoes," worried as she was about things staying in good shape. She watched over everything. She shut off the gas jets and closed the blinds (it seemed to Simon as though they were leaving for several months). The neighbors were astonished at all the activity, but were simply told of the good news, the bar mitzvah, without further comment. It would have been necessary to go into detail about differences in religion and ritual, and no one really felt like it. Except for the baker's wife, who offered them some candy before they set off.

The conventional, general silence that the Christian neighbors kept in the face of an act so meaningful, so revelatory of religious identity, was nothing new to Simon, who had had a clear, sharp perception of it on his arrival in France in 1956. It seemed as though the silence of the others, in the face of something so different (not to mention anomalous or even monstrous), were a kind of respect, a self-contained, mute, unspeakable deference, the mark of a relevant, significant distance. "People" knew! "People" knew that Simon's family (*not* "was" Jewish but . . .) "was-not-Christian!" They were known to be different. And Simon realized this was known.

Nonetheless, Simon suspected that speaking of these differences would allow the real differences, the true ones, to be understood; but he then felt, at one and the same time, shame and the need to keep a distance. Shame because it was not right for a boy of his age, thirteen years old, to teach adults, who perhaps knew the score after all. Perhaps. Distance, a need to keep a distance, because he realized that to speak of the difference would only attract attention. Attention to the difference, not to Simon. And since Simon did not want to attract attention, he preferred to remain silent. Like everyone else. No. Like Simon. Simon, already, did not like to "attract attention."

They jumped into the grey Peugeot 403, crossed the outer boulevards, and arrived at the synagogue of the 18th arrondissement where the bar mitzvah was to take place.

It was near the rue Custine, and Rabbi Judas, his father Joseph's cousin, who lived on rue Stephenson, would be there. It had become more and more difficult for him to get around, because of his age, but Joseph insisted on his being there. He, and none other, would officiate at the ceremony.

They entered a bright, bare, vast room. In the center, towards the front, stood the men; and in back, towards the side, the women took their seats. There was a sort of wooden rostrum, covered with an immaculate embroidered cloth, white and pomegranate-colored velvet. At the forefront were the *sepharim.*

In comparison to the grandiose synagogue Simon had known in Tlemcen, the one here seemed laughable and almost shabby. It made you feel as though Jews had no place in France and hid in order not to call attention to their activities. Were their activities reprehensible? Not as far as I know, said Simon to himself. Why was it so small? The tiny synagogue. The narrow Jew. Shrunken Judaism. European cleanliness and skimpy Judaism. Back there, in Tlemcen, in Algeria, the synagogue took up almost an entire block; here, you went in through the door of a house like all others. This detail mattered. Simon asked his father why and was told that it was a question of "lack of funds." Simon only half-believed him but decided to make do with half a belief. He said to himself, baldly, it may be hard to believe but so it is. Not believing his own eyes, Simon closed them, and believed. Simon would believe. He finally opened his eyes. It was time. It was high time he opened his eyes. That was the very purpose of a communion. Today's the communion. Today?

They began with the short morning prayer, during which a strip of leather is wrapped around the arm. Likewise, a kind of cube, made of the same material and containing biblical verses, is held on the forehead by a band of leather we strap around our heads. The *tephillin*. The faithful Jew, literally tied to the texts, his forehead marked with the sacred seal, devotes himself to the ritual morning prayer—an act of allegiance to God that Simon found hard to accept but took delight in, because of its incongruous, unexpected, almost obscene character. He was on the rostrum. (Strange to think that addressing God was something strictly personal! For a long time, he was obsessed by a problem present in all religions, but more pronounced in Judaism because of its minority status. If God is supposed to be there for all of us, he must "really" be there for each of us. He's "our" solo player. Mine. The great universal dialogue and private monologues. Generalized, pervasive cacophony. Universal harmony. Because we are there and because we speak. It's us.)

Simon wore a new *tallith* given to him by his godfather, the other Simon. He liked the silly material of the prayer shawl and especially the soft white fringes hanging at the ends. You put it on your shoulders and you were covered before God. He also wore a small red velvet skullcap that his aunt Esther, a seamstress, had made from leftover material. But the skullcap annoyed him. It was too small and kept falling off. It wasn't a real silk skullcap, embroidered with Hebrew writing, like the ones adults wore. They helped him. They helped him several times to put it back on.

Simon liked embracing the *sepharim*. It seemed as though he were embracing the entire world and its eternal spirit. He felt like crying when he held the sacred scrolls in his arms. He recited his portion without really understanding it, because he had learned it by heart, over a three-month period, during bar mitzvah lessons at the synagogue. He did recognize some words. Whence his ability to associate or connect words from other languages—Arabic, French, English, even German or Spanish—with their Semitic "roots," when the occasion presented itself. (Thus *zit* in Hebrew, becomes *zeit* in Arabic, keeps the *i* to become *huile* in French, loses the *u* and gains an *o* to make *oil* in English. Languages can transform or keep consonants at their leisure. *Z* stays *z* as one moves from Hebrew to Arabic, it switches from *z* to *h* going from Arabic to French, there's no more *h* in English, *öl* in German turns the *i* into an umlaut on the *o*, ending up with *zeitoun* meaning "olive" in Arabic and Zeitoun as the last name of one of his friends in fifth grade. Zeitoun. *Z* and *t* from the ancient Hebrew disappear, the *i* remains. A straight stick standing up and on the top a point or head. Man walks vertically through history, on the ground. And the history of words goes on, unremittingly, underneath. Languages referring to each other. Words calling words. Our words calling out to each other and beyond.) Whence also the knowing, unspeakable, joy of posting oneself, of being posted at the source of a phenomenon that concerns everyone. Speaking. Writing. Communicating. And using words whose far-removed origins and semantic aura he, Simon, sometimes knew. Semantic. Semitic. Fast-found mimicry among languages. A primitive effect. Writing.

He was rather unhappy when he had to put the *sepharim* back in the lovely ark that looked like a little house. He would have wished to keep them longer or even take them home, so beautiful were they. He liked the little silver towers perched on their very tops and at the ends of which hung little bells of sorts.

What impressed him particularly was the finger you hold on to follow the text. He preferred by far to read from right to left. This was quite a change from his school books that all looked alike with their ugly pictures. Here things were strange and uncanny. Simon felt he was part of an elite. Yes, an elite. Or more exactly a group that resembled no other and that was truly distinctive. Here, he was far from all his friends and even tended to scorn them. Not having had the same experience as he, they would never understand things the way Jews could. They. The others. Simon thus displayed a sureness that quickly turned into superiority. Simon read. In Hebrew, Simon read. He read. Simply enough.

The rabbi helped him follow the text. Simon took special care in reading his portion because what pleased him above all, as though it were his duty, was that no classmate should do so well as he or get so good a grade. Not even the Polish or Russian Jews, whom he learned then to call Ashkenazim, a word he easily remembered because his father's boss in Algeria was named Ashkenazi. Services were different at their synagogues.

Moreover, Simon hardly understood how Jews could be designated by a word with the syllable *az*. The thing seemed impossible to him, even comical, in short: contemptible. Laughable. This contempt Simon transferred onto the Ashkenazim themselves. In his eyes, they were hardly Jews.

He had had, however, more than once, the opportunity of learning that impossible things were indeed possible. So he was not unduly surprised. When Simon thought this way, he opened his eyes wide, to absorb what he saw. Stunned, Simon would absorb and forget. He would forget. Simon would forget. Simon was jubilant, detesting the Catholics. He also detested that notorious Ashkenazi, with whom his father had fallen out because he tried to cheat him of his due.

At the time, paradoxically, the relationship between German and the word "Ashkenazi," despite historical events, was not obvious. The association, hidden in the recesses of the unconscious, was taboo. Only much later did he find out that Ashkenazi meant "German" and Sephardi "Spanish." In this way, certain words conceal in their depths connotations or meanings that emerge later. Certain words, and their chrysalises.

Moreover, Simon liked Hebrew pronunciation, the shin and the beth, the lack of vowels and the greatly condensed vocabulary. It was indeed a communion, a means of communion among members of a minority who assigned to it a unique quality. When the rabbi addressed him—Simon—by name, reciting in Hebrew the names of his father and mother, of his grandfathers and grandmothers, of his great-grandfathers and great-grandmothers, Simon, he, Simon, wiped away tears with a brand-new handkerchief. Brand-new. He heard the women say amen and pray in Arabic as they extolled him. (That the women prayed in Arabic, while the men read Hebrew, added to the confusion, kept Simon from separating Jews and Arabs clearly and distinctly, at least as far as his family in Algeria was concerned. Those women praying, were they Jewish, were they Arab? The question reflected the fact that in Algeria only men were considered fit to learn Hebrew. If a woman knew Hebrew—unless she were a notable scholarly exception—she simply repeated prayers recited a hundred thousand times over. By men!) He turned to the left where there stood a table covered with pomegranate-colored velvet embroidered with gold thread. He continued reading from another book. He thought of all the weddings he had attended, and felt as though he himself were getting married to everyone and no one. Getting married. To everyone and no one.

This idea enraptured Simon, even as it embarrassed him. Only long afterwards did he grasp its exact significance, when he realized that everyone was close to him and no one was close to him, really close to him, to himself, to self. He had married himself having become a man. Communion.

When he arrived at the last lines of his reading, a girl cousin threw sugar-coated almonds at him. He embraced Rabbi Judas, who had a full white beard; his father, Joseph, who stood at his side; his mother, Jeannette, as he came down from the rostrum; his grandmothers, Etoile and Hanna. A member of the synagogue came forward to ask the women to return to their places. Jeannette retorted that she was allowed to kiss her son at his communion, on the day of his communion. God would not mind.

Simon received several gifts. Uncle Jacques handed him a completely white envelope, inscribed with his first name, which intrigued him. He saw the joy, the true happiness, on his family's lips. He remained on the rostrum. Simon. On the rostrum.

It was his brother's turn, his brother Abram, his junior by two years, who liked Hebrew less and whom they had managed to convince that he did not understand why he had to go through the same thing again. The same thing as Simon. After Simon had done it. His *tallith* was on crooked and kept sliding around, the black leather cube made him appear one-eyed, his skullcap rode down his neck. When he pulled up his sleeve in order to wrap the leather strip around his forearm, he seemed half-undressed, as though he were waiting to be examined by a doctor or getting on his pyjamas. His shirttails emerged from his trousers.

He was rather embarrassed and annoyed, he was unsure of his portion and the rabbi kept correcting him because he either read the wrong line or mispronounced words. The worshipers, egged on by Uncle Jacques, began to laugh and make comments. Although absorbed in his reading, Abram raised his head from time to time to cast a curious glance at Judas or to gauge the onlookers' response. His gestures triggered a comic reaction, which then redoubled. So that at the end of a slight half-hour of torture, the rabbi cut things short. Cut Abram's portion short.

Uncle Jacques called out: "We should have said, 'Encore!!!'" "Encore." A legend came to be, which attributed the remark to Abram.

Simon's chagrin, the unspeakable dream, the obvious glance, the future presence, the narrow Jew, the semantic aura, Abram's remark.

. . . .

A few female cousins were in charge of the record player and switched among Arabic songs, rock music and slow dances.

Debates started between partisans of one or another kind of music. Upon hearing "modern" music, Hanna turned to Grandmother Etoile and said, "*Cassement de tête.*" Etoile answered, "*Rass tertek,*" which meant exactly the same thing, but in Arabic.

By listening to his grandmothers, or others, repeat in Arabic what they had just said in French, Simon began to appreciate the differences between the two languages and sense the originality of each. If the phrase meant exactly the same thing in French and Arabic, then there was no reason to say it in both languages. Nonetheless, they said it, repeated it, in both languages. Etoile and Hanna would repeat it. That proved that one language (in this case, Arabic) brought in a nuance that was absent from the other. Here, *rass tertek* added to *cassement de tête* the idea of incessant repetition and irreparable damage. Rock was thus perceived by the two Arab grandmothers as a kind of monotony as well as a sort of smashing, a violent cracking, a total break.

When Simon thought about such things, he liked to go from one language to the other and enjoyed, really enjoyed, the art of nuances. An art of nuances that moved between the local idiolect (the Judeo-Algerian Arabic of Tlemcen) and a mixture of a colonized people's approximate French (which he heard around him) and standard French (which he learned at school). Simon thus had the best reasons to perceive nuances. He appreciated distinctions. He was distinguished. Languages distinguished him. Thus Simon began to forge a language: a language that was not Arabic, or Hebrew, or French. A language. His language. Simon's language.

Others thought that it was not right to play such music on a communion day. This was no ordinary celebration, like a birthday party. The religion had to be respected. So they put Samy el Magrebi back on, along with other Jewish singers who performed liturgical chants in a singsong. The debates stopped. Calm returned.

—Translated by Alan Astro

GLOSSARY

SEPHARIM (Hebrew): scrolls.
CASSEMENT DE TÊTE (French): splitting headache, deafening noise.

CYRILLE FLEISCHMAN

Two from *The Main Attraction**

Following are two short stories by an author who is something of a "crossover" phenomenon, having published both in the Jewish community press and in mainstream literary journals such as La Nouvelle Revue française.

I. BACK FROM AMERICA

Arnold Leibenwitz had two passions: hot *pickelfleisch* and chivalric romances of the late fifteenth and early sixteenth centuries.

He lived on the rue de Birague. He was thirty-five years old, and except for delicatessen and literature, he knew little about the world around him. He remembered having been married for two years to a young English teacher at the Lycée Charlemagne, having perhaps had two or three children by her, whom he thought about with astonishment when he looked at his bank statement from the branch on the rue Saint-Antoine. Every month there appeared on it an automatic withdrawal for alimony and child support, which he otherwise would have forgotten to pay.

Arnold also had a father. Old Leibenwitz had set up shop on the rue du Petit-Musc, on the other side of the rue Saint-Antoine, right after the war. They had come from Russia, where they had wandered through the countryside for nearly four years, having managed to leave Poland in time. Afterwards, the whole family, except for some twenty cousins who made the mistake of staying near Warsaw, came via Germany to Paris, the capital of the enlightened world and the still flourishing center of capmaking.

So old Leibenwitz was a capmaker on the rue du Petit-Musc. His wife died a few years after their arrival, and little Arnold forgot Poland and Russia to become a scholar who pursued research on knights in

*Cyrille Fleischman, *L' Attraction du bal* (Paris: Gallimard, 1987), 55–60, 119–23.

YFS 85, *Discourses of Jewish Identity in Twentieth-Century France,* ed. Alan Astro, © 1994 by Yale University.

fifteenth- and sixteenth-century literature and who ate *pickelfleisch*. Old Leibenwitz understood perfectly his son's passion for *pickel*. In his opinion, it was the only thing normal about him. Sighing in his shop, with tears in his eyes, he would say to his worker, also from Warsaw:

"My son the idiot! With his head in the clouds! And the books! Have *you* ever heard about these Maurice Chivalrics who write stories about castles? No? That's because you're normal. *Him* the Sorbonne pays to study such nonsense! Can you believe it? Neither can I! But what should I do? He tells me, so I believe. What does he do? I don't know. He doesn't take care of his kids. He doesn't buy his clothes wholesale. If he didn't have some *pickel* with me from time to time, I wouldn't even know he existed. My son the idiot!"

Old Leibenwitz need not have worried about Arnold's professional success. He was a shining light in the university world. A specialist. There was not a colloquium held to which he was not invited. Anyone interested in sixteenth-century literature had to cite him. A flattering murmur would rise from the audience, and his colleagues would say, nodding their heads:

"Let's stay to hear the talk on the *Feats and Deeds of the Most Gallant, Noble, and Valiant Huon de Bordeaux, Peer of France and Duke of Guienne*. That Arnold Leibenwitz never fails to amaze us. Where does he come up with such scholarship? His presentations are always elegant, never laborious."

At the same time, old Leibenwitz, stacking up the piles of caps in his shop on the rue du Petit-Musc, would cry out:

"My son the idiot! He never wanted to go into caps. Even if we're doing less well than before, you can still make a living with a shop. Between child support for kids he never sees, and alimony for a wife he's forgotten about, how can he make ends meet? He'll go see the head of the Sorbonne for a raise? He wouldn't dare."

One day, in the middle of the afternoon, Arnold came into the shop and said:

"Pop, I can only stay a minute. I'm about to leave for America. I forgot to tell you. I'm going for a year or two. We'll talk when I get back."

"*We'll* talk? "*You'll* talk. Come see my grave, and as long as you're at the cemetery for me, make sure your mother's stone isn't broken."

"Stop dramatizing. I'll only be away a short while, and we'll have *pickel* together a thousand more times . . . "

" . . . *if* Goldenberg's deli opens up a branch at the Bagneux cemetery, off the first row of graves. Otherwise, you'll eat alone. But as long as you're already here, let's talk about something else. How's the sixteenth century doing? Are you going to America on business?"

Deep down, old Leibenwitz felt reassured. If his son was going to America, he might stop sponging and finally make something of himself. Normally, he would sooner bite his tongue than give a compliment, but he could not help saying:

"After all, if that Sorbonne of yours is sending you there, you must be a serious worker."

"If I'm going there, it's to give courses, lectures . . . "

"I said something else?"

"I still have an hour or two before I pick up my bags at home. We can go get some *pickel* before I go out to the airport."

"You're going by plane? Why aren't you going by boat? You know the pilot at least? Here, take two or three caps, the latest style, to give as gifts on the plane."

"Thanks, pop, it's really not necessary."

"Take. When I give, you take. *Me* you're going to tell how to go on a trip?"

Arnold Leibenwitz kissed his father and left with three caps to become a visiting professor at an American university.

Time went by. Occasionally, Old Leibenwitz received a letter that he would have his bookkeeper read to him, because he never had his glasses with him and he could not understand what that idiot Arnold wrote anyway. Once or twice a month he would see his grandchildren at the home of his ex-daughter-in-law, to whom the bank still automatically paid alimony and child support. He failed to die as he could have just to bother his son. After twenty-one months had passed, Arnold Leibenwitz was back in his apartment on the rue de Birague, which in the meantime his father had sublet to his worker's daughter, to make sure there would be no trouble.

Arnold called as soon as the taxi dropped him off at his place, while his father's worker's daughter graciously packed up her belongings.

He had changed during his stay in the United States. Lecturing on chivalric romances, expertly paraphrasing *The Tale of the Two Noble and Valiant Knights Valentin and Orson, Scions of the Emperor of Greece and Descendants of the Most Christian Pépin, King of France,* Arnold had grown tired, as one suddenly tires of a passion. One day, in the midst of a course, Arnold's personality split into two. Hearing himself speak to his attentive students, he felt the gap widen. What did he have in common with that vanished world? What did young Leibenwitz, whose mother made such good hot *pickelfleisch,* have to do with knights? What was a little Jew like him doing there, lecturing on texts that were so strangely foreign to him?

Towards the end of the course he felt the need to speak more personally. In his perfect English, he surprised his audience by going from a discussion of the daughter of the Duke of Aquitaine to a disquisition on capmaking, followed by another on the Parisian Jewish quarter of the Marais, then by another on Russian pickles, and by yet another on how to make good *pickelfleisch.*

The students looked at him in amazement. Some continued to take notes by force of habit. He extended the course twenty minutes and after making some final points he let the students go, as he let himself go. He came back to France three months before expected.

As he crossed the rue Saint-Antoine on the way to old Leibenwitz's shop on the rue du Petit-Musc, Arnold Leibenwitz felt well for the first time in his life. The dreams were over. It was time to wake up.

He gave up his courses at the Sorbonne. Encouraged by his father, he bought an old delicatessen in the neighborhood. He married the daughter of the worker from Warsaw, who gave him many children whom he learned to love. He finally took an interest in his first children beyond looking at his bank statement.

For many years until he retired, it was at his delicatessen that you could find the best *pickelfleisch* in Paris. He was a happy and successful businessman.

Arnold Leibenwitz had become an adult.

II.   IN HOMAGE TO YANKEL I.

On his passport, where it says "occupation," he could have written: "bar mitzvah gift."

Ever since his *Jewish Stories for Jewish Youth with Jewish Illustrations* had been printed by a Jewish publisher, whenever somebody wanted to give an inexpensive gift—less expensive than a leather wallet or a gold pen—the poor kid had a two-to-one chance of getting Starpletzel's work. The hardcover edition, of course, bound in real plastic.

Which amounts to saying that kids feared like the plague this gift that they couldn't even swap among themselves, since all of them thirteen years old and over already had on their bookshelves three or four identical volumes by the famous Starpletzel—and the booksellers would never exchange one for a comic book.

Abraham Starpletzel himself suffered from his reputation. Whenever he tried to get his editors to accept a new book with stories about goyim, it was always the same sympathetic smile. They would say to him:

"Dear monsieur Starpletzel, you have a specialty, a following, a reputation, why go off after something else? Write stories about Jews for *your* public who loves you. Don't disappoint them. Don't ruin your reputation with these vulgar stories, I could even call them porno-graphic, no offense . . . "

Abraham did not take offense. He understood, but he had had enough. His wife was a goy. His children were goyim. Sometimes, he would have well liked to be a goy himself, a member of the French Academy for example, or even a successful writer interviewed on tele-vision. But he was marked with the stamp of a Jewish writer for Jewish children. And no way out.

He had tried everything. Pseudonyms, but who was naïve enough to publish a manuscript sent through the mail and signed by *Arthur Létoile-du-Métro-Saintpaul*? Or contacts, but people would say to him in a friendly manner:

"Don't waste your talent. Think of the story about the pirate rabbi that meant so much to me when I was about ten, just after the war. That's your speciality, my dear Starpletzel."

Abraham was now sixty-eight years old and the war had been over for so long that he could not remember exactly which story or which war was being referred to.

He had enthusiastic readers among adults because children are not naïve. The priest of his wife's parish was Abraham's most enthusiastic fan. He liked the Jewish stories so much that Starpletzel was embar-rassed: all catechism classes were required to read Starpletzel. To get a feeling for the origins of Catholicism, said the good priest.

It was the priest who had encouraged him to go on emphasizing the Jewish side of his characters, and starting in 1946 Starpletzel was the rage not only among left-bank intellectuals, but also in the neighbor-hood of the Bastille, at the République, wherever parents wanted chil-dren to reacquire a taste for the Jewish legends that had suffered so much during the war, having been misinterpreted by the Germans.

People had stuck the proper label on him and he had become the Starpletzel everyone knew.

The only time he was able to get away from literature for model children was when a literary prize was conferred upon another writer, a writer for adults. I no longer remember which magazine devoted a special issue to the laureate, a Yiddish author.

Starpletzel had been asked to contribute an article on a subject like "Childhood in the Work of Yankel I.," or something similar.

Starpletzel was thrilled. He managed to write ten typed pages where I.'s name appeared only twice: once in the beginning, and another time on the last line. The rest was about something else. Not about childhood, which Starpletzel, to tell the truth, was not at all interested in; nor about I., who in Starpletzel's opinion was famous enough to live without the obligatory homage for his jubilee prize, the Yovel Prize.

On his ten typed sheets Starpletzel spoke about goyim, about science fiction, about the Grand Duchy of Luxemburg where I. had perhaps never set foot, and about everything else that was close to Abraham's heart, including eroticism.

Since no one reads this kind of special issue before setting it out on a bookshelf, Starpletzel had been able to indulge himself completely.

At last, he had written what he wanted to. He said to himself that it was too bad I.—or someone else for that matter—had not gotten the prize earlier. The chance to express himself freely, and to be paid for it into the bargain, gave him happiness of a sort he had not known for forty years at least.

In his article, Starpletzel took personal revenge against everyone.

No one read it. Except I., who received a translation in New York.

He did not hesitate to come to Starpletzel in his sleep:

"So you're the French author who dares to write articles about me that don't talk about me? I've already seen chutspah among my friends at the cafeteria, where I meet monsters, but you, the Jew from Paris, are worse than a monster. What demon got into you?"

"Reb Yankel, Mr. Yovel Prize, keep a sense of humor," dreamt Starpletzel.

"Yovel Prize, Shmovel Prize," said I., calming down. "But that's no reason to ruin the special issue of a magazine in Paris that was paying me homage for once in fifty years."

"Yankel, if I may call you Yankel, what difference could it make to you that I don't speak of you in your special issue?"

"It bothers me to be famous and unknown. But that's not the problem. What else do you write?"

"Usually, stories for children. With rabbis who fly, *chazanim* who sneeze, *shochetim* who cut themselves, schnorrers who become princes, just about everything children aren't interested in."

"That's already been done," said I., annoyed, getting bored. "What do you write in? In Yiddish, in Polish, in. . . . What language do they speak in that Luxemburg of yours where you went to see a blond *shikse* in a house, as you write in your article?"

"I write in French. In Luxemburg, I was nineteen years old and didn't stay, but the girls there, Yankel, you would have liked them too!"

"Of course, I like all women. Why not the women from Luxemburg or wherever? What's your name again?"

"Abraham. Abraham Starpletzel."

I. took on a meditative air:

"Are you sure we don't know each other? Your name and your story ring a bell. Didn't I write a tale about you in *The New Yorker?*"

"Not as far as I know, Yankel. But I read very little English, and in Paris you can't get *The New Yorker.*"

"Really? And why not?" said I., surprised. "After all, you're perhaps right, it must have been in *The Saturday Evening Post*. Okay, we'll forget about it this time. But next time, please, speak a little about me, still and all, in your homage. You know the way we storytellers are."

—Translated by Alan Astro

GLOSSARY

PICKELFLEISCH (Yiddish): corned beef.

PICKEL: short for *pickelfleisch.*

LÉTOILE-DU-MÉTRO-SAINTPAUL (French): literally "the-star-of-the-Saint-Paul-subway-station," a pseudonym that transforms the name "Starpletzel." The Saint-Paul station serves the Marais, a traditionally Jewish neighborhood in Paris, referred to in Yiddish as the *pletsl* ("little plaza").

YOVEL (Hebrew): jubilee. Here, an obvious play on "Nobel."

CHAZANIM (Hebrew): cantors.

SHOCHETIM (Hebrew): ritual slaughterers.

BERNARD FRANK

An Age of Excess*
(Excerpts)

The following are from a volume of autobiographical, literary, and political reflections, originally published in 1970.

I have no idea what an "assimilated" Jew is. It's an ugly term, useless, indigestible—a word only a boa constrictor could love. It is my sincere hope that I—who am French and love this country for a thousand reasons that should be of no concern to it—am not a Jew assimilated into France. My identity papers suffice to prove I am as French as anybody else; there is no great honor in that. It's true that I was born in Neuilly, that my father fought in World War I, that my great-grandparents left Alsace in 1870, abandoning their forests, their thickets, their blueberry bushes where children love to roam and stain their shorts and white shirts with red. Does all of that make me any more French? More French than who? Could anyone possibly imagine that non-Jewish Frenchmen are model Frenchmen? Who would even ask them to be? It's not because you've grazed on the same grass and chewed the same cud in the same village for generations that a country is yours or you its representative. Most French people are French out of a sense of obligation. The only Frenchmen who have a clear idea of France[1] are those who have experienced their homeland as a place of exile.

*Bernard Frank, *Un siècle débordé*, rev. ed. (Paris: Flammarion, 1987), 67–72, 73, 93, 110–12. The title is taken from Montaigne, III:9: "L'écrivaillerie semble être quelque symptôme d'un siècle débordé" ["Scribbling seems to be one of the symptoms of an age of excess" (*The Essays of Michel de Montaigne*, trans. M. A. Screech [London: Allen Lane/Penguin, 1991], 1071)].

  1. "Les seuls Français qui se soient fait une certaine idée de la France . . . ," a phrase that echoes the beginning of de Gaulle's memoirs: "Toute ma vie, je me suis fait une certaine idée de la France" ["All my life I have thought of France in a certain way" (*War Memoirs of Charles de Gaulle: The Call to Honor, 1940–1942*, trans. Jonathan Griffin [New York: Simon and Schuster, 1955], 3)]. [*All notes in this piece are by the translator, except as otherwise indicated.*]

YFS 85, *Discourses of Jewish Identity in Twentieth-Century France*, ed. Alan Astro, © 1994 by Yale University.

My dear Jews of France, always worried lest you not be sufficiently French, you bore me to tears. Stop trying to imitate your neighbors. The devil take your military crosses and other medals, your relatives who gave their lives for our country, and your generosity to boot. Be ugly, stupid, and nasty if such is your desire, if that's the way you were born. Your virtues will never disarm your persecutor, that wretch named Xavier Vallat.[2] (Why Xavier Vallat? Because there are names that creep up in your throat like heartburn from rotten eggs.) Xavier Vallat would have you believe that France is the Jockey Club, that he is its president, and that a blackball from him amounts to a yellow star of David on your chest. Yes, this fine gentleman and those like him may luck out and get a chance to embody the law. They can help send us to the ovens, but for that to happen, their beloved country first has to be up to its ears in shit. They are truly French only when France is defeated. The swastika had to be flying over the Arc de Triomphe for me to be convinced as a child of Xavier Vallat's superpatriotism.

I am well aware that for the Jewish bourgeoisie, being Jewish is rotten luck. They would have liked nothing better than to doze their lives away along with the rest of the French bourgeoisie. Jews are the only people who have well-founded reasons to be anti-Semitic! Unfortunately, or rather fortunately, they can't be that way any longer. Do you think the Jewish bourgeoisie wants anything different from what the rest of the bourgeoisie wants? That they look down their noses at money, nice apartments, houses in the south of France, Citroën DS 21's, yachts, the *Figaro*, the *Express*, wealthy matches for their children, good relations with the United States? That they aren't put out by strikes in the public sector? That they are well disposed to Arabs and blacks? What the bourgeoisie has, they have; what the bourgeoisie thinks, they think; what the bourgeoisie dreams of is their dream too.

The only hitch is that since 1940 their hearts aren't in it. The Jewish bourgeoisie has become the sick bourgeoisie of Europe. Everything they appreciate has been spoiled for them. They no longer harbor that hostility, those prejudices, or explode into those holy fits of absolute, dense ire that are so reassuring. Even the most obtuse Jews suspect that virtues like stupidity and avarice, which go so far in helping their neighbors deal with the difficulties of life, would be of scant aid to them should misfortune strike. Being Jewish is a kind of baptism: it

2. Xavier Vallat, as readers of this book may have forgotten, was the first Commissioner of Jewish Affairs for the Vichy regime. Apparently, he is still living and writes for the weekly *Aspects de la France*. That's all pretty hard to unravel. [*Author's note.*]

makes you think. Don't get me wrong! I'm not saying Jews are saints, I'm just saying they can no longer be total bastards in all good conscience.

It's exhausting, intolerable, to be forced into becoming something other than you would have wanted to be, than what you are, simply because of some invisible trait. It's enough to drive you crazy. The European Jew reminds me of Argan, the bourgeois protagonist of Molière's *Le Malade imaginaire,* who wishes to punish his daughter. A mischievous maidservant keeps repeating to him: "Come now, sir, you won't do what you say, you're too kind for that. You're just joking, making idle threats." Argan grows impatient, stamps his feet, stammers: "Won't I? You'll see whether I won't. I don't want to be kind, darn it. I'm not kind, I'm nasty!" Though unlike Pascal and Paulhan,[3] I don't believe in a proper use of illness, I'm not far from thinking there is a proper use of being Jewish.

And you, Roger Ikor (Is no luminary. Doubtless a fine fellow. Wrote one of those sagas on Jewish families throughout the ages, to which the French public is definitely partial and which are generally unreadable. Received the Goncourt Prize for *Les Eaux mêlées* in 1955, the same year I published my last novel, which explains that feat of memory. As Clemenceau might have said: "When they crown one, they usually choose the stupidest."[4] Author of an essay on the Jewish question, published by my most recent editor.[5] The excerpts I have read in *Le Figaro littéraire* seem rather clumsy. They reveal the kind of dull thought that makes critics and the public alike proclaim Ikor a man of good will with whom it is a pleasure to exchange ideas. Ikor is a socialist, a true one, of the Mollet variety[6]), would like to do away with that slight uncertainty, as fine as a gossamer veil, as infinitesimal as a grain of sand, in favor of a bovine assimilation, the sense of which, moreover, is inapparent to me. Or rather, I understand all too well what you mean by that, Roger Ikor, despite the thousand detours you take. You, as well as Cau (we'll get back to him later), would like to have a bunch of poor

3. Jean Paulhan, French writer active in intellectual circles of the Resistance.

4. In order to diminish the power of the chief executive of the Third French Republic, statesman Georges Clemenceau suggested a strategy of "voting for the stupidest" candidate for the presidency. In 1920, he fell victim to his own ploy, when he lost his bid for that office to the intellectually inferior Paul Deschanel.

5. Roger Ikor, *Peut-on être juif aujourd' hui!* (Paris: Grasset, 1968).

6. Guy Mollet, a moderate socialist statesman during the Fourth and Fifth French Republics, attempted to crush the Algerian independence movement and supported de Gaulle's return to power.

Jewish devils chew on the same stupid words, pour forth the same rabid hatreds as the rest of the French tribe.

The greatest good a Polish Jew can do for France, should he take up residence on her grounds, is to remain Jewish, Polish, or whatever else he might be for as long as possible. It takes someone who knows nothing of this country wracked by civil strife to imagine for one instant that the inhabitants of some village in Corrèze, Brittany or Corsica have *assimilated* into France. One day, alas, we'll all be assimilated, not into the effluvia of the French soul but into the civilization of the *brave new world*[7] we know all too well.

In turn, Cau's recent pamphlet, the title of which escapes me,[8] takes the form of a monologue addressed to a Jewish woman of humanistic convictions, a real idiot, who believes that people are basically alike. He proceeds to demolish both her and her opinions by his brilliant common sense. He's above such claptrap, Cau is; he doesn't pussyfoot around. Arabs disgust him and anti-Semitism he considers a plague, but people being the way they are, Jews have to disappear lest they be annihilated.

For Cau and Ikor, things are clear: either you're Israeli, which is fine; or you're French, and that's perfect. Your name is either Horowitz or Bertrand. I'm oversimplifying. Ikor, like the old regionalist writer he is, has nothing against ancestor worship, which indeed has inspired his finest pages. Cau, who is in favor of complete camouflage, has little use for Ikorian literature. He sees things as they are, and they're not good: "Jews, into your hiding-places!"

Ikor, as befits a socialist, is optimistic. He's quite happy Israel exists, since that way all those Jews who do not live in France, where he was so fortunate as to win the Goncourt Prize, have a decent homeland as a consolation. Ikor speaks of Israel in the glowing terms a rich industrialist might use to announce to his workers the imminent completion of a "luxury" housing project. After tipping his hat to Israel, this dense, obdurate burgomaster urges his coreligionists to set their sights on France alone, so bounteous in exquisite prizes and prestigious degrees.

It's useful to have Cau around, because he often says or writes what you would like to say or write yourself, but he does so in such a way that you feel you've gotten off easy by keeping quiet. What I don't like

7. In English in the original.

8. Jean Cau, *Lettre ouverte aux têtes de chiens occidentaux* (Paris: Albin Michel, 1967).

about Cau is his indifference to possible mass murder, his good humor in the face of crimes against humanity, as though he really imagined his writings could peacefully coexist with crematoria. He seems to offer French Jewry the kind of advice a knowing father gives his children: "Change your names, change your noses, stop circumcising your sons. People being the way they are, it's still your best bet. Now, if you don't feel like listening to me—and you have every right not to—don't come whimpering back to me, afterwards, if they exterminate you. Remember I warned you."

Curiously, that old-fashioned, stubborn desire to remain Jewish is starting to look quite honorable to me, even if the word "Jewish" designates no more than an imaginary quality, a kind of reverse nobility, nothing in fact, any longer. If others are bothered by the Jewish desire to remain Jewish, it is they who are detestable, not those who let themselves be considered Jewish by others. I can't imagine what comfort French Jews could derive from knowing that their children, kept in ignorance of their fictitious background, might end up as mass murderers. If the sole advantages of being Jewish, of belonging to a minority, were to prevent you from entertaining stereotypical ideas and to stir within you extreme disgust at the sight of savagery, then I, for one, would be delighted to find out there shall be Jews (even if that word no longer designated any religion, race or people) until the end of time, preferably dispersed if that's not asking too much.

Let no one see in these remarks any racial pride or hidden mysticism. I am merely cautioning against the simple-minded attempts of well-meaning philo-Semites, who in order to deflect attention from those they take under their wings, seek to prove that Jews are in no way different (different from whom? as regards what? who knows!), that Jews aren't so rich, so intelligent, aren't all doctors, philosophers, bankers, aren't the Rothschilds, Bergsons or Dassaults that people think. All of which simply makes anti-Semites sneer to themselves, for they never go anywhere without the professional listings of the phone directory under their arms and can recite to you, without skipping a beat, the number of Weils in Paris who are furriers. That's their way of laying a wreath at the monument to the martyrs of the death camps.

Of course, Jews are different, even if they feel love, jealousy and pain, are greedy or generous like everyone else. They're different, because they've been made to be different. History can't deal you one right smack in the kisser, the way it has them, without leaving a trace. You can't have been *considered a Jew* between 1939 and 1944 and not remain one for life. But I don't see why anyone should feel guilty for not having been exterminated. What matters is not to come up with arguments against anti-Semitic idiots, but rather to make good use of the extra trouble visited upon us by Divine Providence (for want of a livelier term, which it seems I have no right to use).

. . . .

You may be astonished not to encounter in my writings a vigorous critique of the State of Israel. The sins of that state qua state do not appear as clearly to me as to Vidal-Naquet.[9] I'm not a paradoxical Jew. I know how Israel was built. I didn't expect any miracles from it and I don't see how any country can harbor ill will towards Israel for being a country like any other. I *would* be surprised to find out that it isn't like every other country. The majority of the Jews who so greedily snatched up those grains of sand had no other choice. When I see right-minded people nod their heads and mumble, "It was folly for them to settle where they did," I'm sure the same folks would unreservedly approve of their taking hold of the Beauce plains, Andalusia, Yorkshire, the Ukraine with its granaries, the Carolinas, the pampas, or while we're at it, Cochin-China.

Israel is not El Dorado, my long lost homeland, my mother. I would never speak of it as Camus, Jules Roy, Emmanuel Roblès and so many others have spoken of Algeria.[10] When those who have escaped death have only one way out, when that way out is historically reasonable, when in fact it hurts no one (I'll develop that point later[11]), when it has been recognized as legal by a majority of nations, it would be madness not to take that way out. Those more fortunate Jews are despicable who, now that the storm has passed, declare out of a kind of skittish snobbery that the Israelis are not their cousins.

. . . .

When de Gaulle, in his famous press conference, called the Jews "an elite people, domineering and self-assured," he was attacked most of

9. For some examples of classical historian Pierre Vidal-Naquet's positions regarding Israel, see his *Les Juifs, la mémoire et le présent* (Paris: Maspéro, 1981).

10. Like their fellow writer Camus, Emmanuel Roblès and Jules Roy were born in Algeria.

11. All points of Frank's argumentation regarding the State of Israel are not translated here.

all for his belief in a Jewish essence.[12] But no one batted an eyelash when a week later Maurice Clavel, a well-known philo-Semite, sallied forth, spear in hand, in his column in the *Nouvel Observateur*.[13] Unabashedly, he committed an identical sin, in order to defend those in need of his patronage. Only the way he had it, Jews were not an object of envy (how ridiculous!), but of pity. Clavel was indignant: how could the general dare to treat those frightened, abject, almost revolting creatures as a bunch of tough customers? The nerve! Clavel, a little worried lest people misunderstand, quickly added that it was God's will that had made Jews that way for so long. As a Jew, what should one prefer: de Gaulle's envy or Clavel's pity? I, for one, have made up my mind.

History swept through the general's head in a mighty rush. No doubt he saw himself alternatively as Richelieu and as Louis XIV, and pushy minorities were not to stand in the way of the necessities of state. We mustn't forget that the only politician whom de Gaulle admired was Stalin. Admiring Stalin is never a good sign, whether you're Vailland,[14] de Gaulle, or some second-rate writer. In the Technicolor films that raced through the general's mind, I'm sure he more than once revoked the Edict of Nantes.

. . . .

I remember a visit from a Zionist writer, Arnold Mandel, in the rue des Saints-Pères, where I was living at the time. He came to ask some questions on behalf of a Jewish magazine, *L'Arche*. A royal pain, that Mandel, quite the cleric.[15] I imagine he suspected me of being a *camouflaged* anti-Semitic Jew; he wanted to force me out and hound me into a corner, at whatever price. He could not understand why I failed to practice the religion of my forbears and, even less, why I had never been so curious as to visit Israel. Obviously, he was unaware that I

---

12. The phrase from de Gaulle's press conference of 27 November 1967—which was actually "an elite people, self-assured and domineering" (with the epithets in that order)—is discussed in the contributions by Annette Wieviorka and Michel Abitbol to this issue of *Yale French Studies*.

13. Maurice Clavel, novelist, playwright, and journalist, was a supporter both of the Gaullist regime and of the May 1968 demonstrations against it by students and workers.

14. Roger Vailland, French writer, was a member of the communist party from 1952 to 1956.

15. A recent collection of Arnold Mandel's articles for *L'Arche* and other Jewish periodicals—*Une mélodie sans paroles ni fin: Chroniques juives* (Paris: Seuil, 1993)—presents perhaps more interest than Frank's polemics would suggest.

detest travel as much as I do hot weather and that I wasn't in the habit of feigning interest in shoe factories, wheatfields, or farming collectives. It would never occur to me to visit or inspect such marvels, even if they were just a stone's throw away and the climate far more temperate. I find Barrès's churches boring enough,[16] without having to applaud Sartre's incomparable knowledge of sugar-cane production in Cuba or Simone de Beauvoir's equally impressive familiarity with the blast furnaces of Han-k'ou. The reasons for preferring Castro's Cuba to Barrientos's Bolivia are sufficiently clear and need not be obscured or put to the test by statistics.

Mandel, at wit's end, asked if I would agree to be included in an anthology of *Jewish* writers. That was his cleverest trap.

"Gladly, if the editors would like to have me in it."

"Nonetheless, you live in France, you are French, you have no connection to Judaism, or at least you claim not to; the State of Israel bores you; no, no, don't deny it, I can tell you're infinitely more interested in Guez de Balzac than in kibbutzim"—and how right he was![17] "Isn't there some contradiction?"

"And even if there is, what difference could it possibly make?" I said, as softly as possible, for Mandel was a slight, frail man and I had no desire to see him fall out of his wicker chair, which certainly he would have, had I breathed too hard. You can't be a descendant of those Alsatian Jews with necks like butchers' and expect nothing to come of it.

My God, those clerics, what a bunch! It was simply impossible for that man to grasp that I had no need to justify myself, that such an activity was unhealthy, and that I already engaged in it quite enough. Certainly, I was rife with contradictions (as they might say in some literary manual) and eyed them as an old cat does a fresh litter of mice. I felt like saying to him, screaming to him—too bad, if this time he fell—that I didn't give a damn if a band of detectives, all too curious and naïve, wondered why I was in an anthology that didn't even exist yet, simply because I wasn't wearing the proper number of yellow stars of David on my chest. I was more interested in France than in the State of Israel, because that's the way things were. It was an old story, quite a natural one at that, and my concern alone. It hardly provided me with an alibi or a safeguard, and it was no great glory to be French in the eyes

16. See, for example, the descriptions of churches in *La Colline inspirée*, a volume appearing in 1913 by the far right-wing Maurice Barrès.

17. Jean Louis Guez de Balzac, sixteenth-century man of letters, was one of the original members of the Académie Française.

of other Frenchmen. Among Frenchmen who would ask me whether I was French, I'd no longer feel like being French. You had to choose: if people of that kind were French, I'd personally ask for a leave of absence from France. It's no accident that they note on police records whether you're French, when France is defeated and the bastards are in power. If displaying my "Jewry" saddened and exasperated so many right-thinking souls, I could never exhibit it enough.

I believe I had come to a realization. Like so many French Jews, I was Jewish in my imagination and French in reality, but for a Jew to call himself French or to assert his French identity was something redundant or vulgar. Frenchmen who boast of being French are dangerous or sick. Like the Jew who pretends to be Jewish, they too experience as part of reality something imaginary: France, or their French identity. However, what they imagine is quite hostile and can lead, under the proper circumstances, to denunciation and murder. Conversely, when you know nothing about Judaism (I won't say such ignorance is praiseworthy, but I'm as unreceptive to religion as to painting), and when you have no desire to become a citizen of Israel, pretending to be Jewish is still a good way of revealing other people's stupidity and an excellent means of combatting one's own unintelligence. Being a Jew, even if it has become a kind of lie (a harmless lie, except to oneself) enables me to take an interest in others. It constitutes my sole ethics.

—Translated by Alan Astro

PAULA JACQUES

Aunt Carlotta's Legacy
(Excerpt from a Novel)*

On Saturday, 4 September 1976, Mother received a letter from the
Home for the Elderly of Cairo, announcing the death of Carlotta Sonsino, her eldest sister.

. . . .

On letterhead from the Baladero Home for the Elderly of Cairo, the
director, Nahass Abou Nahass, regretted to inform us of the demise of
his dear resident on 9 June 1976, in her sixty-sixth year. Her death, he
further specified, occurred without excessive suffering. "Carlotta Sonsino (May God have mercy on her soul, and surely He does!) departed as
she lived, in the affectionate embrace of the President of the Jewish
Community of Cairo, and accompanied by my own high regard and the
love of her fellow residents, at her bedside in her last hour. May God
have mercy on those she has left behind! Glory to the Lord who will
renew the world and raise the dead!" The carefully handwritten letter
was composed of some ten pages, all equally optimistic. The Director
expounded on the qualities of the deceased, her piety, and her cheerful
willingness to die. He lingered over the merits of a life so complete that
nothing remained for her to do but expire, to be reborn in the assembly
of God. He described a vision of paradise which burst forth like a spring
in the yellow harshness of the desert, and enumerated the incorrupt-
ible guardians of the Gate where at last would appear the Almighty,

*Paula Jacques, L' Héritage de tante Carlotta (Paris: Mercure de France, 1987; Galli-
mard, Collection Folio), 9, 11–25.

YFS 85, Discourses of Jewish Identity in Twentieth-Century France, ed. Alan Astro,
© 1994 by Yale University.

41

who would bend down to receive the passing soul of the most excellent Carlotta.

The epistolary style of the Home's Director was already familiar to us. On a regular basis, just before the High Holy Days, Nahass Abou Nahass bombarded us with letters which mixed the sacred and the profane, Talmudic allegory with accounts of high finance. He exhorted us to "offer a check for which God gives the receipt," and implored us to make preparations for our salvation: "Bring to the Treasure House your tithes and offerings and I will open to you the gates of heaven (Mishnah, Chap. IV)." He lambasted the selfishness of the "neglectful diaspora," praised our sense of filial duty, and ended with "the detailed balance sheet, figured down to the piaster, of the residents' expenses for the year which (by the grace of God!) has just passed, and the Projected Annual Budget (quite modest indeed), which you will find enclosed."

"And Carlotta's funeral expenses?" asked Mother, "Oh, I already see it coming."

Nahass Abou Nahass promised to apprise us of the costs upon receipt of the estimate from the Ascher Funeral Home, the last one still serving the Bassantine cemetery. At the moment, he said, his desire was to share (at least in spirit) the family's pain ("What? Does he mean that the bill will be coming to us?" Mother exclaimed), and to express his own grief: with Carlotta gone, the centuries-old line of Egyptian Sonsinos was erased forever from the land in which they had lived.

Mother showed clearly that she had already realized this.

Leaving her chair, she went to stand in front of the Louis XV mirror budded with phosphorescent morels. Dreamily, she examined her features, still fresh and rosy, and stretched her wrinkles toward her temples—a gesture I knew well and which called for a contradiction. None of us uttered the least word of comfort. Annoyed, Mother assumed a theatrical stance, her palms held up to the ceiling.

"Soon it will be my turn, I feel it inside."

"Don't believe it," protested Aunt Melba. "I . . . I'll be the first to go even though I'm the youngest."

"Leave together, but do it quietly," growled Aunt Marcelle. "I'll continue with the letter. No, I'll skip some irrelevant things, and get to the postscript. Ah, look, a proposition: "Do the French relatives—that's us—desire repatriation of the dearly beloved's remains? In this case. . . . "

Aunt Marcelle stopped.

"Repatriation, does that mean return to France?" asked a frightened Aunt Fortunée.

"Where do you think, to Lapland?" retorted Aunt Marcelle angrily. "Without asking the impossible, Fortunée, I beg you to think just a little bit."

"But still, repatriation. . . . "

"Be quiet, you imbecile. One more ridiculous outburst and you leave!"

Aunt Fortunée kept quiet, but her distracted gaze showed the rebellion of an unjustly reprimanded child. She sniffed, wiping her nose on the back of her sleeve. Mother jumped up to make the others let the innocent one have her say: she who could not get a word in edgewise, so zealously did her sister defend her. Of the four Sonsino sisters, Mother was the only one who dared to confront Marcelle, the youngest, whose slight moustache shaded her upper lip.

"Will you finally stop trying to be Haman?

'C'est lui et j'en frémis ma soeur,
A sa vue mon coeur de crainte se resserre,'"[1]

recited Mother, who had a love for the classics.

"That's enough arguing," intervened Aunt Melba. "Let's think. If Abou Nahass suggests repatriation, it's to hint delicately that our Carlotta hasn't been buried yet, and won't be unless money changes hands. Cold storage, cold storage, that's what he's getting at. What calculation and scheming!"

"God help us," groaned Aunt Fortunée, restraining the beating of her formidable bosom. "In cold storage, Carlotta's delicate feet? Her sewn eyelids, on ice? But what did she finally die of?"

The Director had not seen fit to enlighten us on this point. We began to explore the possibilities: illness, accident, natural catastrophe? Our debate made clear that dying of old age was the privilege of pure souls.

"Purity is the esthetic of the innermost heart," explained Aunt Melba. "I'm serene about our Carlotta; she has no need for an advocate at the court of Last Judgment."

"I too am completely serene," sobbed Aunt Fortunée.

---

1. Camélia's mother is misquoting verses from Jean Racine's play *Esther* (1689): "C'est lui-même, et j'en frémis, ma soeur, Mon coeur de crainte et d'horreur se resserre." (Act III, Sc. 3, vv. 934–35) [It is he himself, and I tremble, my sister, My heart shrinks with fear and horror].—Trans.

"Great sorrows are mute," said Aunt Melba, and, tapping her brace-lets, she burst into tears. The jangle of gold and silver kept time with the soft cries of the Sonsino sisters, and through the open window wafted stale odors from trash cans. I felt the moment coming when the mourners would begin to scratch their cheeks and beat their breasts, and might even tear out a few hairs.

"Well, shall we go ahead with repatriation? What do you think?" I said, and obtained the desired effect. Ceasing the wringing of her hands, Mother rebelled.

"Why in the world repatriation? Why are you interfering, Camélia? Do you all hear how my daughter wags her tongue? Carlotta never set foot in France and you want to repatriate her? Don't be ridiculous!"

My aunts, with the exception of the brave Fortunée, concurred: repatriation was not appropriate! Repatriation was offensive! Repatria-tion presumed the act of repatriating! Repatriating meant having a homeland! As far as Carlotta was concerned (May she rest with the angels!), there was no native land but Egypt (May she die of white leprosy!), even if Egypt had proved herself a poor mother to her Jewish children. That was an established fact; we were not going to go over that again! It was an old story, an old injustice, one for the elderly to worry about! All told, the lamentable discrimination hardly affected more than a hundred survivors of the community, a group which at one time numbered more than eighty thousand souls. Nowhere on earth is the Jew at home. It's the will of God!

"Yes, no doubt," said Aunt Fortunée timidly, "but those who are left are so badly off. We have Paris; they have our worst nightmares. Famine, physical cruelty, children throwing rocks, adult Moslems spit-ting, torments of every sort, not to mention the worst!"

"We will not discuss it," said Aunt Marcelle, cutting her short.

We discussed it for a good dozen minutes. Imprecations fell on the heads of the Egyptians, cursing the marrow in their bones and the fresh semen in the wombs of their women. As we recalled Moslem barbar-ities, the specter of Nazism raised its head. Aunt Marcelle reminded us of the practices of Hitler and Nasser, joined in such a way that common decency prevented a more detailed description. Her diatribe against sodomites inflamed her, and the walls shook. A neighbor banged slowly on the partition, then more forcefully. Mother became fright-ened. With her mouth pressed against the brown velvet of the wall-paper, she begged the protester to calm down, respectfully offering apologies and finally promising a tomblike silence. Exile had instilled in her the humility of those who feel superfluous. This was, however, a superficial sentiment, which she exaggerated to the point of servility, and for which she took revenge surreptitiously through mockery and curses for a thousand years to come.

"Be quiet, for pity's sake," implored Mother, "or that louse is going to call the police. The bastard begrudges me even the air I breathe; he's ill-bred, a nobody, just a night watchman. During the day he sleeps above my head. May he have his last sleep!"

"May he sleep in Carlotta's place," agreed Aunt Melba. "Is he a handsome man, at least? I'm thirsty, darlings. . . . I'm burning up. . . . But wait, I smell something. . . . An odor of gas. . . . It smells of gas in here, Louna; my headache is never wrong. But gas is very dangerous, isn't it? Do you have a leak?"

"Just a little one," said Mother. "My heater is giving up the ghost, and I have to replace it. But where can I find the money? You get used to it; I keep the window open."

"Then you can't replace it?" asked Aunt Melba in a mocking tone.

"I can't! But is it any of your business? Let's talk about Carlotta."

"Let's speak softly," said Aunt Melba. "Let the living commune with the dead. I don't feel at all well. If only she had agreed to die in our arms. If only she hadn't insisted on settling in over there. Why, why, Lord, does the stubborn mussel cling to the bare rock?"

"She couldn't leave," moaned Aunt Fortunée. She rolled her thoughtful, gentle eyes. "Cairo, that was her life, her city, her calling."

"What can you know about callings, poor Fortunée?" retorted Mother, shrugging her shoulders. "Carlotta's calling was to love Arabs, natives, fez-wearers."

"How could that be?" asked Aunt Melba "ARABS. . . ! As for me, even if they paid me my weight in gold, I. . . . "

"Someone paid you?" sneered Aunt Marcelle. "He must have been blind."

"What, what?" protested Aunt Melba. "Do I embellish the truth, invent things, make up stories to brag about? Me?" She was choking with indignation. "Look, just the other day, a Lebanese man came into the store, to buy some perfume for his wife. He took a gander, noticed me, and forgot the gift he came for; I slew him with my charms. He refused to leave unless I let him whisper sweet nothings in my ear. Ah, if only he were free! He was free, for the evening. He invited me to tour Paris in a river boat, then to dine at the Café de la Paix. My dear sisters, believe me or not, as you see fit: I paid him no heed; gave him no smile except a professional one. I threw him out. 'Go home to your wife!,' I said. I did this with no regrets; that's the way I am. Sensible, reserved, shy. And yet nowadays men are like movie stars: you can't get near them! But all that's over for me; I've given up. I don't want to turn heads anymore. Starting tomorrow, it's only herb tea for me. I'll be fifty-five, and. . . . "

"You mean a good sixty," said Aunt Marcelle. "Every birthday Melba gets ten years younger; soon it'll be time for bibs and kindergarten. But we're getting off the subject. We're supposed to be discussing Carlotta."

"Wait a minute, excuse me," cried Aunt Melba. "I'm turning fifty-five tomorrow, why would I lie? Me, I'm not Carlotta, I'm not man-crazy!"

"Carlotta was crazy," conceded Aunt Fortunée, "but not about men. Crazy about Cairo, I'd say. There's quite a difference."

"Poor dear Carlotta," said Aunt Marcelle. "I don't mean to speak ill of the dead, but throughout her lifetime she loved gloom. Prefer Cairo to Paris? That's insane! Is there anything more beautiful than sunlight dancing on the Loire?"

"The Loire? You, Marcelle, you know about the Loire?" scoffed Mother. "You sing the praises of France? A dinner party where the host and the guests are both absent, that's France for you. As for the Parisians, may God rip out their souls through their tongues. Have you forgotten Marcelle? Have you forgotten that in Paris a stateless person is worth less than nothing, and that anything is worth more than a stateless person? For me, the wound is still fresh. Every time I have to renew my residence permit, I bleed. The last time, the clerk at the Aliens' Bureau (May God make him alien to his own mother!) addressed me so rudely; you can't imagine what it was like. . . . "

"What, what?" asked Aunt Fortunée worriedly. "Were his intentions less than honorable?"

"What intentions? It was a full-scale assault. He spoke to me as if I were black. Using familiar language, his nose all wrinkled up, his finger pointing like a machine gun; he treated me worse than a wild animal. And yet I was stylishly dressed, with my grey suit and my blue fox."

"That's no longer in fashion," said Aunt Melba. "Furriers pay you to buy them. No, I myself would really like a small ocelot, cut. . . . "

"You must understand," interrupted Mother. "The wife of Gaspard Belrespiro, treated as if she were the straw that broke the camel's back, no better than a maid. I, who used to command a regiment of servants and. . . . "

"Prejudice once again, Mother; that's racism, I think. Let's get back to Aunt Carlotta."

"What about you? Whose daughter are you," grumbled Mother, "the offspring of a giraffe and an elephant? You make me ashamed, Camélia, calling your own mother a racist—me, who sacrificed so much to bring you up, who. . . . "

"Enough," said Aunt Melba. "Are we at a colloquium on racism? We're talking about Carlotta."

"Carlotta, do you hear us, dear?" sighed Aunt Fortunée. "May the dust of your ears be poured into mine and may you be able to hear once again. I'll give up my life. What life? I'll give up my death for Carlotta. Why aren't you by my side, oh voyager in the infinite? Come into my house, come into my heart. But that's impossible. Carlotta had no warm feelings for France. She didn't want to leave Egypt. She didn't want to be deported to the land of no return!"

"It was an obsession," conceded Aunt Marcelle. "Frankly, it was the only one the poor woman ever followed through with."

"Don't treat her like an idiot," wailed Aunt Fortunée. "She's dead!"

"Who mentioned idiocy?" bellowed Aunt Marcelle. "But it's true that you could search for a long time, and among Carlotta's great qualities you'd find everything except intelligence."

"What would you find?" asked Aunt Melba absent-mindedly.

"Faithfulness," said Aunt Marcelle.

"Faithfulness to the country of Father and Mother, of Grandfather and Grandmother, of. . . . "

"Please, Fortunée, don't go all the way back to the Inquisition," said Mother. "I warn you, I have nothing to serve you for dinner. Faithfulness? Nonsense! Mental retardation, I'd say, and quite a serious case. That explains Carlotta's behavior."

"You're exaggerating, Louna," said Aunt Melba. "Why this abuse all of a sudden? Let's say that Carlotta had the herd instinct, like a sheep held in a pen. Did you know, Camélia, that your aunt couldn't stand even the thought of taking the train from Cairo to Alexandria?"

"How many times did we beg her to join us?" added Aunt Marcelle. "To enjoy the warmth of our homes, to share our humble fare? How many times? Ah, I can't go on; I can't keep track of all the selfless efforts we made, I can't do it!"

"She was deaf as a post," Mother went on, "and if you want my opinion, our poor departed was quite stupid, a very common person, with a pea-sized brain, no concern for her own welfare, and no savings to get her through the ravages of old age. That's just not done!"

"Don't throw out any more garbage, Mother, the courtyard is already full."

"What courtyard? . . . Oh, yes, now I get what you mean . . . that's a French expression. It's very good of you to take up your aunt's defense, but I know what I'm talking about. Carlotta had about as much common sense as that chair you're sitting in—and stop rocking, you'll break it, and who will pay to have it fixed?"

"How many times did we offer Carlotta room and board here in Paris?" continued Aunt Marcelle. "And now this little girl criticizes us! But go on, Camélia, make us feel remorse. You're dying to do it, we can see that in your frozen face. Louna, the way your daughter turned out so quiet, you'd have to say she isn't your daughter; she doesn't have your sharp tongue. Go on, Camélia, speak, tell us what you think you know about your Aunt Carlotta."

"Well . . . she was your sister, after all, not mine."

I had always suspected that my Egyptian aunt was afraid of trading her residence in an old folks' home for a place in Paris, where her life would have been even more miserable—if you could believe the picture the Sonsino sisters painted of it. Their letters told of exaggerated tortures and perpetual hardships; in short, of an existence that would have brought tears to the eyes of a condemned man. With some allowance made for hyperbole, it was true that our family was not rolling in money. Aunt Fortunée worked at home as a seamstress for a wholesaler in the Sentier garment district while Aunt Melba was employed in a specialty perfume shop in the Place de l'Opéra, in the duty-free section for tourists. For fifteen years Mother had been an assistant accountant with Madame Chocolat, a subcontractor for an automobile firm, who exploited her shamelessly, all the while showing her "special fondness and consideration," as Mother put it. On the other hand, Aunt Marcelle, in our eyes, embodied a type of success. She ran a laundromat in the Barbès quarter; though poor, the people there had a sense of hygiene, thank goodness; processing their dirty clothes brought Aunt Marcelle an apartment spacious enough to accommodate the eldest sister. But Aunt Marcelle refused to feed an extra mouth, "especially since the mouth in question does not come with eyes," she used to say. Indeed, the thought of Carlotta pacing up and down the corridors of the subway or showing up at the Aliens' Bureau was utterly ridiculous; she would not have been able to find her way around, much less to spell her own name. The fact is that my Aunt Carlotta did not know how to read or write. The alphabet was a mystery to her; moreover, ever since adolescence she had felt no need to write because the use of her body had made learning and a regular livelihood unnecessary.

Let us now praise this remarkable woman.

Aunt Carlotta enjoyed the notoriety of being "the youngest Egyptian dancer in Cairo." At an age when her sisters were still playing with dolls, she plied her trade in a nightclub of rather ill repute, and yet the cosmopolitan and fashionable clientele of that time flocked to applaud the "Jewess with the Arab navel." Needless to say, the Sonsino sisters rarely ventured there. Carlotta besmirched their name; her hypnotic performances would have sullied the reputation of any family. Ours observed a modest silence regarding "the great indiscretions of that shameless woman," who did not even have the decency to pick out a pseudonym. Carlotta's name was displayed in large letters on the walls of Cairo, when she made her first film with the famous singer Gamal Gamil. Her affair with the producer Rachid ("An Arab who isn't even Christian!" growled Mother) virtually filled the papers. Not a day passed without the radio's mentioning Carlotta, or the gossip columnists' inventorying her assets, her clothing, her lovers, and—wonder of wonders—the hundred mirrors that lined the walls of her Moorish villa. Every day, people came to enjoy the cool air of the Nile around that beautiful home, in the hope of catching a glimpse of Carlotta, Carlotta's butler, Carlotta's dog. The Sonsino sisters could have put up with the dancer's glory—after all, no one can be blamed for success and such a considerable fortune—but then Carlotta refused reconciliation. She sent her little sisters, and their acquired bourgeois respectability, back to their own kind, and seemed afterwards to take even greater pleasure in defying convention. She flaunted her passion for money and for furs ("A bit too much for the climate," grumbled Mother), as well as her lover of the day, of the day before, and of the day after. Her sisters, novices in affairs of the heart, no doubt credited her with twice as many lovers as she really had. It was true, however, that quite a few men of both noble and common birth declared themselves willing to kill each other for this cruel woman. The dethroned monarch of the Kingdom of Albania—a certain Zog the First, who in the Ashkenazic quarter was colloquially called "The Sock King" ('zog' in Yiddish des-

ignating the part between the ankle and the heel)—was politely dismissed, in spite of the jewels he laid at her door. King Farouk, fed up
with hopeful expectation, dispatched his henchmen to the back door of
the cabaret; it was said that they kidnaped the dancer and drove her to
Abdine Palace, where she remained a prisoner for an entire night. It
should be pointed out that her art and her beauty won her songs and
ballads which she would have been at quite a loss to figure out. Roger
Vailland, passing through Cairo, was supposedly inspired by Aunt Carlotta to create the heroine of his *L'Orgie,* while rumor had it that Jean
Cocteau dedicated to her his famous quatrain:

> Quand ton corps d'Orient tu déploies,
> Comme ample éventail de fine soie,
> Dans la nuit des nuits d'après-minuit,
> Ta lune, ô statue, est un soleil qui luit.[2]

—Translated by Michael T. Ward

2. "When you unfold your Oriental body, Like a broad fan of fine silk, In the night of
nights after midnight, Your moon, oh statue, is a shining sun."

SALIM JAY

A Star is Worn*

The writer Emmanuel Berl, a friend of Proust's, of Drieu La Rochelle's and Malraux's, who in the first weeks of the Vichy régime wrote speeches for Pétain, noted in 1968 that the government of his former employer

> inscribed [his] name upon a list that . . . made [him] part of a community distinct from the community of Frenchmen. That was a source of great difficulty hardly compensated for by the yellow medal that was handed out.[1]

That medal—the yellow star of David—was to have been worn by my mother's mother, Gabrielle Moscovici, born to Rumanian parents, and brought up in Paris, where the fortune her father had made allowed her to live on the Place du Palais-Royal. Her brilliant social relations led her to join not just any Resistance network, but one called "The Honor of the Police"—an honor quite necessary to safeguard, since all too often members of the Parisian police arrested Jews for the Gestapo.

In place of the yellow star intended for my grandmother by the Nazis and their collaborators, she was posthumously awarded by the French Republic a piece of parchment proclaiming officially that she had "died for France." She probably never imagined her grandson would be named Salim Jay. That would have occurred to my other grandmother, whose son was to be the national poet of Morocco. You

---

*Salim Jay, "Une étoile est portée," text written especially for this issue of *Yale French Studies*.

1. Emmanuel Berl, *Nasser tel qu'on le loue* (Paris: Gallimard, collection Idées, 1968), 12. [All translations here are my own, unless otherwise indicated.—Trans.]

YFS 85, *Discourses of Jewish Identity in Twentieth-Century France*, ed. Alan Astro, © 1994 by Yale University.

can read all about that in my *Portrait du géniteur en poète officiel.* For example, there you'll learn that my mother was quite happy to live in Morocco, where "no one ever wore the yellow star. It's a detail that, all things considered, could make the sky even bluer. . . ."[2]

I am not the only French writer to mention the yellow star in his or her work. Naïvely having asked, since my tenderest years, of literature that it teach me how to live, I trusted it as well to demonstrate if not its sanctity, then at least its lack of complicity with crimes against humanity. My expectation has not always been met.

It was not only my ability to see myself in any book, but also my parents' divergent backgrounds, that led me to identify with the Proustian narrator's friend Bloch, when Swann found he resembled the portrait of Mahomet II by Bellini.[3] Did my friend Bernard Frank resemble that ruler as well? The rulers of Saudi Arabia, had they taken a look, might not have refused him a visa; and the French diplomat he was to accompany might not have felt strangely obligated to go along with his hosts' ostracism. But it is truly an ill wind that blows no good. If not for all that, I might not have been convinced that repairing this injustice demanded that someone with a Moslem name—mine in fact—write the first monograph on Bernard's work.[4]

That incident, which France refused to raise to the level of a diplomatic one, met with the reprobation of my Swedish friend Claude Kayat, the author of *Mohammed Cohen.* Like his protagonist, Claude is the fruit of a union between a Moslem woman and a Jewish man. Born in Tunisia, he lived in Israel before residing for the last twenty-three years in Stockholm. His hero's lamentation is at one with mine:

> "It revolts you from both sides?" he inquired with an equivocal
> smirk normally reserved, no doubt, for victims of advanced
> schizophrenia. "Both sides, precisely," I replied, without a trace of
> humor. "Such a waste of life for nothing makes you want to
> vomit. . . ."[5]

Of course, this was before the recent handshake between Arafat and Rabin, which makes me hope that the Mid-East will live as happily "as

2. Salim Jay, *Portrait du géniteur en poète officiel* (Paris: Denoël, 1985), 44.

3. Marcel Proust, *Du côté de chez Swann,* ed. Antoine Compagnon (Paris: Gallimard, collection Folio, 1988), 96.

4. Jay, *Bernard Frank* (Paris: Rupture, 1982). [See the translation in this issue of *Yale French Studies* of excerpts from Frank's *Un siècle débordé.*—Trans.]

5. Claude Kayat, *Mohammed Cohen: The Adventures of an Arabian Jew,* trans. from the French by Patricia Wolf (New York: Bergh, 1989), 196.

God in France," as they say in Yiddish and German. (My father had me take German as a foreign language at the French lycée in Rabat, because of his admiration for Einstein and Werner von Braun; the language of those scientists' second home was to be my twin brother's domain, which is why this essay has to be translated.)

My mother often told me how much she liked glimpsing, from the window of her family's apartment on the Place du Palais-Royal, their prestigious neighbor, the writer Colette. In memoirs translated as *The Evening Star*, the author of *The Pure and the Impure* describes the shock provoked by the arrest of her husband, Maurice Goudeket, who was Jewish. She managed to have him freed after seven weeks of detention at the Compiègne internment camp:

> A ring at the bell still afflicts me, to a lesser degree, with nervous shock, a twitch of the mouth and the corner of the eye, of the shoulder raised to the ear. Will one never get over it? Yet many women who suffered the same experience at the same time change so as to obliterate these reflexes. . . . But I . . . I'm too old to get over it.[6]

What happened to me, as a citizen, a reader, a walker, is that I have not managed to accept, placidly, that I was too young to know those terrible times. The desire neither to deny nor minimize that terror has given it a sense of reality that is the vitiated form of my notion of time and space. The yellow star has become the totem of my quarrel with the world, the motif of my mistrust, the cause of my disillusionment.

The obsession sometimes recedes, when I read about an attempt to save a Jewish life. Colette speaks of her husband, an "Israelite who is dear to me,"[7] whom a poor woman in the neighborhood offered to save if the Germans came for him:

> Run to my room, it's not bolted, and go on, hurry, don't be ashamed, snuggle up with me in my bed! You can be sure they won't think of looking for you there! [24]

I imagine snuggling in that bed intended for my mother's neighbor's husband. It's a rather regressive identification, considering it would demand my having left her womb not three months before term (which was the case), but rather nine years and six months pre-

6. Colette, *The Evening Star: Recollections*, trans. David Le Vay (Indianapolis: Bobbs-Merrill, 1973), 19–20 (ellipses in the original).

7. Colette, 24, modified as per the original: *L'Etoile Vesper: Mémoires* (Geneva: Milieu du Monde, 1946), 30.

maturely. However, I am almost delighted by my polymorphous obsession with the time when there were, as Henri Amouroux put it, "forty
million Pétainists," without an equally great number of Gaullists, out
of a population of far fewer than fifty million.[8]

The exclusion of Jews from the community of France was one of the
ways Marshal Pétain gave his country "the gift of [his] person," as he
declared on 17 June 1940. The violence of Pétain's words is made clear
by psychoanalyst Gérard Miller, quoting Lacan: " 'I give myself to you,'
says the patient, 'but that "gift of my person"—as the other fellow
said—mysteriously turns into an offer of shit.' "[9]

Wearing the star, the poet Max Jacob made a kinder offer to others,
before his death in a French internment camp in 1944. One of his last
prose poems was called "Amour du prochain" [Love of One's Fellow
Man], an expression that, in Jacob's writing, is certainly no antiphrasis.
The mocking tone reflects the elegance of despair, a desire to give the
reader the most exact idea possible of the station of hell to which this
lover of his fellows has been brought. Now he must envy a toad that
passes unremarked. Previously, no one had noticed him on the street
either: "Now children make fun of my yellow star. Happy toad! You
don't have the yellow star."[10]

The cruelty of children is recalled in Annette Muller's account of
the reaction that greeted her at school after her release from a French
internment camp:

> They placed themselves in a circle around me and pointed to my
> shaven head and my star. I heard them laughing and making fun.
>
> In despair, I felt myself beginning to pee. I couldn't hold it back.
> The warm liquid flowed down my thin legs and spread out in a
> puddle on the ground.
>
> That caused my classmates' joy to redouble, as they chanted "The
> Jew-girl peed in her pants."[11]

In *La Dispersion*, novelist Serge Doubrovsky speaks of schoolmates
who reacted differently, "those to the right, those to the left, who have

8. Henri Amouroux, *Quarante millions de pétainistes* (Paris: Robert Laffont,
1977).
9. Quoted in Gérard Miller, *Les Pousse-au-jouir du maréchal Pétain* (Paris: Livre
de Poche, 1988 [orig. ed. Seuil, 1975]), 220.
10. Max Jacob, "Amour du prochain" in Jacques Eladan, ed., *Poètes juifs de langue
française* (Paris: Noël Blandin, 1992), 99.
11. Annette Muller, *La Petite Fille du Vel' d'Hiv'* (Paris: Denoël, 1991), 111.

eyes not to see, who have washed the stigma off me, gotten it off my chest."[12]

In "Histoire ancienne: Sigrand et Sip'tit," Jacques Lederer recounts the experience of a seven-year-old, acutely aware of danger:

> On the corner of the rue Saint-Paul, there was a urinal that I used as a changing-room. In the blink of an eye, I pulled my sweater off and rolled it up into my schoolbag. The star lay there, curled up in its wool, a wakeful nightmare awaiting its moment.[13]

Another school scene: in *Un Sac de billes*, Joseph Joffo tells how he ripped his star off his shirt when a classmate asked him to trade it for a bag of marbles. His novel is an epic account of the kind of *débrouillardise* [resourcefulness] we French pride ourselves on. As Fred Kupferman remarks in his preface to Joffo's novel: "At the age when a schoolboy learns his lessons, a Jewish child learns to survive."[14]

Not only the *système-D* ["the D-system," with a *d* for *débrouillardise*], but also the pranks of the *poulbot* [a streetwise Parisian youngster], show just how French these children were, who were marked as different from others their age. Henri Szwarc is a witness who does not fear showing himself in a bad light in order to recreate the past accurately. He recalls the "horrible times," to which corresponded "horrible games":

> We invented one called "The Persecuted Jew." My friends pretended to beat me up in the street, and when someone tried to intervene, I would tell him to mind his own business, and to get out of the way. . . . The best outcome was when this person who had tried to defend a Jew ended up calling me "a dirty kike." We soon stopped playing this game. . . .[15]

Szwarc's game [*jeu*] corresponds to the double-crossing [*double jeu*] that the Nazis and their collaborators engaged in, as imagined by Simone Veil, former president of the European Parliament, herself an Auschwitz survivor:

> How can we explain that some Jews wearing the star were able to stay in Paris until the Liberation? Was there an attempt to deceive

12. Serge Doubrovsky, *La Dispersion* (Paris: Mercure de France, 1969), 222.

13. Jacques Lederer, "Histoire ancienne: Sigrand et Sip'tit," *Les Temps Modernes* 551 (June 1992): 5.

14. Fred Kupferman, "Postface" to Joseph Joffo, *Un Sac de billes* (Paris: Livre de Poche, 1982 [orig. ed. J.-C. Lattès, 1973]), 379.

15. Henri Szwarc, "Souvenirs: L'Etoile jaune," *Annales: Economies, Sociétés, Civilisations* 48 (May–June 1993): 631.

the general population as well as the Jews into believing that as long
as the latter followed the rules they had nothing to fear?[16]

"At the end of July 1944," writes Szwarc, "I was finally able to
remove my star" (633). Only five months earlier, Szwarc's mother was
arrested and deported to Auschwitz. She survived, unlike Annette
Muller's mother:

> "Stand up straight. Keep your posture," murmured Mother. Her
> arrogant gaze seemed to defy those who looked upon us in silence.
> She wanted to show everyone a young Jewish mother proud of her
> four Jewish children. . . .
> Wouldn't it have been better for her to throw the stars in the
> garbage and flee as far as she could with her children? A few months
> later, she was dead. She would have soon turned thirty-four years old.
> [75–76]

On 15 July 1942, one day before Annette Muller, her mother, and her
sister were arrested by the Parisian police, Léon Werth made this entry
in his diary:

> The Christians in Paris who for a few hours wore the Jewish insignia
> as a sign of protest and defiance felt humiliated by this obligation
> imposed upon Jews, all the more so than had they been Jews. Thus
> they spared themselves a personal humiliation.[17]

In 1943, in *Le Petit Prince*, Antoine de Saint-Exupéry apologized for
dedicating this children's book to Léon Werth, an adult, but explained:
"This grown-up lives in France where he is hungry and cold. He needs
to be consoled."[18]

Jean Cocteau had offered consolation of a different sort to the Jews,
as Galtier-Boissière records in the 12 June 1942 entry to his *Journal de
l'Occupation*:

> Dinner at Mademoiselle Valentin's bistrot, with my usual crowd,
> plus Auric who told a nice anecdote about Cocteau, to whom a Jew
> had bemoaned being forced to wear the yellow star:

16. Simone Veil, "Réflexions d'un témoin," *Annales: Economies, Sociétés, Civilisations* 48 (May–June 1993): 693.
17. Léon Werth, *La Déposition* (Paris: Grasset, 1946), 238; volume republished with different pagination (Paris: Viviane Hamy, 1992).
18. Antoine de Saint-Exupéry, *The Little Prince*, trans. Katherine Woods (New York: Harcourt Brace Jovanovich, 1971 [orig. ed. 1943]), modified as per the original: *Le Petit Prince* in Saint-Exupéry, *Oeuvres* (Paris: Gallimard, Bibliothèque de la Pléiade, 1959), 407.

"Console yourself," said Jean. "After the war, you'll have us wear false noses."[19]

But after the war, the Jews didn't stop wearing their stars. "The yellow star is one of those that are not extinguished when day arrives," as we read on the back cover of Serge Doubrovsky's *La Dispersion*. "All of sudden, that stigma sewn on last night, worn since this morning, instead of burning, has started to shine" (208). Jews and non-Jews are not only under different stars, "we no longer inhabit the same planet: France, capital Drancy" (222). Not the spa of Vichy, but the Parisian suburb of Drancy, where Jews were held before being sent to Auschwitz.

But now that France's capital is once again Paris, Prime Minister Edmond Balladur has declared that not just Jews, but all France should be consoled for the yellow star: "France remains inconsolable over this terrible drama," he proclaimed fifty-one years to the day after Annette Muller and her mother and brothers were arrested.[20] Is France inconsolable—or ashamed? As early as 1943, the writer and resistant Vercors was not afraid to admit such things. His narrator recounts meeting an old man with a star, whom he had known before the war:

> I lacked the courage necessary to confront the endless disgrace, those flags, those posters, those newspapers, and, later on, those stars. . . .
> On a fine June morning, one of those came towards me. As always, I turned red (not once have I been able to come across one of those without turning red).[21]

The wearer of the star was a francophile from central Europe who did not believe his adopted country could betray him. In *Autobiographie de mon père*, my friend Pierre Pachet recounts the attitude of another immigrant, also a lover of France, but a more lucid one: his father, whose voice he takes on. "Little by little, France revealed the face I always feared might appear: frivolous, passionate, xenophobic."[22] He knows he must never

> forget those Gothic letters awarded by Hitler; their complicated, threatening form; above all, that monstrous writing: the word JUDE, embroidered or painted on the yellow stars. Those letters were in

19. Jean Galtier-Boissière, *Journal de l'Occupation* in *Journal 1940–1950* (Paris: Quai Voltaire, 1992), 104; orig. ed.: *Mon Journal pendant l'Occupation* (Garas: La Jeune Parque, 1944), 136.
20. *Le Monde* (18–19 July 1993): 6.
21. Vercors, *La Marche à l'étoile* (Paris: Minuit, 1946 [orig. ed. 1943]), 71.
22. Pierre Pachet, *Autobiographie de mon père* (Paris: Belin, 1987), 48.

Gothic style, but their hateful, pseudo-medieval contortions were meant to evoke the traditional form of our Hebrew letters. [98]

Whereupon Pachet offers this subtle analysis of the exclusionary function of the yellow star:

The insane marriage that Nazism rendered nearly indissoluble between our death and its power was figured in those ambiguous characters. On the one hand, they brought forth among the conquered peoples a healthy sense of terror in the face of Germanic barbarism . . . ; on the other, by designating a preferential victim, already trapped by these letters that seemed to twist in a painful fire, they reassured the Aryans by promising them protection and peace. . . . [98]

By the age of fourteen, I had already found a yellow star in the work of a writer who would someday be a friend of mine. I was reading the first enormous volume of my career as a bibliomaniac: Jacques Borel's *L'Adoration*, which had won the 1965 Goncourt Prize. The narrator, a figure for the author, was hardly three years older than I at the time that he was bringing back to life:

I remembered well the first Jews with the yellow star. . . . , that old man in a black hat who was walking along the curb just before the corner of the rue de Sévigné. . . . My mother and I were squeezing against each other, saying nothing, wondering whether we should avert our glance from that man . . . , lest he think we had set him apart from others . . . , or whether we should on the contrary address a timid or tearful smile to him: we didn't know whether it would hurt or, perhaps, comfort him for an instant.[23]

Borel does not content himself with recounting the unease felt by his mother and himself, which made them move closer to one another; he also bears witness to the feelings of those around them:

We seemed to detect, emanating from other passersby, the same feeling that had overcome us simultaneously; pity, indeed; and a kind of embarrassed tenderness; but also, perhaps, at the same time, an undefinable doubt, an unavowable desire to recoil. [447]

They recoiled in order to protect themselves from contamination, fear, the reality of the violence. Borel recounts that the violence did not really dawn on him until

the day, long after, when a Jewish girlfriend I cared greatly for told me, as we passed in front of the Saint-Sulpice Church, that it was the

23. Jacques Borel, *L'Adoration* (Paris: Gallimard, 1965), 446–47.

first church she had ever entered: it was in 1942, she wore the yellow
star on her pea-jacket, and she prayed there. [448]

The young man whose feelings are being explored was a sixteen- or
seventeen-year-old student whose mother worshiped him. The Jewish
girlfriend entering a church to pray could have been his schoolmate,
but a hounded one:

> She was my age, and while I was playing the big shot at the Lycée
> Henri IV—feeling up my cousin Paulette and trying to convince
> Geneviève that I loved her and that she should be my mistress—she
> packed and hastily repacked her bags at night, with her mother and
> her sisters, looking for another precarious shelter in which to catch
> their breath. As others have staircase wit, I had staircase suffering,
> staircase stupor, or staircase remorse. [448]

Twenty-eight years after the publication of *L'Adoration*, this remorse returns in *Le Déferlement*. Borel explained to me how he invented this monologue by a Jewish poet:

> An act of love and compassion for the Jewish victims of
> persecutions, pogroms, and death camps—that's how I conceived *Le
> Déferlement*, dedicated to one of my closest friends, the Jewish poet
> Pierre Morhange.[24]

B., who represents the author of *Le Déferlement*, listens to his
friend Joseph Saverne, a professor of philosophy and a poet, like Morhange. B. thus becomes the "twin mirror" of the Jewish poet in whose
"body, voice, heart and soul" Borel says he wished to enter. Saverne
plunges with painful irony into his friend's past, as he refers to himself
in the third person:

> So that neighborhood of yours, that parish—eh?—Saint Paul, was
> crawling with yellow stars . . . . You would have thrown yourself at
> Saverne, would you? I know full well you didn't know his poems yet.
> Would you have even shaken his hand, had you come across him
> with his yellow star on his lapel, as he walked on the rue Saint-
> Antoine . . . ?[25]

That handshake cannot be taken for granted, as we know from the
passage from *L'Adoration*. Remorse has thus given us a book that recreates some of the forceful [*déferlant*] black humor of Pierre Morhange
(1901–1973), who was alternately a mordant ironist and a bard with a

24. Personal interview, summer 1993.
25. Borel, *Le Déferlement* (Paris: Gallimard, 1993), 168–69.

scalpel-like precision. Morhange must be reread, lest his particular quality go unremarked amidst the vast poetic production on the humiliation of France at the hands of the Nazis and their collaborators. Let us simply quote his poem entitled "Juif" [Jew] from the 1966 volume *Le Sentiment lui-même:*

> J'ai vu mon visage
> L'étoile d'un miroir brisé
> J'ai serré ma poitrine
> Dans mes bras solitaires
> J'ai serré dans mon coeur détesté
> Le diamant de la justice.
> [in Eladan, 183]

> I saw my face
> The star of a broken mirror
> I squeezed my chest
> In my solitary arms
> I squeezed in my detested heart
> The diamond of justice.

How can one remember the diamond of justice? That's the question Elisabeth Gille invites us to consider in her book about her mother, the novelist Irène Nemirovsky. It takes the form of memoirs she imagines Nemirovsky having composed, before her arrest on 13 July 1942 and deportation to Auschwitz four days later. "According to a German encyclopedia," this French writer who was a Russian Jew died a month after arriving at Auschwitz.[26]

Gille, who was five years old in 1942, portrays her mother and older sister:

> Denise, sitting on the ground next to me, in her black pinafore that makes her yellow star stand out, memorizes her lesson:

> France, mère des arts, des armes, des lois
> Tu m'as nourri longtemps du lait de ta mamelle.
> Ores, comme un agneau qui sa nourrice appelle
> Je remplis de ton nom les antres et les bois. [227–28]

> France, mother of arts, arms, and laws
> Thou hast long nourished me with the milk of thy breast.
> Now like a lamb who calls for its nurse
> I fill the caves and the woods with thy name.

26. Elisabeth Gille, *Le Mirador: Mémoires rêvés* (Paris: Presses de la Renaissance, 1992), 265.

Nemirovsky was betrayed by those she befriended and the country she loved, all the more so as she moved in a "brilliant" milieu, where men and women of letters rubbed elbows with politicians. Thus Joseph Caillaux, head of the Senate's Commission on Finances, sent her a copy of his memoirs with a warm dedication. In its pages, she could read such words as these: "In general terms, the Jew, in whatever sphere he operates, carries within him a taste for destruction, a thirst for domination, the appetite for a precise or vague ideal . . . " (quoted in Gille, 228).

During the Occupation, anti-Semitism found expression among progressives and moderates as well as ultras. But the honor of poets was safeguarded by some, as we see in *La Patrie se fait tous les jours: Textes français 1939–1945*, edited by Jean Paulhan and Dominique Aury. They include these lines from Max Jacob:

On a vu de partout l'étoile des Rois mages
laisser tomber du sang comme tombe un orage.
A jamais, cette main, la mienne, en est tachée
et par deuil, sauf de Dieu, de tout bien détachée.[27]

We have seen from everywhere the star of the Magi
Letting blood fall as a storm falls.
Forever, this hand, mine, bears the stain
And by mourning, from all goods but God detached.

—Translated by Alan Astro

27. Jacob, "Reportage juin 1940" in Jean Paulhan and Dominique Aury, ed., *La Patrie se fait tous les jours: Textes français 1939–1945* (Paris: Minuit, 1947), 85.

GUSTAVE KAHN

One Yom Kippur*

For a long time, Slimsohn had been saving considerable time and money on food. He had started by limiting himself to just one meal a day, towards evening, then delaying it until that undefinable moment when a snack of coffee and a croissant can take the place of dinner, if at that solemn moment when soup is normally served one is careful to think about something else. Thus for several months, the content and duration of Slimsohn's dinner and his breakfast were exactly alike. That balance was upset when it suddenly dawned on Slimsohn that he couldn't pay the rent on his garret at the end of the month. He was fond of his garret, although not because of its furnishings, which consisted of the thin seaweed-stuffed mattress and bolster he used to separate his dreams from the tile floor of his lodgings. His rented recess spread out oddly under one corner of a roof where the architect had daringly married a cupola with a pagoda. When this headgear was placed atop the tenement building, the architect, together with the owner, gazed from across the street and decided it didn't look so bad after all. They might have to make a few monetary concessions, though, in renting some of the garrets, since these were lopsided, low at the door, higher under the gutters, with no more than a small oval window. The walls sloped. Near the door a square chimney-shaft rose, but ironically, the unbroken wall left no opening for a fireplace or grate. On certain wintry days, however, Slimsohn would receive a few gusts of tepid air in his hovel, in much the same way he might have heard the faint echo of a

*Gustave Kahn, "Un jour de Kippour," in Contes juifs (Paris: Grasset-Fasquelle, 1977 [orig. ed. 1925]), 127–36.

YFS 85, Discourses of Jewish Identity in Twentieth-Century France, ed. Alan Astro, © 1994 by Yale University.

confidential conversation whispered on the ground floor. In this horn of poverty, Slimsohn had a few books he wouldn't have parted with even under the worst of circumstances. But that would have been utopian, so great was the weariness they exhaled from their broken bindings.

Slimsohn's poverty was not the fruit of his indolence. He was a hard worker, but he had chosen his career without giving any thought to material considerations. Just as a ten-centime coin dropped into the slot of a vending machine brings forth a token or candy, a question about an erudite trifle placed into Slimsohn's ear would yield a long, precise, detailed answer from his mouth. But who needs erudition in this world? Every morning the newspapers furnish factual errors so contradictory on all subjects and in such numbers that they seem like mere nuances of opinion to be chosen at will. Slimsohn had no market for his products. So he did without his roll for breakfast, and the balance between his two little meals was broken.

Newspapers couldn't have recourse to his superior knowledge. The alphabetically arranged errors in encyclopedias supplied enough background for their reporters. As far as magazines were concerned, Slimsohn had wisely snubbed them. In magazine offices they're more sympathetic towards shiny hats or multicolored jackets, less exacting when a question required handling a book or two. The editors there preferred a footnote or a little article for which the wage was equivalent to that paid to a fashion-house apprentice.

But at the precise moment when Slimsohn had succeeded in publishing a long article on Cossack messianism during the Middle Ages in the scholarly review, *Danube et Volga*, Duger, the editor, stopped paying cash and started paying by draft. The banks hadn't yet equated these two instruments. With every effort to cash Duger's note, which Slimsohn kept inside the moleskin holes he used for a wallet, it bore a greater resemblance to a wrinkled railroad ticket to La Châtre.

As ill-suited as Slimsohn was for any financial considerations except those having to do with historical deeds, he realized the weakness of this claim to universal exchange. But hunger calls for bold moves. At one point in Slimsohn's quest, the owner of the local café referred him to a wine merchant, who sent him to a liquor dealer, each one eager not to endorse the note, but careful to conclude their discussion with this polite petitioner by giving him some more or less chimerical information or superfluous recommendation. Which is what led Slimsohn to Charley Dicky, maker of bicycle bearings.

Slimsohn found Charley Dicky in his office, two meters square set off from the store by a glass partition. Dicky was alone. He had already read the morning newspapers. It was eleven-thirty.

His correspondence was finished because, having only received demands from creditors, he found it pointless to respond. His mood was composed, even cordial, since he hadn't yet exhausted a small profit gleaned at the races the previous Sunday. No clients had come to see him, so Slimsohn's arrival made it seem as though he had a visit. As soon as he saw Slimsohn's frizzy hair and noble, aquiline nose, he remembered that he, Charley Dicky, had originally received the name Isidore Lehmann from his people. After Slimsohn had produced his letter of introduction and as he was disclosing the reasons for his visit, Charley thought back, somewhat joyously, to some love poems he had penned in his youth. He had Slimsohn explain the matter over and over, appeared to be looking for a solution, then abruptly changed the subject and asked Slimsohn to tell him about himself. Slimsohn became so engrossed in telling his story that he forgot all about his request, going so far as to confide in Dicky his plan for the future Jerusalem, immediately achievable, just as in the Golden Age, including the reconstruction of the Temple, merely an easily solvable problem of financing. Dicky went back to his newspaper, consulted a calender, then interrupted a splendid disquisition on the industrial capacity of the Jews during the Middle Ages, simply saying, "I'm not sure what to advise you. Let me think about it. Perhaps you could leave me your draft."

"Here it is," said Slimsohn, with a trusting flourish.

"No, I'll think about it, we'll see, but hold on, why don't we discuss it over lunch?"

Slimsohn suddenly felt dizzy. Lunch! How could he possibly pay? Had Dicky invited him?

"I'm inviting you for lunch," continued Dicky. "I find what you say most interesting. One rarely comes across anyone as interesting as you in the business world."

"Not really, I'm just . . . "

"It's clear to me that you have an educated and inquisitive mind."

"No, just a bit well informed, actually. All of that is its own reward, I mean, it's not very rewarding financially," muttered Slimsohn with melancholy. "No, I'll come back. I can't accept such a kind offer."

Dicky realized that Slimsohn was proud and wouldn't want to appear to be cadging a meal for anything in the world. He felt esteem for this poor fellow, who was certainly as awkward as he was unlucky. He began to look for a scheme.

"Listen, Monsieur Slimsohn, please have lunch with me. Maybe over dessert I can ask you to help me correct this brochure I'd like to send out for my business."

"We'll do it right away. You don't need to invite me to lunch for that!"

"Now you're making me uncomfortable."

All the same, for the past several minutes Slimsohn had been listening to the chiming of two differently pitched bells in his head. One, deep and sad, rang in his ears like a knell, resonating through his entire body! It was the knell of hunger! In contrast, a whole set of small emphatic chimes, like stacks of dinner bells in palaces and castles and doorbells in apartments, babbled, "Eat! Eat!"

"I accept," he said, with simple straightforwardness, like someone resolving to act inhabitually.

Dicky was concerned about calming his guest's lingering sensibilities. He understood their sincerity.

"Nothing fancy, you know, just the corner bistro."

Slimsohn bowed with serious nobility.

"I am especially touched by your kindness."

Slimsohn was happy. In the evening at his café (when he could afford to go), even at night when the lateness of the hour makes numb ears more indulgent, as he tried to outline to his companions his plan for the future Jerusalem, immediately achievable, they would reach for their hats and overcoats, making up excuses about waiting wives or an urgent business meeting at dawn. So it was neither the cutlet nor the Beaujolais that had put Slimsohn in a mood of fond candor and winged enthusiasm as he confessed to Dicky his adherence to the faith of his fathers.

After the coffee and the cognac, offered with graceful insistence and accepted after an intricate defense, Dicky said off-handedly, "Yes, I'll bring up your matter to my friend Blum, the tire manufacturer. Perhaps you have heard his name mentioned?"

"I'm afraid I don't know who he is."

"You might have met him. He associates with Jewish circles, although he hasn't practiced the religion since he was young. Back then, on Yom Kippur, when he couldn't get a bite to eat at home, he would get me to treat him at my little restaurant. On this day twenty years ago, it would have been easy for me to introduce you to him. True, he wouldn't have been very useful to you. Twenty years ago he would have been asking me for a cutlet today."

"Today?" asked Slimsohn, horrified.

"Yes, today is Yom Kippur. Didn't you know? I read it in the newspaper."

He handed the folded page to Slimsohn, who sputtered, "Yom Kippur! Lunch!"

He was very upset.

"By the way, Monsieur Slimsohn, tell me, did you eat lunch yesterday?"

"No," Slimsohn said weakly.

"Or dinner?"

"No. I didn't."

"And the day before yesterday?"

"Well, no . . . yes . . . a little lunch, no dinner."

"Then you were early, that's all!" murmured Dicky, savoring the double pleasure of having treated a coreligionist to lunch and made him miss Yom Kippur. . . . "A cigar, Monsieur Slimsohn?"

"Well, yes," answered Slimsohn, crushed, his voice fallen.

—Translated by Glenn Swiadon

SARAH LÉVY

My Beloved France*
(Excerpt)

In this novel published in 1930, the narrator, a Jewish woman from Paris, has married a French nobleman, had a son with him and moved to his ancestral home in the provinces. Ghislaine, a friend visiting from Paris, is a writer. Another friend is Rosen, or "Rosenlafeuille," which can be translated as "rose leaf." No doubt he originally bore the common Jewish name Rosenblatt, of the same meaning in German.

Have I made it clear how much I indulge my husband? Seven years of love had been simply one long series of concessions, joyfully made in a whirl of happiness. I adjusted to everything, all the Christian customs, so long as they didn't compromise my loyalty to Judaism. I even came out here to find out more. The consequences were just now dawning on me. Upon arriving home with Ghislaine, I collapsed on the sofa, confessing, "I can't go on like this anymore. . . . "

That night, Ghislaine returned to Paris. The next day, my mirror, reflecting a tense, pale, and older face, certainly older, kept repeating, "Hussy, hussy. . . . "

Then, the days went by. My daily routine covered up what had happened. I didn't speak about it. Better to avoid mentioning it. Until one morning, in a stack of brochures and unimportant letters, I recognized Rosen's handwriting on a long, heavy envelope.

Poor friend! It had been days since I had called him. What could have caused him to write? The envelope contained ten or fifteen sheets, covered with Ghislaine's hieroglyphic scrawl. Notes written with a blue pencil, in large, despotic letters, were sprinkled throughout the margins. The last one, at the end of the final page, especially caught my eye: "We must get you out of there. DO YOU NEED MONEY?" This was underlined three times.

*Sarah Lévy, *Ma chère France* (Paris: Flammarion, 1930), 81–91.

YFS 85, *Discourses of Jewish Identity in Twentieth-Century France,* ed. Alan Astro, © 1994 by Yale University.

Here is what Ghislaine had written:

Dear Monsieur Rosenlafeuille,

Since last week I have been staying at our friend Sarah's house. The visit has been enjoyable. The countryside is charming, so is the house. You know my hosts better than I do, and you have been friends with Sarah longer. I feel that the close friendship you and she have shared for so long obliges me to call upon your help.

I must inform you that Sarah is unhappy. Much to our surprise and in spite of our warnings, she married a Christian. That was her business. Then, she dazzled us with her happiness, her entrance into a new world, her marvelous social life. No one was happier for her than I. Seeing her now in her present situation, nobody feels worse for her. I'm not the type of person to lord it over her by saying, "I told you so." But she had it coming, all the same.

Why should she come here, of all places, three hundred kilometers from Paris, the end of the world as you will soon see? When I ask her, she answers langorously, "I did it for him!"

It was something else, though, that caused her downfall. I am too accustomed to unraveling the motives of others to be wrong about this.

You know how she is, haughty at times, like a man who makes a successful business deal, sometimes humble like a woman who has succeeded in love. She is too proud to confide in either of us. She certainly won't ask her lord and master for help; that's not how the game is played. Like all men, he is completely selfish, all the more since—given their respective origins—he imagines he is doing her a favor by shutting her up in his horrid little village shanty. Does she still love him? Yes, her love for him endures. You know how our women use their submission to buy affection. That is how our Sarah, so bright and refined, has ended up in the muck heap, the endlessly boring routine of a village whose five hundred inhabitants—devious and sullen by nature—are all she has for company. It is a radical change; from the heights of Parisian civilization she has fallen upon the bleakest soil. When I think that it will be months before the poor dear will set foot in a theater!

Well, I am sure Sarah has fancied herself the lady of the manor. She loves flowers, trees, creatures of all kinds! You can't possibly imagine, my dear Monsieur Rosenlafeuille, how she has pledged herself to living out the absurd drama she has created. Before she arrived, the peasants had already declared all-out war on her. They torture her with stories about an old woman who always goes to mass and never eats meat on Friday. The whole village has united against the Jewess, the vague and faraway symbol of money, worldliness, cosmopolitan pleasures.

Oh, my dear Monsieur Rosenlafeuille, we control the press, the Parliament. You have banking in the palm of your hand, and I literature. We enjoy the right to vote and run for office, and yet we are denied entry into the sweet garden of France.

If a fortuitous combination of events had not brought me here, I never would have imagined the scandal of Sarah's mustering up, after a miserable day, a welcoming smile for her master, who, as you well know, simply hides his villainy behind a benevolent appearance.

(In the margin: DO I KNOW YOUR HUSBAND? AND HOW! BETTER THAN YOU DO!)

Yes, I openly admit it! In the interest of her happiness, I eavesdropped on them. I wanted to plumb the depths of their souls. I hoped, nay felt sure, that behind their bedroom door, Sarah would be the same energetic Jewess, passionate and strong in her fight against injustice, delighting in uncovering her heart.

Really, Ghislaine had listened in on our conversations! What a dangerous little snake!

And so, what do you think I heard? No screams, no tears, no stamping feet. I swear to you, Monsieur Rosenlafeuille, they were hardly alone for two minutes before she threw her arms around his neck! It broke my heart.

(In the margin: MEN, JEWS OR NOT, ALWAYS NEED TO BE RULED WITH AN IRON HAND.)

I believe, Monsieur Rosenlafeuille, that we are witnessing an unacceptable deterioration. I find it inadmissible that a Jewess be scoffed at, as in the worst moments of our history, and happily accept it.

I bring the matter before you, as one of the most powerful representatives of our race in the City of Lights: Paris! Paris, where the highest honors at school were rightfully awarded to a handful of Jewish students, to nobody's surprise! Paris, where teachers and schoolmates silenced their prejudices, in deference to true merit! Paris, where one is treated fairly at all levels of society! Parisians would burst out laughing, then cry out indignantly at the news that a place mired in medieval ways still exists in France. I cannot imagine what form your intervention could take, but I know that you will act as befits your strong character. Those bumpkins need a lesson, as does the husband. Blinded by her female submission, Sarah needs to be shaken up. But while it is true you must save a coreligionist, your first responsibility is to uphold the banner of civilization.

(In the margin: INDEED.)

Here is a task all the more worthy of your efforts. You know our friend so well. She cannot be left in such a dazed stated. Deep down, she is intact. Even when she was young, we were struck by her sense of pride. Someday soon, instinctively, she will rise up full of spirit against the unfortunate fellow who was playing for high stakes when he married her. I would feel sorry for him if I did not know how unpleasant your dealings with him have occasionally been.

I think that, rather than concerning yourself with their happiness, you should let your friendship for Sarah inflame your sense of indignation in these unprecedented circumstances. I know Sarah has not always reacted favorably to your attentions. In the future, a man of your character shall certainly enjoy more consideration. The Jewish gentleman in you, as well as the generous-hearted man, will soon find an opportunity to collect on a debt that has been deferred for too long.

And, no less, she finishes with protestations of friendship for me! I paled with rage as I read her scribbling through to the postscript.

P.S. I think I can work passages of this letter into a book I am writing. Please hold on to it for me!

Here, I burst out laughing. Rosen's note claiming to know Henri better than I do would have done much to relieve the bad taste left by such racial intransigence and female jealousy, to use the authoress's expression, if some remorseful feelings for my old friend hadn't troubled me. In his eyes, my love for a goy makes me more beautiful, especially since this particular goy has shown himself to be quite clever in the business dealings Monsieur Rosen arranged for him. Monsieur Rosen never thought I would marry Henri, and once I did, never imagined I would stick it out. His admiration of these exploits has intensified feelings on his part that were not strong enough to be voiced at the appropriate time. He stirs within me indulgence of the kind one has for an old friend who has underestimated one's character. I imagine him trying to seek sweet revenge from this turn of events, as a financial wizard profits from overly optimistic prognostications.

I can just see him. His beard must have become even redder, his jaw harder at each page, his eyes glazed over, and at the last line, who knows, a smile may even have lit up his features. I'm genuinely fond of him, this dear friend, especially for not rushing to see me. He didn't want to gloat over my troubles. His triumph was modest, and yet it would have done me good to talk to this former apprentice of my father's, who used to accompany me to temple every Friday night. I could have told him of the confusion in my mind, of my loneliness and chagrin, of my humiliating error. He could have understood how deeply they cut.

The image of Ghislaine, writing cholerically, sweeps aside that of Rosen sighing for my, or rather his lost happiness. What a liar she is! If this is how she writes her novels, they must make for fine reading.

I could have disregarded all of this, but as Henri says, life is a question of ebb and flow. According to him, knowing how to live means figuring out the right moment to jump in the surf so as to be carried along without a struggle. An irresistible wave is taking my life further and further out. Now I know it for sure. The movement has strengthened with the arrival of another letter corroborating Ghislaine's.

It took weeks for my aunt and uncle Alphonse from La Chaux-de-Fonds to digest the news of my arrival at Saint-Félicien. They were sure I would finally benefit from their experience:

> We cannot understand why you foolishly insist on living in that
> backwater. You must realize that such places are not meant for us. I,
> who understand life, intend to take advantage of my next visit to my
> clients in Paris to warn you once again. . . .

They too disapprove. This compilation of various opinions has finally made things clear to me. The peasants' sly gestures towards my house as they pass on their way to market ("That's where the Jewess lives . . . how could Monsieur Henri . . . "): *rishes*![1] The mailman's refusal when, imitating my husband, I offer him a glass of wine in the kitchen (this civil servant is in the church choir): *rishes*! The shopgirl's indignation when I, insisting on paying cash, flout the traditional trust extended to my husband's family; the refusal to repair my car or my roof, to sell me the best cuts of meat; the disdain for my hygienic recommendations; that Planchenault woman and her insults; the disobedience of the servants; a thousand veiled threats, and a thousand insolently precise replies: *rishes*, all of it! I knew this, and it made me

---

1. *Rishes*: a Yiddish word of Hebrew origin, meaning "ill will," used to denote anti-Semitism before that term gained currency in Yiddish. See Arnold Mandel, *Une Mélodie sans paroles ni fin: Chroniques juives* (Paris: Seuil, 1993), 49–50 [special editor's note].

laugh. It's not as easy as I thought it would be to put up with. Indeed, it's quite impossible to endure this latent anti-Semitism, this unanimous disapproval in my daily dealings with others which, while I was growing up, we denounced with the Hebrew word *rishes*.*

—Translated by Glenn Swiadon

*I'm not even mentioning here the disparaging allusions to my relationship with the country doctor, unfortunately neither old nor unattractive, whom I had made a point of meeting in case I took ill. Coming from eastern France, he had brought a spirit of social progress to the region. He was the only person kind enough to let me know what everyone was saying behind my back. He told me all so that I might have the strength to resist. Given his combative spirit, his ardent soul and fiery pronouncements, he too ended up leaving the area. He had no choice. He couldn't take them all on.

ARMAND LUNEL

Nicolo-Peccavi, or The Dreyfus Affair at Carpentras* (Excerpt)

In this chapter from a 1926 novel, Jewish women from Carpentras board a bus, in the hope of glimpsing Captain Dreyfus, who is resting there from his trial.

It was, in fact, our aunt who had commissioned the bus. Madame Léa Josué Chanaan was our aunt and we called her Aunt Chanaan, just as we called her husband, Monsieur Josué Chanaan, our uncle, although none of us in the Jewish community of Carpentras was really their niece or nephew. They must have had real nieces and nephews somewhere—but who knows where?—just as they were reputed to have sons and daughters even farther away. But a certain Chanaan, a French diplomat in China; his brother, a correspondent in New York for the great Paris newspapers; their youngest brother, the director of an emigration agency in Palermo; and their sisters, married to rich bankers from Amsterdam, Berlin, or Constantinople—these were the kind of people who could not admit that they were born in Carpentras or in Landerneau, as if these small towns existed only in the legends of *Pêle-Mêle* or *Charivari*.[1] (For you see that while Carpentras has given birth to personalities eminent both in Paris and throughout the world, no one is aware of this, and no one will pay her homage.) It should be noted that the elderly Chanaans, after having enjoyed a considerable fortune amassed in the madder-dye industry under Napoleon III, were almost ruined by the advent of artificial colors. But all the Jewry of Carpentras, admiring the philosophical attitude with which they had withstood the vicissitudes of fortune, showed them a concern and kindness which gave them almost complete consolation. There was hardly a family in which they were not treated as if they were members.

*Armand Lunel, *Nicolo-Peccavi ou l'Affaire Dreyfus à Carpentras* (Paris: Gallimard, Folio Collection, 1976 [orig. ed. 1926]), 196–208.
    1. *Pêle-Mêle, Charivari*: satirical journals of the time. [All notes here are by the translator, unless otherwise indicated.]

YFS 85, *Discourses of Jewish Identity in Twentieth-Century France*, ed. Alan Astro, © 1994 by Yale University.

Judging from what could be learned at the Agricultural and Musical Union from the pictures in *L'Illustration*, Chanaan looked exactly like Francisque Sarcey—which at that time and in our city, brought a kind of glory.[2] That handsome old man, blunt, rustic, and full of aphorisms, was noteworthy as well for the birthmark on his right hand, to which he owed his nickname of Red Hand. It was a broad stain, startling, bright in color and awe-inspiring, at which we gazed with a religious dread, for it reminded us that we had before us not only the greatest retired dye-maker of France, but also the man who had performed the *milah* on all the young male Jews of the Comtat region, and still did so.[3] People say that for many generations before our own, Red Hand (like Abraham, when he inaugurated this practice on his son) operated with a sharpened flint—taken from a flintlock, the old man used to say, without noticing the anachronism, as he showed his cannibal-like teeth. This Judeo-Comtadine joke, far from provoking laughter, brought forth a shiver along the spine, especially among those who heard it for the first time. It is understandable, in any case, why so many of us called Monsieur Chanaan Uncle, and had such respect for him, after our eighth day of life.

If we had the greatest respect for Uncle Chanaan, what we felt for Aunt Chanaan was love, admiration, adoration, and veneration, because it had always been common knowledge that she was as much lovable, admirable, and adorable as she was venerable. This elderly lady, to whom growing old was something foreign, had more youth and life in her than many young girls, who would have paid dearly to obtain her charm and sprightliness. There were still men younger than forty who practically courted her, not that she had maintained the slightest physical seductiveness (it would appear that she had never had any), but she still had lightheartedness, insouciance, and mischievous naïveté of another age, in all their freshness. Wherever Aunt Chanaan appeared, her charm bracelet jingling, there was of course wit, excited talking, plays on words, good humor, and surprising stories. If in those days we laughed at everyone, she was the first to laugh at herself, her past grandeur, the servants she no longer had, and especially her carriage, put up for auction; it was after this that, for lack of anything better, she hired the city bus for her afternoon visits.

This time, however, it was not for her own purposes that Aunt

2. Francisque Sarcey (1828–1899), theater critic.
3. *Milah*: circumcision, in Hebrew. [Author's note.]

Chanaan had ordered the bus. Just as she used it for herself, for lack of anything better (that is to say, a carriage), she had requisitioned this humble and plebeian vehicle for the use of the oldest Jewish women of Carpentras. But you would have sought her in vain among the passengers: because of her rheumatism, she had felt it sufficient to be represented by Léonide, her old cook. Léonide had been given the duty of knocking on doors and introducing in turn each invited guest, in accordance with the list (a duplicate of which had been given to Jean-Hilare).[4]

. . . .

Beginning on the day that the pardoned Dreyfus—instead of seeking refuge in England or Alsace, as was believed at first—came in search of peace and quiet to the outskirts of Carpentras, where part of his family lived (our neighbors, the Valabrègues), all we Dreyfusards and anti-Dreyfusards, through the amazing effect of local patriotism, were reconciled little by little, with the same feeling of restlessness and pride. All of France, and the world with her, were going to have—indeed, already did have—their eyes fixed on the Captain's place of refuge, and might even discover a noble and peaceful town, beneath the slander of humorists. As the *Comtat Sentinel* wrote so elegantly: "Our dear town, taking its turn after Rennes and Devil's Island, found itself at the forefront of current events. Mr. and Mrs. English Tourist, coming and going from La Fontaine de Vaucluse, will soon see a side-trip to our small, ancient town as a must." But a certain caution was necessary! We had to remain calm, maintain our dignity, and under no circumstances give a handle to the malicious curiosity of journalists or the satirical indiscretion of photographers—all people from the North, whose disagreeable manners hid under apparently harmless exteriors, and who could not register or even eat a steak at the Grand Hôtel de l'Univers et d'Orient without everyone's finding out about it and being secretly titillated.

The shock was particularly strong in the rue Vitrée, also known as the Passage Boyer, which constitutes the barometer of public opinion, since the Carpentras character is particularly strong there. Strangers who ventured into this famous street during that time carried away with them the memory of those dark and often angry glances they received from its residents—"the same terrible look," they would say

4. Jean-Hilaire: the driver of the bus.

upon returning home, "as if we had unknowingly entered their bed-rooms and trampled on their bedside rugs." For you see, the shopkeepers—and their wives even more so—regarded the Passage as their private property, and kept watch from morning to night on the thresholds of their shops, in order to prevent violations of their home-steads; only their neighbors and well-known customers, whom they could name and tell stories about, had the right to go by without raising an alarm. These impertinent people, however, these indiscreet strangers, who were they? Where were they from? How long would they keep up their little game? It was the custom for everyone to re-main at home. Would we have moved in on their territory? The in-vaders were seen as unlikely reporters, agents of the secret police, maybe even spies—in any case, they were certainly obtrusive. Was all this wrong? Certainly, the presence of a good Sardinian Republican (who, it was decided, bore a resemblance to Garibaldi) was very cu-rious, as was that of a rather ridiculous delegation of Danish socialists. All these odd types came to greet Dreyfus, and took an interest in his case or feigned to do so. It is true that the sale of *berlingots* did not suffer one bit.[5]

We were not at all mistaken in thinking, that evening so long ago, that the Dreyfus Affair would put forth a new branch in our Carpentras. We were not, however, the only ones to realize this, and the unexpected cutting produced foliage and fruit of very amusing kind.

My grandfather had been asked by an old and very dear friend of his, an editor at *Le Figaro*, to keep him apprised every day of the comings and goings of the Captain, as well as of the reactions of the natives. My grandfather thought that his friend was making fun of him, but after receiving no word, the editor repeated his request by telegram. Abranet then responded with a week's worth of telegrams of this sort: "Dreyfus has taken a bath." "Dreyfus has smoked a pipe." "Dreyfus has drunk a bottle of beer." The joke—which, of course, had not really been one, since this was all that could be reported to the Parisians—was consid-ered to be exceedingly funny in the provinces.

The Jewish bus (as it came to be called) was precisely the last of those events of local history which, tied more or less closely to the Affair, saw Carpentras in turmoil just before 1900. It was much ado about nothing. No one today thinks about it at all. As I attempt, after a period of twenty-five years, to clarify my childhood memories by com-

---

5. *Berlingots*: a hard candy for which Carpentras is known.

paring them to authentic evidence, when I interview survivors of that grand time, I find nothing—nothing but shrugs and a feigned or real indifference, I am not sure which. Was there in fact no Dreyfus Affair in Carpentras? Was there also no Peccavi scandal, grafted onto the Dreyfus Affair? What about the bus?

If you go to Tarascon, you will at last be shown, after much reluctance, Tartarin's house.[6] If you go to Rouen, you might still find some very old people whose parents witnessed the hurried passage of Emma Bovary's hackney, with its silver lanterns—and they will describe it with guarded words. But you will find no one in Carpentras who can speak of the Jewish bus, in which Aunt Chanaan gathered the matrons of the Jewish quarter in order to make it possible for them, as for the Parisians (and these women deserved it just as much), to go see Captain Dreyfus. It was, to be sure, a collective demonstration of Israelitic solidarity, but also a simple visit, motivated by courtesy and sympathy, with a good dose of curiosity. If one of those accursed journalists still prowled our avenues on that Wednesday, he suspected nothing, and even today the citizens of Carpentras continue to deny the existence of that bus. How can this conspiracy of silence be explained? Could it be fear of ridicule? Just wait for what comes next.

It is for these reasons that, though I believe I am faithfully reconstructing my memories, as carefully as one arranges a jigsaw puzzle, I am afraid lest I put in inauthentic pieces and create a veritable novel, a work of pure imagination—because I am absolutely alone before the truth. I fear not being believed. I'm sure that no one will believe me. But that's life. Beside, I've gone too far. I can't stop. . . .

Now comes the time to recall without error the identities of all our travelers; then—as if I had before me the roll given to Léonide by Aunt Chanaan—to put each one in her proper place in the bus.

What were they called? Like the names of most Jews, theirs derived from the places their families had first settled in.

There are Israelites who bear the names of great cities and even capitals, proudly, as if this were an unquestionable sign of their importance and social position. "Yes, I am nothing but a pauper, and it is my fault," said a Monsieur Amsterdam, "but you can tell just from my name that my ancestors were diamond kings in Holland."

At least in Carpentras, especially in the bus (and with few exceptions), names differed only in degree of unpretentiousness. There were

6. *Tartarin de Tarascon*: a novel by Alphonse Daudet (1840–1897).

names most often of small southern towns (many in France, some on the Iberian Peninsula and in Italy) or of almost unknown villages or hamlets in the area nearby. Perhaps we should also recall Biblical names; nevertheless, I know that by examining a gazetteer of Provence and Lower Languedoc I could pick out the names of a good third of my ancestors.

I have already recognized the wives of Samuel Orange, David Perpignan, and Joseph Caylar, seated to the right of Léonide. Even if their ancestors, thank God, neither figured in the records of the stock exchange nor traded in precious stones, some of the most distant were surely among the philosophers and poets who composed the glorious school at Lunel during the Middle Ages. Renan has certainly referred to them in his *Histoire littéraire de la France*, although their great-granddaughters knew nothing about all this. Yet with their thin faces and fine, immobile wrinkles, these women gave an impression of ingenious patience, and behind their huge metal-rimmed glasses their eyes shone with a light so penetrating that popular wisdom (which is never mistaken without knowing, however, why it is right) had called them for some time "the sages." Yet Madame Orange traded in sewing notions; Madame Perpignan was only a linen dealer; and Madame Caylar sold nothing but candles, wax, and small brooms. But all three ladies brought unconsciously to their humble dealings the same subtle ardor shown by their ancestors in disputes regarding the views of Maimonides.

Immediately after them came the cousins, Vonvoune and Franquette Carpentras, still formidable despite their unpretentious names; formerly attendants at the ritual bath, these two shrews, with their dragon voices and Amazonian bearing, continued to inspire awe of a kind reserved most often for religion and the army.

I can see them all, sitting on the bus seats in small intimate groups, just like at a public meeting. There were eternally inseparable couples, former students at the Muscat Boarding School, who visited each other every day and always left with a ceremonious "Let's get together one of these days." There too were the bonneted Esther Beaucaire and Bellette Tarascon, and a solid block of grandmothers: the two sisters and two brothers of the Roquemartine family had married the two brothers and two sisters of the Sisterons. Next, alone in a corner—wishing to be with all the others, however, but not daring to offend anyone through an unwarranted preference—was the discreet and obliging Madame

Sinigaglia,[7] smiling and nodding almost imperceptibly right and left, unceasingly.

All were dressed soberly in black, some hatless with a plain kerchief over their bangs, others wearing aprons like the two bathhouse attendants, all proper, often elegant, and almost uniformly small and of slight means, talkative, restless. Showing here and there remnants of gracefulness despite their age, there they sat, the old Israelitic women of the town; some among them, those who had been the most beautiful, were reminiscent of ancient Oriental Mireilles.[8] Lyonette, the widow from Lyons (small as a comma); Miette David (the little *e*, or the ant); Méliton Milhaud (called Milhaudette); Fénella Mossé (called Mosséchonne); Précile Narbonne . . . ; and Bengude, Blanquette, Astruguette, Isaquette, Belle-Bottine. . . . Last names, first names, nicknames collided in the rocking of the bus. "Is it believable, is it possible, that so many Jewish women were there?" you might ask. Am I mixing them up? Am I adding some? Am I mentioning some who had not been out for twenty years, centenarians, who might have even been dead? Could the bus not even have been that big? How could it have held them all? Of course, three or four small Jewish women can sit in the space occupied by a fat commercial traveler. No, that remarkable magic bus is not yet full, and it still rolls on, meandering through Carpentras.

I know full well that today in Carpentras there are hardly a dozen Jews and that the temple has been closed for lack of members. But 1899 was still a different century; everyone flocked to temple on the sabbath and the decline of the great Jewish community had scarcely begun.

"Let us be counted, and re-counted," said our elderly ladies.

Each in turn spoke tirelessly of another era, even further removed, in which they had been more numerous, another century in which "the Jewish quarter" had not been an empty phrase, when the temple was kept in its full splendor. That time of the Popes, so longed for by Jean-Hilaire in his driver's seat, was almost longed for as well by the Jewish ladies in the bus.[9]

---

7. Sinigaglia: a small port in the province of Ancona, on the Adriatic. [Author's note.]

8. Mireille, the heroine of the poem of the same name by Frédéric Mistral (1830–1914), principal figure of the Provençal literary revival. Armand Lunel recounts his grandfather's correspondence with Mistral in *Les Chemins de mon judaïsme et divers inédits*, ed. Georges Jessula (Paris: L'Harmattan, 1993), 91–93.

9. When the Popes ruled Carpentras, as they did nearby Avignon, Jews were toler-

Have patience, poor Jean-Hilaire! A few more turns, a few stops, some sips of local wine at the more hospitable houses, and your task, with the receipt of the hard-won coins, will come to an end.

"Two seats for the Azulaï sisters!" cried Léonide, and there arose an entire Jewish chorus calling, "Azulaï! Azulaï!"

What a beautiful name! How exquisite! Before seeing them, merely upon hearing their name, one thought of something very poetic, very sweet, such as *azure*, of course, but infinitely more rare; then, of the beauty of pearls and a distant sky, exotic and perhaps still showing the blue, shaded freshness of Spanish gardens.

"Please take your seats, I beg you, ladies."

And in the presence of these Jewish women, imported to Carpentras from Gibraltar, one could admire the loveliness of Hispano-Arabic pottery, but their beauty was in truth too unusual, showing too frequent mending and a glaze marred by flakes.

—Translated by Michael T. Ward

---

ated but subjected to diverse humiliations. See Armand Lunel, *Juifs du Languedoc, de la Provence et des Etats français du Pape* (Paris: Albin Michel, 1975).

RYSIA POLONIECKA

Herring Story*

You can take life in any number of ways. Today, I'll take it by the herring.

It recently occurred to me that my life was full of herrings. I hadn't realized it until then.

In one sense it's a bit surprising. It's not something I eat every day, there's no print or painting of it adorning my walls, and yet, no doubt about it, my life is strewn with herrings the way others' lives are strewn with flowers. Lately the herrings have returned. There are lots of flowers in my life, but they are artificial, whereas the herrings are real. Let me clarify: my flowers, the ones I plant on the balcony or in the kitchen, the ones I buy, the ones I give as gifts, are always real flowers that have grown, blossomed, faded, and for a while even smelled good; but for me apart from poppies, cornflowers, daisies (which I pick from the edges of wheatfields and a bunch of which I have—the only bunch composed of artificial flowers—on my nightstand from my native Poland), the other flowers aren't actually real. I've never had hollyhocks, fragrant peonies, velvety irises, or double lilacs or forsythia thriving in my garden; I've never had a garden and perhaps I'll never be able to have one, unless somebody gives one to me, though it's not a question of the money involved. In my heart I've planted a garden, with florists, marketplaces, a terrace, and thefts of flowers along the bushes and hedges.

But let's return to the herrings. I, or my ancestors, have had quite a few of them. Could herring be the emblem of my family tree (as almost

*Excerpted from Rysia Poloniecka, "Nourritures," *Les Temps Modernes* 536–37 (March-April 1991): 97–116.

YFS 85, *Discourses of Jewish Identity in Twentieth-Century France,* ed. Alan Astro, © 1994 by Yale University.

everyone knows, herrings climb trees, and are painted blue, red, green to make them harder to notice), as the emblems of other families are a unicorn or two lions sitting on their haunches? The only difference is that it wouldn't occur to me to wear a herring as a signet-ring. I wear it directly on my hands, and it smells.

It's because of this familiarity with herring that there's almost no difference between Jewish men and women. Both have been acquainted with herring continuously and through successive generations. Women, however, have learned to differentiate between male and female herrings by weighing them in their hands, fingering them, trying to distinguish hard-roed and soft-roed herring. Men, less well informed, eat more of them because they drink vodka with them.

Herring no doubt was itself rare but real, a marvel that graced a poor man's table.

Of course, there is a fundamental difference between flowers and herrings: the smell. The former can be sweet, refined, soft, marvelous, intoxicating; the latter unpleasant, even unbearable. I do not like the smell of herring on my hands after I've prepared some, but I know it well, so well, in fact, that one day when there was neither smell nor herring to be found, I realized that I would have liked to marry a man because of a fuss over herring. But it didn't happen. The time wasn't right.

He was a very elegant man, the most elegant man I've ever met (and I'm no longer a kid in the gutter, even if I do like herring): an American Jew, intelligent, sensitive, seductive, who moved only in the WASP circles of Paris (WASP: White Anglo-Saxon Protestant, having arrived—and how—with the first immigrants to America, definition provided for those who have not tried to leave behind their herring or their stew by learning foreign languages). He had his coffee only at Fouquet's[1] (he had never made it to whiskey in his stiff climb, having found his way, in thirty-five years, only from tea with lemon to black coffee) and since he was penniless, it was the others, the WASP's of Paris, or those passing through, who paid for his coffee. They would just as well have bought him the best cigars (cigars? what for?) and the best whiskey, so great were their admiration and regard for him. Sometimes he had enough to pay. Then he invited everyone, and everyone accepted.

One day, he told me how, when he was a little boy in the family-

1. A café on the Champs-Elysées. [All notes here are by the special editor.]

owned Jewish grocery, run by his mother, a tub of herring had fallen on his only pair of shoes, which he happened to have on. For weeks and months he had to wear those stinking shoes, and with what shame. When he was in a closed room, he moved from one corner to the other, looking for a way to open a door or a window to lessen the odor slightly. I would have rocked, I would have hugged, I would have married the man who was telling me all this so simply, with such feeling, years and years later, when he wore only the best shoes from Bond Street. All the same, we had herring in common; yet this wedding never even contemplated (though he was a bachelor, and I was free), never took place. Really, I could describe a geography of my love life through herring.

So I married a man for whom herring was an intimate part of family custom. I discreetly started giving him, after a first son, marinated herring (forgive the repetition of the word, but you have to call a spade a spade; there's no getting around it). The recipe had been given to me by an old Jewish woman I did not like at all, so silly did she seem, but herring and intelligence have nothing in common.

Don't go thinking that we ate herring for breakfast, lunch, and dinner, and that in between we made love. No, it wasn't like that at all, although looking at it that way does have a certain charm. We were apt then to eat herring together, but this proximity didn't sufficiently sweeten our lives (it's true that the choice of this plain and salty food may not have been sensible in this case), and we separated.

The children were too little to take over the herring eating.

Then I found a goy (any non-Jew to Jews), a very good man, who had the unfortunate peculiarity of liking herring in all its guises. I half lived with him; then, after an adequate time mourning my official married life, I again happily made marinated herring. But what had to happen happened, and after a few years we separated, having eaten too much smoked salmon, served to him with brown ale, in the course of a trip. Following a certain euphoria, then sadness, I again felt up to making marinated herring, preferably soft-roed (two thirds water, a third vinegar, carrots, onions, salt, pepper, bay leaves, a little sugar), for myself. The children were still too little!

Well, it wasn't meant to be. For months, years, of my life, there was no man who liked herring: either the dish was a failure though I never ruin a dish; or else, most often, it was a success, but remained in the refrigerator for weeks without my touching it until it went bad and had to be thrown out. It got to the point where the young woman who helps me at home would say, when I started making herring, "So when will it be time to throw it out?" (The same thing happened with jellied feet, but that is a culinary concern outside our topic.)

I've temporarily given up on home-made marinated herring, but I've not lost hope, and marinated herring has stopped troubling me for the time being.

On the other hand, I have turned to real *herring*[2] soaked in pickling brine. The switch took place imperceptibly from Baltic herring at one or two restaurants, then to the purchase of commercial marinated herring.

Now I know all about them: Russian ones in big round steel cans, which barely need to be put to soak, hard to find (when will we start lining up for it? Yea to herring! Nay to Mercedes!); Dutch ones in barrels of brine of different quality depending on the stores, more or less salty, more or less firm, more or less big. The ones I prefer come, of course, from the rue des Rosiers[3] (the street in Paris where there are the most herrings), from a little grocery run by a couple from Poland (you can stop neither progress not the evolution of customs, the men no longer spend their time studying). They're no longer young at all (neither am I). The woman with a big smile of dentures and gold, sinks her red hands up to her elbows in the brine, does me a favor by looking for the biggest ones with soft roe (from which I make a salad: soft roe, oil, hard-boiled eggs, green apple, a little sugar). The prices go up from month to month, apparently the size of herring too, ever since they noticed the simultaneous rise in my fortunes and my voracity. The woman always tries to sell me something else—anything; anyway, they have a little of everything. Sometimes I buy, and in addition to the herring I leave with eggs, beets, cans of peeled tomatoes, kvass for the borscht, slivered and powdered almonds. Each and every one of my sons has come and admired the store and its owners. Only the elder (I have only two, but if I say each and every one, for an instant I can believe, and make you believe, that I have four, five, six, seven; a wonder, in short) said to me one day at home: "I should really start liking herring." Naïvely, I asked him: "Why?" Seriously, he answered: "Because otherwise the tradition will be lost."

Coming home with the herrings wrapped in newspaper is a little difficult: first they mustn't drip in the car (the smell again) and then especially, once they're out of the brine, the herring cycle begins anew and continues no matter what, demanding immediate attention. You can't ignore it. To remove the salt, you must put the herring to soak

2. In English in the original.
3. In the Parisian Jewish quarter of the Marais.

right away in a vat more or less reserved for this purpose. I know all about the time needed to remove the salt depending on quality, seasons, origin: it's precise and can neither be cut short nor increased, lest the result be too salty or too bland. At the imperative (or imperial) moment, at the end of the soaking process (yes, you can allow yourself a half hour's leeway, but no more), the unpleasant moments begin: draining, peeling the skin, removing the backbone and especially the small bones, drying the fillets, finally cutting it up into pieces and placing it properly into jars, with the right amount of oil.

These successive operations bring to the surface each time all the constraints necessary for a single moment of pleasure. They take place most often in the evening in the kitchen, which is also where I sometimes write. I am alone there with an extra lamp from my room (so I can see better), many copies of *Le Monde,* plenty of Sopalin paper towels for delicate tasks, and no small number of swear-words: "Never again!" Lately, I have resigned myself to fine surgical gloves. My taste for untouchable tradition didn't survive the enduring smell, resistant to everything (including lemon) on my hands. My horizon has widened, and yet I can't get out of this mess, but do I really want to? I've tried, though I don't go out much, to go have herring elsewhere: once or twice at the Maison du Danemark (peacefulness and white porcelain), and at the deluxe fast-food restaurant on the Place Dauphine where a friend took me. The taste is almost there, but the atmosphere isn't. I miss home, and how can one eat herring anyway at a time decided upon beforehand?

To do so is to feel nothing, understand nothing about immediately satisfying the need for a mild, salty, and firm herring that melts in the mouth. The amount necessary to quiet this hankering can vary greatly: sometimes returning to the haven (*havre* in French, nothing to do with the port, or the girls, or even the coffee) of my home, and before I start to work again, a single piece is enough to quell my hunger. It satisfies me like a lavish meal; it fills me up. Sometimes I need much more to arrive at the same result, and although I'm usually careful not to help along my atavistically round hips or (to be done with euphemisms, it must be said) my buttocks, I need three, four, indeed seven pieces (like the sons above) to achieve my purpose.

My horizon has widened a little, but does not leave the rue des Rosiers. There, it was into another store, a bigger store, with blue tiles on the exterior, called Klapisch, that my aunt sent me as a child to fetch smoked sprats, which had to be *fraîches, brillantes et bien pleines* ("fresh, shiny, and nicely plump": in speaking of them at home it was

thought fitting that the word be of the feminine gender[4]) and pickles
that were firm and not too salty (herring being almost, paradoxically, a
personal creation). These days when I am there, I buy small jars of pink
cherry-flavored Danish herring already prepared, which I eat at home
with delight.

Once, while I was trying his pickled herring straight out of the
barrels (I search for a man in whatever way I can), the salesman told me,
pointing to the pink Danish ones (Denmark, the only country where
civil rights are 98% respected and which supplied me with warm milk
and cod-liver oil during recess, as well as a red explanatory and promotional handbook for that country right after the war on my arrival in
France): "Those are the ones I prefer." I said to him: "Why?" He said to
me: "It's a matter of taste." It's true that we had the same taste, and the
same after-taste.

But the way out was much narrower than it seemed. One day, I saw
from afar one of the K. nephews whom I had heard mentioned when I
was little (my uncle had been deported by the Nazis and had come back
with his uncle). I saw him for five minutes, he didn't even see me, he
lived far away, elsewhere. Well, for some time, I thought he was the
only man on earth who would suit me. (Of course, the story is much
more complicated. Sometimes you have to simplify in order to embellish a little.)

I'll close with this since I'm somewhat tired (as are you?), sick of
removing from my guts fatty and nourishing fish, even in the form of
small neatly cleaned morsels. One day, the salesman from that store,
who reminds me of Woody Allen (among others), told me at length—
while I was running as usual to buy two jars of cherry-flavored Danish
herring and he was burning a commemorative candle in an iron goblet
on the counter—about the life, arrest and death of his father, deported,
returned, "deceased," whose *yortzeit* it was (anniversary of his death),
as well as all the questions he had not asked him. It had been impossible for me to remove myself from "my" herring.

All of which could just as well be called, *Of Marination in Pickling
Brine*, or better yet, *On Happiness Found in Herring*.

WINDOWS

After I wrote the story about herring, I no longer needed the ladder to
fill in the gaps in the window every evening and to hang the double

---

4. Actually, the word is masculine: *le sprat*.

curtains. It was summer. The connection doesn't seem obvious. Every-one, or almost everyone, knows how herrings painted in several colors climb trees so as not to be recognized right away. Until only a few days ago, they also climbed my windows. They? Who? Herrings? My win-dows? Another woman's? What bothers me when I tell stories is that the topics repeat themselves. Maybe it's because the stories begin in several similar places where the herrings meet double curtains while laughing up their (black) sleeves.

It was while trying to tell stories that I realized how limited my personal hardware, my own bric-à-brac is: a few objects (far too many for an apartment), a few pictures, a few ideas, a few feelings, a few people who meet up, misjudge, then get to know one another. However, my story with the windows is serious. I would like only to allude to this seriousness. The Warsaw ghetto is burning; the houses fall, red in flames; people jump out of the windows; live torches disappear into the air. I am a little girl who sees all of this from outside the walls. The grown-ups have gotten me out; above all, the child had to be saved. My parents stayed. I can believe they're still there, even though I see the tremendous blaze. Years later, whenever I was happy for a while, phrases came to me like "I want to leave," "I want to go away," "I want to jump out the window." It took me years to put the two together, and the windows apparently have quieted down in me.

But nothing really disappears, and real windows have refreshed my memory. I live in an old apartment, the wind blows in and I can't get around to having any repairs done, even to having the double curtains sewn. In summer it's pleasant; there's natural ventilation. In winter it's cold, especially since the boiler is defective and I lost the estimate I'd managed to ask for in order to get it replaced last year. As soon as spring is here, the light of day awakens me very early. (Day! What an admirable word!) Still, when I bought a light-weight aluminum ladder on sale at Inno, the situation did improve.

In May, after I put two wooden rings (from my reserve of notions of all types) on the big brown bed-cover that for years had remained folded, each evening I was able to hang this would-be curtain on the pegs of the curtain-rod of the window, and in this way sleep until after daybreak.

The advantage was much greater in winter. Instead of being abso-lutely cold, every evening I'd climb the ladder (the same model used in all seasons for gathering all kinds of fruit) and with the help of a sharp kitchen-knife I'd fill the cracks with absorbent cotton. It's rather effec-tive. In the morning or every other morning (one does have to air a room for reasons of hygiene), pieces of cotton would fly into the courtyard when I opened the window, no matter what precautions I'd taken during this operation. The superintendent of the building, who also helps me out at home, told me, laughing (we share our little secrets) that some tenants had asked her, "Where *does* this cotton come from?" Of course she answered, looking surprised as they did, that she had no idea. It did become irritating, though, on Saturdays and Sundays when, since I was at home during the day too (on Sundays anyway) I discreetly had to replace the cotton in the morning, after having of course unfolded the light-weight ladder. I admit that in the long run these practices had become tedious. Finally a friend who is a cabinet-maker, a *compagon du Tour de France*[5] who now does something else, but who despite his financial difficulties had a pleasant disposition, agreed to take care of the repairs on the windows and in particular the one in my room. (With or without money, no repair is considered by me but from within a network of trusting acquaintances; thus the house is falling apart.) It's comfortable when it's not too cold. In addition to having meticulously repaired the window, he put in a joint, but polyester is not a noble material, so its use was not taught in the fellowship of the *compagnons*, at least in his day. So the joint is not put in right. With time the wood warped a bit and gave (as opposed to humans and dogs, who with time give rather less). I hoped all the same that I wouldn't have to climb the ladder every night to secure a continuity. (You do what you can when your name isn't Jacob[6] and you're a woman without a husband and have only two sons who are still young, if anything intellectuals and artists rather than handymen.)

Meanwhile, when the warm weather returned, the problem with my early morning awakenings reappeared. I used the ladder (made of aluminum) until the day I went to Aligre (a kind of combination flea- and fruit- and vegetable-market in Paris that I've visited frequently and where I've set myself up with a past, as one sets up a household) and bought second-hand pink double curtains of the worst kind but which miraculously fit my bedroom window. They stayed folded in a pile for a year, then I had them cleaned. A rod was needed to hang them; curtain rods never work very long in my house, they may even be among the

5. *Compagnon du Tour de France*: a member of one of many groups of itinerant workers who travel around France, offering their services in various localities in order to train one another in their skills.
6. In a section not translated here, the author mentions that in Yiddish her name is Rifka, i.e. Rebecca, the mother of Jacob in the Bible.

things that work the least (with the casters on the legs of the television to go from one room to the other on the torn carpet). The strings get stuck, break, and I never did understand or try to understand anything about how to put them back together. I went to the Bazar de l'Hôtel de Ville. I hate buying curtain rods. By nature, I hate or nearly do people who say BHV (or Samar for the Samaritaine department store). I get angry with myself for categorizing like this, but to me it's another world and it scares me. People who are sure of themselves, of their privileges, of their stupidity (I have my own, and my privileges I doubt, even the privilege of living), claim to have small means and I believe them to have great potential means for extermination. All these terrible associations in my head from an abbreviation! It could be the SS coming back. The persecutor's power consists in having the persecuted remain so, even if only by a hardly lethal ridiculousness, even if it means you get caught up in curtain strings (and must tighten your purse strings), as well as in your rods and abbreviations of all sorts in order to continue your own life, to make certain that something from that time, the time of persecution, remains, that it didn't die then, that it lives on in its new-found freedom. Also, camouflaging windows was something we knew something about.

I bought those wooden curtain-rods with large rings that one puts right on the pegs already installed in the wall, with all the useless accessories that go with them. It took me only a month or two to put them up! I can, whenever possible, sleep a little later in the summer and be a little warmer in the winter. What a victory!

One victory—since the stories I used to tell myself when I was very little right before the war while looking at the curtain-rod on the high window of my bedroom, where a whole magical world made up of extraordinary characters, animals, trees, flowers, meadows, bedrooms, princes' castles, came alive for me and which no curtain-rod since has been able to recreate.

What moves me most about windows is when they face each other from one end of a house to another. All at once, the absurdity of the whole construction comes to me, of all the houses men build to keep in air and emptiness. There, in these windows that cut across the walls, you can see it all, beautiful, laughable, full of hope. Of course, glass walls don't produce the same effect, you need the alternation of the opaque and the transparent and the meeting of the transparent with the transparent. Windows must be in proper doses, like salt in ordinary soup.

While writing this story I understood why—even though it's for my eyes only, hidden from everyone else's—I had placed a postcard in my study of a painting by an artist with whom I'm entirely unfamiliar, one J.-P. Pincemin (pinch me, pinch you), which is simply of a window closed on an almost blue sky. I am alive. The windows had something to do with it. It's from a window that I watched for the ever uncertain return of my parents in the room where I stayed locked up all day. I still have all the equipment in my bedroom: ladder; small sharp knife; cotton, of which I put some back in, just from time to time. For this year, in any case, weather-stripping is out of the question. Windows, too, need to live.

—Translated by Anna Lehmann

HENRI RACZYMOW

Tales of Exile and Forgetfulness*
(Excerpt)

In this passage from the end of the novel, Matthieu Schriftlich, a young Parisian Jew whose name means "written" in German and Yiddish, mulls over the fragmented memories of his family in Poland and France: stories from before, during, and after the Second World War.

She's good and dead, the wondrous grandmother who could have sated Matthieu Schriftlich's tiresome curiosity about Szlama Davidowicz waking up, back there.

"Quick, let's take a look in at the hens." Had the hens ever existed? Who could tell him now? That all took place in prehistoric times.

"Ah, let's don our *bonjourke*, that's right, let's put it on." In those days, Matthieu, Jewish *valiskes* were never out of reach. When we shut those *valiskes*—May God spare you such a fate—it wasn't, as you know, to go off on a wildly carefree holiday. It was usually a one-way trip. Yes, they exiled you from your place of exile, and you left your home, your furnishings, and sometimes even other *valiskes*, too heavy to carry. Afterwards, there was no point in following proper procedures, dispatching others to retrieve even part of your belongings. It wasn't worth the trouble. The predators had already stripped your home. A rolling stone. . .

What happened in Poland happened in France. The same scenario. In 1941, four "Polish" nationals by the name of Davidowicz (father Szlama, mother Matl, son Herschl, and daughter Anna) were relocated by the Sûreté Nationale to Fontafie in the Charente. Forced to leave their residence at 4, rue Dénoyez, Paris, in utmost haste, they tried to have their belongings looked after. From the concierge at No. 4 of the aforesaid rue Dénoyez came the following undated letter:

*Henri Raczymow, *Contes d'exil et d'oubli* (Paris: Gallimard, 1979), 114–24.

YFS 85, *Discourses of Jewish Identity in Twentieth-Century France*, ed. Alan Astro, © 1994 by Yale University.

FROM   Madame Marchander
       4–6, rue Dénoyez
       Paris 20

TO   Monsieur Davidowicz
       c/o Monsieur Hude
       Greengrocer at Chasseneuil, Charente

Paris, 1942

Dear Sir,

    I have had news of you from Monsieur Kurtzner. Moreover, I often have news of you. From many people, some of whom we don't even know. Madame Szaphir gave everything to Monsieur Mager, your niece's father-in-law. Two large wicker trunks. Another gentleman came on your behalf. We don't know the people you have sent. Your belongings have gone off, two small suitcases full. Monsieur Mager took care of them. He got them from the Parcel Service. Your overcoats and the rest. So see Mager and that other gentleman. By now, I've had more than my fill of you. If you send me anyone else, I'll throw the bastard out. You don't even know the people you send. Anyway, Madame Szaphir is going to write to you. As for me, I've already got my hands full with my sick husband and feel no need to bother myself with your business. All the more so since by now you've surely gotten your belongings. Anyway, the doors are padlocked. We have been forbidden to enter.

Madame Marchander must have taken all the Davidowicz family's possessions, for when they returned after the war, they found nothing. The name "Marchander" caught Matthieu Schriftlich's eye. At first he thought it concealed a Jewish identity, but he was wrong. As for Monsieur Hude, he had originally read "Monsieur Jude." Among those whom Szlama Davidowicz had sent to the rue Dénoyez was a certain Maurice Davidovici, no relation despite the name:

FROM   Monsieur Maurice Davidovici
       34, rue Bisson
       Paris 20

TO   Monsieur Davidowicz
       c/o Monsieur Hude
       Greengrocer
       Chasseneuil, Charente

Paris, 9 September 1942

Dear Friends,

    I have received your two cards and am very glad to know you are in good health. You have asked me to retrieve your belongings from your home, but your concierge will not allow it. Please be so kind as to instruct her to let me in. Only then will I be able to look after your things. Tell me what you need.

At Szlama Davidowicz's burial in the Jewish section of the Parisian cemetery at Bagneux, in February 1968, Matthieu Schriftlich thought of Shüffra Rozenbaum and of the letter dated 24 August 1942 that she sent to her "dear little Anna," Matthieu's mother. But what's there to report, what's there to Rappaport, mutters Matthieu. (When the Davidowicz's crossed the demarcation line, Szlama wore new shoes that squeaked with every step he took. In the woods through which they secretly passed, they urged him to take them off. Telling this story, Anna Davidowicz never fails to break out laughing.)

"Voy, voy, *Monsieur le Gendarmke,* I am a pure Catholic. Everyone here is Catholic. My wife, my children, we're all Catholics. The rabbi who circumcised me without consulting me beforehand was also Catholic. I swear to it on the Holy Cross of the King of the Jews who died and rose from the dead for our salvation."

FROM Mademoiselle Rozenbaum
         12, rue Ramponeau
         Paris 20

TO   Mademoiselle Davidowicz
         c/o Monsieur Hude
         Chasseneuil, Charente

Paris, 24 August 1942

My dear little Anna,
      I received your card three days ago. Excuse me for taking so long to answer. I wasn't doing very well. I hope you are in good health, and likewise your parents and brother. Esther's illness remains the same. I am in despair over your mother's having been sick. As for me, dear Anna, nothing has changed. I have news from my sister. My brother is working, as is my father. Madame Szaphir sent you two *valiskes* a good while ago. Regards from Suzanne Zlotystik, whom I see from time to time. I miss you and find myself bored without you. Every moment of the day I think of you. From your little friend, with love and kisses.

Railroadke, bonjourke. Railroad and *bonjour.* The bags are packed.

FROM Madame Sarah Zask
      34, rue Bisson
      Paris 20

TO   Monsieur Davidowicz
      Salle des Fêtes No. 21
      Fontafie via Genouillac, Charente

Paris, 10 January 1943

Dear Friend,
        I sent you two packages by express mail on 7 January. Write me if
you have gotten them. Tell me if you need anything. I can't find
cereal for my baby. I can't send you the trunk for I haven't a key or
any string. Neither can I send you dishes for I haven't any and can't
find any. My little Berthe has been sick. I left someone with her in
order to send you the packages.

Who is Sarah Zask? Where is Berthe Zask today? Who is Madame
Szaphir? Where is she? O dear ladies of long ago. "Sweet stabbed faces
Dear flowery lips," wrote Kostrowitzky, who Matthieu knows was not
Jewish, despite the charming name. And who is Matthieu Schriftlich
and whither goes he?

Zise geshtokhene penemer Tayere lipn vi blumen

Nowadays, for the gentile Christmas, Matthieu would have given
his grandfather Szlama Davidowicz guess what: a *bonjourke*. Perhaps
each morning he would have donned it to look through the windows,
not at the hens, no, but at the damage caused by the Parisian pigeons.
And perhaps he would have remembered the whipper of the Konski
carriage, let's say somewhere in Volhynia, in prehistoric times. It took
travelers to the train station, up there, beyond the new factory. Watch
out for the Polish stones, about a mile and a half down a muddy serpen-
tine road. The graceless face of Haim Beinfeld, the *railroadke* with the
pantrylike beard. Is he drunk already? Perhaps, unbeknownst to him,
Szlama Davidowicz would have turned around and blurted to Matl
Oksenberg: "Come see, Matl, quick! There's the *railroadke*." Well,
Matthieu, you know, if there are no longer carriages that take you to
the train station, there are still train stations and *valiskes* that are shut
in haste and anguish. Times have changed, but somewhere, for us, for
others, tragedies occur, houses are abandoned and pillaged.

Bonjourke railroadke.
Bonjourke railroadke.

Children, repeat after me the lesson of time, murmurs Rabbi Schlomo Grünenflamm, the cantor of Kaloush, in Galicia let us say. But on this hot Polish summer morning, Schlomo's grandchildren must have had a good deal of trouble getting up. Lazybones! Schlomo is alone on the terrace above the Kamenetz lake, in those improbable, happy days when there had been a lake in Kamenetz. He fears lest the nightmare he senses come to pass. He strokes his beard without thinking and puts his hand before his eyes.

"Take your hand away from your eyes, *kochany panie* Gorbatchev. Look. Listen. Don't hold back the words. Let them come forth. I beg of you."

No, muses Matthieu, in those days, in the Austrian Poland of Franz Josef I, or in the Tsarist Poland of our Little Father Nicholas II, our Tatenyu Nicholas II, in Poland of those years, dispossessed of Poland, the star of day did not emerge from the tops of the fir trees solely for the Poles. Gorbatch recounts: as he awoke in the morning, Rabbi Schlomo Grünenflamm's first glances may have happened upon the two copies of the Book of Psalms that he possessed, but his first thoughts were for the weather they were likely to have. He foresaw, one after the other: a sky gray like the ripples of the lake; or a blue sky, rocks caressed by the brilliance of the sun; or even the innumerable circles that the rain would bring forth on Kamenetz. So where was the second Book of Psalms that his grandfather Mikhal Grünenfeld had handed down to him when he came to bid him farewell on his deathbed? In the common room, exposed to the indifferent glances of visitors? In the wicker trunk under the rafters of the *isba*? One would have to ask Rywka. Perhaps she is reading it by the light of the Sabbath candles, during one of her mysterious vigils as she waits for him, for Schlomo, on a Friday evening. So much for the first thoughts, the first glances. But what about the first thing he felt, wonders Matthieu about Szlama Davidowicz. Would it have been the hot, sweet sensations of Rywka's breakfast roll with honey? Wearing a nightshirt of coarse white cloth, and a sleeping-cap, he would be savoring the maternal warmth of the full-bellied down quilt. He murmurs the morning prayer:

> I have laid myself down and fallen asleep
> I have arisen, for the Eternal One sustains me,

but he is thinking of Rywka, of the breakfast roll, of the lake, of his cigars, of his grandchildren. Today he plans to tell them the story of the seven beggars, by Rabbi Nachman of Bratslav, the great-grandson of the

Baal Shem Tov of blessed memory—if only he could recall the ending. What then, the children will ask. What then? Then nothing. Everything turned out well.

Instead, everything turned out quite badly, as some years later his grandchildren were to learn, alas, and pay the price dearly.

How about questioning Matl Oksenberg, just once more, even at the risk of disturbing her? Matthieu Schriftlich's hands move hesitantly under her arms upon which her long, stiff hair has fallen. Once more he grips her, he hoists her yet again over the lake, towards the east of Europe, in Volhynia let us say, towards the part of the world that has cast out its Jews. There are many such regions. You leave the place where you reside only when you are forced to, repeats Simon Gorbatchev. Living somewhere for years and years, you pretend to believe you belong. You grow accustomed to exile. You are a stranger in exile, but you fool yourself into believing that you have become like the others. You lose nothing for the wait, Matthieu. Trouble comes anew. The earth fissures, cracks, bursts. Separation occurs. From the other side of the wall children point at you. You are the weeds of the world. So an uncle, a sister, beckons from afar and you pack your bags.

"If indeed they give you time to leave, *panie* Gorbatch. You know, I'd gladly have a shot of vodka, just a drop, a teardrop. That's it, a teardrop. . . . But how was it again?"

—Translated by Alan Astro

GLOSSARY

BONJOURKE (Polish): a kind of dressing gown.
VALISKE (Polish, Yiddish): a small suitcase.
SÛRETÉ NATIONALE: a French police force.
GENDARMKE: the French word with a Polish diminutive suffix.
RAILROADKE: renders Raczymow's *chmindferké*, which adds the Polish suffix to the French term for "railroad," *chemin de fer*.
ZISE GESHTOKHENE PENEMER TAYERE LIPN VI BLUMEN (Yiddish): "Sweet stabbed faces Dear flowery lips," which renders "Douces figures poignardées Chères lèvres fleuries," the first verse of *La Colombe poignardée et le jet d'eau* by Guillaume Apollinaire, *Calligrammes* (Paris: Gallimard, Coll. Poésie, 1966), 74. Raczymow refers to the poet by his real name, Kostrowitzky.
KOCHANY (Polish): dear.
PANIE (Polish): sir.

TATENYU (Yiddish): little father.

ISBA (Russian): a small house made of fir.

BAAL SHEM TOV (Hebrew): "Master of the Good Name" (ca. 1700–1760), founder of Hasidism.

HENRI RACZYMOW

Memory Shot Through With Holes*

This is the text of a presentation entitled, "Exil, mémoire, transmission," which was read at a colloquium of Jewish writers held at the Sorbonne on 12 January 1986.

My place here is somewhat paradoxical. I am supposed to speak, yet I have nothing to say. No lesson to teach, no advice to give, no message to deliver, no strategies to propose. I bear tidings neither of war nor of peace. Like everyone else, I have opinions about everything, but my opinions are no more interesting than anyone else's.

There is one thing of which I can speak: my work as a writer. I do not necessarily believe that a writer is best suited to speak of his work. A careful, somewhat impassioned critic can do just as well, perhaps even better. But I can shed some particular light on one aspect of my writing: the Jewish concerns that run throughout.

The paradox I mentioned—my speaking while not having anything to say—is not simply a more or less gratuitous rhetorical figure. The paradox becomes clear to me as I think of when I began to write, or rather, first decided to write. I had an overwhelming desire to write, which has never left me, yet at the same time I felt I had nothing to say. The theories of the "new novelists" appealed to me. They took delight in repeating that they had nothing to say, that they needed to devise new forms of fiction. I thought I was attracted to such theories for purely ideological or esthetic reasons, but that was not at all true. Some years later I came to understand that I did *not* have *nothing to say*. Like many others I could have said, or written, just about anything. Rather, I had *to say nothing*, which is not the same thing. As the years went by, as I wrote more, I discovered that the nothing I had to say, to write, to

* Henri Raczymow, "La Mémoire trouée," *Pardès* 3 (1986): 177–82.

YFS 85, *Discourses of Jewish Identity in Twentieth-Century France*, ed. Alan Astro, © 1994 by Yale University.

explore—the nothing I turned into sentences, narratives, books—the nothing I could not escape saying as a positive nothing, was my Jewish identity.

My Jewish identity was not nothing, it was *nothingness*, a kind of entity in itself, with its own weight, value, stylistic possibilities, contours, colors, moorings. It might seem that my view is similar to the one expressed by Alain Finkielkraut in *Le Juif imaginaire*, but that is not the case.[1] Unlike Finkielkraut I would not say that Jewish identity is necessarily defined by absence, that it has to be an empty category, something imaginary. For some years now I have been teaching in an orthodox Jewish school, and my students, as becomes immediately apparent, are anything but imaginary Jews. I, however, am one, and I believe that the Holocaust has nothing to do with that. The figure of the imaginary Jew predates the Holocaust. It has been around for a while, having emerged in the *Haskalah*, the Jewish enlightenment, with the secularization of the Jews.[2] If Alex Derczansky were speaking instead of me, he could address the subject quite knowledgeably.[3] He might tell you about Bialik's poem, *On the Threshold of the Beit Hamidrash* [House of Prayer] which portrays the warmth within and the cold without.[4] The warmth within is the warmth of the *beit hamidrash*, and as a *maskil*, an "enlightened" Jew, Bialik remains on the threshold:

> On my tortuous path
> I have known no sweetness
> My eternity is lost.[5]

The lost eternity of which the poet speaks is Judaism itself, at least traditional Judaism. For Ashkenazic Jewry, eternity was lost well before the Holocaust, well before emigration to the West. I could say, "We

1. Alain Finkielkraut, *Le Juif imaginaire* (Paris: Seuil, 1980). [*All footnotes to this piece are by the translator.*]

2. The *Haskalah* ("enlightenment" in Hebrew) was the movement of nineteenth-century Eastern European Jewish intellectuals, called *maskilim*, who disseminated Western ideas of progress among their coreligionists.

3. A well-known scholar in the field of Yiddish, Alex Derczansky has taught at the Institut National des Langues et Civilisations Orientales, Paris.

4. Chaim Nachman Bialik (1873–1934) is a foremost figure of modern Hebrew poetry. A clanking, rhyming translation of *On the Threshold of the House of Prayer* appears in *Selected Poems of Hayyim Nakman Bialik*, ed. Israel Efros (New York: Histadruth Ivrit of America, 1948), 29–33. The original, *Al Saf Beit-Hamidrash* can be found in Bialik, *Collected Poems 1890–1898*, ed. Dan Miron (Tel Aviv: Dvir and Katz Research Institute, 1983), 253–55.

5. Vv. 41–43. We translate from the French version that Raczymow quotes.

are all German Jews," as the student slogan had it in May 1968.[6] But here that would mean that we are all modern Jews, all orphaned Jews, bereft of Judaism. We would not have seen, in the last few years, such a forceful return to the Judaism, to the Talmud, to Jewish languages, if precisely all that had not been lost. To return implies having left. Nonetheless, some fragments had been transmitted. "An I-don't-know what and a next-to-nothing," as Vladimir Jankélévitch would say.[7] But a few words of Yiddish do not constitute a legacy, but merely a remnant, the "next-to-nothing" that remains of what was lost. It is the proof or the mark of the loss—its trace. So a trace remains. In turn, we can lose the trace. Lose loss itself. Lose, if you will, the feeling of loss. And dissolve into nothing.

At the end of the 1970s, I made a voyage. I did not know then that I was not the only one. It was an imaginary voyage. I went to Poland, to the Jewish Poland that my grandparents had left. From this imaginary trip—I have never set foot in Poland—I brought back a short book in which I attempted to explore the "next-to-nothing" in my own memory.[8] A memory devoid of memory, without content, beyond exile, beyond the forgotten. What did I know about Jewish life in Poland? What had been told to me? Once again, nothing—or next to nothing. The unsaid, the untransmitted, the silence about the past were themselves eloquent.

Itzhok Niborski and Annette Wieviorka, in their work on *Les Livres du souvenir*, attempt to explain why immigrants from Poland could not or would not transmit their heritage.[9] They write: "The *shtetl* generation possesses a treasure that they are unwilling or unable to share. They feel that those who did not know life in the *shtetl* cannot

6. During the May 1968 student uprising in Paris, this slogan became a popular protest against the planned explusion of Danny Cohn-Bendit, a German Jewish student leader.

7. Vladimir Jankélévitch is a contemporary French philosopher whose works include *Le Je-ne-sais-quoi et le presque-rien* (Paris: Seuil, 1980).

8. Raczymow is referring here to his *Contes d'exil et d'oubli* ["Tales of Exile and Forgetfulness"], an excerpt of which is translated in this issue of *Yale French Studies*.

9. Annette Wieviorka and Itzhok Niborski, *Les Livres du souvenir: Mémoriaux juifs de Pologne* (Paris: Gallimard-Julliard, 1983). "Livres du souvenir" and "memorial books" translate *yisker-bikher*, the Yiddish term for the volumes of commemorative texts, maps, and photographs published by survivors of Eastern and Central European towns whose Jewish populations were decimated. For a presentation in English of such works, see Jack Kugelmass and Jonathan Boyarin, trans. and ed., *From a Ruined Garden: The Memorial Books of Polish Jewry* (New York: Schocken, 1983).

understand or identify with anything about it."[10] After the Holocaust, for that generation and even more so for the second and third generations born in France, the prevailing feeling is one of nostalgia, something very ambiguous. Nostalgia is an ambiguous sentiment because it is rife with mythology about a lost paradise, an idyllic "before," summed up here in the word *shtetl*. But well before the Holocaust, the *shtetl* was a world already belonging to the past and falling apart.

You have to distinguish between two kinds of nostalgia. The nostalgia of the generations of Jews born in France is not the same as the nostalgia of the generation born in Poland. That generation, as Niborski and Wieviorka have shown, has to imagine their place of origin beyond death, beyond the extermination of their families, towards whom they feel a debt. The "memorial books" they produced after the war to commemorate their towns take the place of graves for those who had no graves. Those works embellish the past simply because it was the past, the world before the Holocaust. In some way, the authors are lying to themselves, for they knew that world only too well. Roman Vishniac's photos of Jewish Poland, taken in 1938, hold no secrets for them.[11] How could they be nostalgic for the filth, the wretchedness, the poverty shown in those pictures? In turn, those born in France, especially the third generation looking back to the vanished world of their grandparents, also mythologize the past, but they do so unconsciously. We are submerged in mythology, and in their case even their nostalgia is mythical, for it is for something that they never knew, that no longer exists and that will never again exist. Their nostalgia is devoid of content, like the memory devoid of content I spoke of earlier; it is motivated by the very fact that the world they long for is no more, having been entirely reduced to ashes.

However, it is not the world Vishniac shows us that is missed, but rather the community, the "warmth within" (to repeat Bialik's phrase), a world where Jews truly formed a people whose very language was Jewish. They were a people, not a lobby, or a fad, or a topic for cocktail

10. *Les Livres du souvenir*, 174. The term *shtetl*, a diminutive of the Yiddish word *shtot* ("town" or "city"), is commonly used to designate the semirural localities in which many Jews lived in Eastern and Central Europe. Folklore on the *shtetl* has fostered a largely romanticized conception of Jewish history, exemplified by the musical *Fiddler on the Roof*. Actually, on the eve of World War II, great numbers of Jews lived in large cities such as Warsaw, Odessa, Kiev, Budapest.

11. Roman Vishniac's photographs of Polish Jews were republished in *A Vanished World* (New York: Farrar, Straus and Giroux, 1983).

party conversations, or learned symposia. Emigration has excluded us from that world, from that life, which themselves were wiped off the map.

It is only after something has taken place that we can measure its importance. After writing the slender volume in which I tried to recreate a Jewish Poland, I realized that my book formed a kind of parenthesis. I opened the parenthesis on a Poland that I knew led directly to Auschwitz or Treblinka, and I closed it on a portrayal of the place of immigration, the Parisian Jewish quarter of Belleville in the 1950s. In the center of this parenthesis stood a blank. Even later, quite recently in fact, I discovered that this blank had a name, but I could not bring myself to utter it. My first book, *La Saisie*, devoid of Jewish subject matter, had portrayed absence, emptiness.[12] A few years later, my first "Jewish" book, *Contes d'exil et d'oubli*, reiterated this absence, this blank, but inscribed it in a Jewish space. A parenthesis was formed by the before and after, the prewar and postwar; it was a frame in whose center lay silence. For me at that time, only silence could evoke the horror. A taboo weighed upon it.

I could, though only in my imagination, conjure up life before, claim to remember a Poland unknown and engulfed, whose language I had heard but never spoken. I could also portray what happened afterwards, in the semblance of a *shtetl* that Belleville was in the postwar years, with its simulacrum of *Yiddishkeit*.[13] It was a *shtetl*, a *Yiddishkeit*, shot through with holes, with missing links: the names of the dead. But what happened between the before and the after, when the drama was played out, when all disappeared, was off limits to me. I had no right to speak of it. Unlike Elie Wiesel, I could not ask how to speak of it, how to find the words for it. For you can always figure out how to speak, you can always find the words, in accordance with your ethics. My question was not "*how* to speak" but "*by what right* could I speak*," I who was not a victim, survivor, or witness. To ask, "By what right could I speak," implies the answer, "I have no right to speak." However, as any psychoanalyst will tell you, the time comes when you have to speak of what is troubling you. That was the point of my last book, caught in the abyss between my imperious need to speak and the

12. Raczymow, *La Saisie* (Paris: Gallimard, 1973).

13. *Yiddishkeit* (literally, "Jewishness") is a Yiddish word that can denote either Orthodox Judaism, or a Jewish way of life defined less in terms of religion than of culture. Raczymow is using the term in the second sense.

prohibition on speaking.[14] It is inscribed in what English-speaking psychoanalysts call a double bind.

What I name the "pre-past" or prehistory, along with the Holocaust, was handed down to me precisely as something *not* handed down to me. That was my case, but I believe it was quite common. Writing was and still is the only way I could deal with the past, the whole past, the only way I could tell myself about the past—even if it is, by definition, a recreated past. It is a question of filling in gaps, of putting scraps together. In my opinion, or at least in my case, "Abraham's memory" does not exist.[15] It is a myth. Abraham's memory is shot through with holes. The memory has burst, as a balloon bursts, but we spend out time sewing it back up. Sewing is an old tradition among us. In fact, sewing scraps together is every writer's task, a hypothetically endless task, an impossible task. That is why my work consists in presenting the scraps in all their diversity, in their disorder, in their dispersion, in a kind of diaspora—if I may use that well-worn metaphor.

In a remarkable essay, Nadine Fresco speaks of the "diaspora of ashes."[16] The hopeless attempt to trace down the ashes, to follow the trains (think of the recurring trains and tracks in Claude Lanzmann's film, *Shoah*), is the only thing that give me roots.[17] Mine are superficial roots, along the railroad tracks across Europe, through the paths of emigration and deportation. But I neither emigrated not was deported. The world that was destroyed was not mine. I never knew it. But I am, so many of us are the orphans of that world. Our roots are "diasporic." They do not go underground. They are not attached to any particular land or soil. Nor do they lie, as portrayed in David Shahar's work, at the

14. Raczymow, *Un Cri sans voix* (Paris: Gallimard, 1985). A translation by Dori Katz, *A Cry Without a Voice*, is to be published by Holmes & Meier. For a study of this and other novels by Raczymow, see Ellen S. Fine, "The Absent Memory: The Act of Writing in Post-Holocaust French Literature" in Berel Lang. ed., *Writing and the Holocaust* (New York: Holmes & Meier, 1988), 41–57.

15. This is a reference to Marek Halter's *La Mémoire d'Abraham* (literally, "Abraham's Memory") (Paris: Laffont, 1983), a best-selling romantic saga of Jewish history since its beginnings. It was translated by Lowell Bair as *The Book of Abraham* (New York: Holt, 1986).

16. Nadine Fresco, "La Diaspora des cendres," *Nouvelle Revue de Psychanalyse* (Fall 1981): 205–20.

17. Claude Lanzmann's nine-hour-long film on the Holocaust, entitled *Shoah*, has been discussed in many American publications. See, for example, "Seminar with Claude Lanzmann: 11 April 1990" in *Yale French Studies* 79 (1991): 82–99.

bottom of a well in Jerusalem.[18] Rather they creep up along the many roads of dispersion that the Jewish writer explores, or discovers, as he puts his lines down on the paper. Such roads are endless.

In a well-known passage, Kafka suggests that if Moses did not reach Canaan, it was not because he had sinned, but because his life was merely a human life.[19] We never reach Canaan. Canaan is only in sight. But for the writer, Canaan is the book that he is writing and that he dreams of finishing. Once it is finished, another Canaan is in sight, as he dreams of finishing another book. To reach Canaan would be to die. You surely know Luria's theory in the Kabbalah.[20] In order that creation could come to be, God withdrew himself from one point, so as to form a void. In my work, such a void is created by the empty memory I spoke of, which propels my writing forward. My books do not attempt to fill in empty memory. They are not simply part of the struggle against forgetfulness. Rather, I try to present memory *as* empty. I try to restore a non-memory, which by definition cannot be filled in or recovered. In everyone there is an unfillable symbolic void, but for the Ashkenazic Jew born in the diaspora after the war, the symbolic void is coupled with a real one. There is a void in our memory formed by a Poland unknown to us and entirely vanished, and a void in our remembrance of the Holocaust through which we did not live. We cannot even say that we were *almost* deported.

There are holes as well in our genealogy. We have no family trees. At the most, we can go back to our grandparents. There is no trace of anyone before. Whose graves can we go visit? What hall of records can we consult? Everything was burned. It seems that what was transmitted to a whole generation of Ashkenazic Jews was anything but a full body of knowledge. It was more like a cloud of neurosis in which the individual cannot orient himself. He must discover his own path, but through one of the perverse tricks that history plays on us, he experiences a kind of *déjà vu*. Strangely, he finds himself in the well-known, oft-discussed situation of the German-speaking Jews between the two world wars. Kafka despised them as he despised himself, a Western Jew,

18. Raczymow is referring here to a work by the contemporary Israeli novelist David Shahar, *The Palace of Shattered Vessels*, trans. Dalya Bilu (Boston: Houghton Mifflin, 1975).

19. Franz Kafka, *Diaries 1914–1923*, ed. Max Brod, trans. Martin Greenberg and Hannah Arendt (New York: Schocken, 1949), 195–96.

20. This theory of Isaac Luria, the sixteenth century Kabbalist, is discussed in Gershom Scholem, *Major Trends in Jewish Mysticism* 3d rev. ed. (New York: Schocken, 1961), 261.

but he also felt pity for them. He wrote to Milena, "I am as far as I know the most typical Western Jew among them. This means, expressed with exaggeration, that not one calm second is granted me, nothing is granted me, everything has to be earned, not only the present and the future, but the past too—something after all which perhaps every human being has inherited, this too must be earned, it is perhaps the hardest work. When the Earth turns to the right . . . I would have to turn to the left to make up for the past."[21]

So much for what Kafka wrote at the beginning of the 1920s. Since then, the earth has turned, and we know in what direction. But recapturing the past, trying to pursue it as we do the horizon, has been the purpose of my work as a writer. Of course, people will say to me (in fact, they have already said it, or I have read it here and there): "Well, that's all quite disappointing. You're always looking back, caught up in nostalgia, brooding over the past, a past dead and buried that no longer interests anybody. Why don't you follow the example of the American Jewish writers who tell us about their day-to-day lives as American Jews in the here and now? They don't bore us with stories about Poland and exile." To which I reply: "The Jews who came from Eastern Europe are inextricably tied to the past. Their world has been destroyed and the Jewish blood that was shed pollutes the entire European continent, from north to south and east to west. America is free of such pollution. Even those of us who did not live through those times tread every day upon ground where trains rolled towards Auschwitz, every day. . . . "

I spoke earlier of a cloud of neurosis, our only legacy. I believe it has to do with the feeling all of us have, deep down, of having missed a train. You know which train. What Kafka wrote to Milena at the beginning of the 1920s—"When the Earth turns to the right. . . . I would have to turn to the left"—is truer for us, more concrete and more essential. Out of the impossibility of recapturing the past, some forge the very meaning of their writing, well aware of how ridiculous the pursuit of the impossible is.

—Translated by Alan Astro

21. Kafka, *Letters to Milena*, ed. Willy Haas, trans. Tania and James Stern (New York: Schocken, 1953), 219.

OSER WARSZAWSKI

A Contract*
(Monologue)

> This text was written in Yiddish in 1943, a year before the author
> was murdered at Auschwitz. It tells of Jewish refugees in Grenoble
> who had escaped French internment camps. They suspected an even
> worse fate were they to be deported.

A well-dressed fellow, barely past thirty, with his hair carefully parted
on the side and a pleasant voice: that's B. Cinejdek, Pola Cinejdek's
brother, whom I've seen and spoken to just once in my life.

He's the guy with the contract. Pola arranged the meeting with her
brother. "He's got a proposition for you," she said, "a jewel of a proposition, for these days."

She's a jewel of a girl herself, that Pola. Twenty-eight or twenty-nine
years old, looks no more than twenty-six. A jewel of a girl. On the index
finger of her right hand she wears a diamond the size of a two-franc
piece and on her two ring fingers she has diamonds enough for four
betrothals. That's what she says her darling brother B. has "scraped
together" in the scarce two years the war has gone on.

"Scraped together?" In just two years? She must be kidding. Occasionally, some mortals do "scrape together" a fortune according to the
mathematical law of geometric progression. You know, the way mi-
crobes, bacillae and other microscopic organisms multiply. Take a
sum, let us say ten francs, and let it double overnight. The next morning, you have twenty. Let it double again. The morning after, you have
forty. How much do you think it comes to after twenty days, huh, how
much? You couldn't figure it out. A schoolboy knows that trick.

B. Cinejdek was a millionaire, a multimillionaire. And his sister
Pola was an acquaintance of my wife's, which means that up to the war

*Oser Warszawski, "A kontrakt" in Y. Spero et al., Yisker-bukh: Tsum ondenk fun
fertsn umgekumene parizer yidishe shrayber (Paris: Afsnay/Union des Juifs pour la
Résistance et l'Entr'aide, 1946), 101–05.

YFS 85, Discourses of Jewish Identity in Twentieth-Century France, ed. Alan Astro,
© 1994 by Yale University.

she worked as a seamstress like every other Jewish immigrant girl. The miracle was that despite her diamonds, she had not taken on cultivated airs. And that bothered my wife. "Pola? Even before the war she was flirtatious and flighty. Artists? She sneered at them. She preferred the company of our young Parisian doctors and merchants." That's what my wife told me and she knew Pola as one knows family.

My wife and I live in one room with our two children, whose ages all told add up to three and a half years. It was a miracle to have found even one room in G. No small matter, finding a vacancy in G.!

Why am I dragging the story out?

It's summertime. My wife has taken the children out to the square for fresh air. There she sees Pola, a Pola with diamonds! "She even pretended not to recognize me," my wife kept on saying. "But when she saw the two children, her eyes popped out of her head, as though she had never seen anything like them." There's the rub! She literally threw herself at our children. She became a daily visitor. One day, she brought candy for the older one, the next day one of her own dresses for my wife. (Our wardrobes, never quite worthy of the name, had been reduced to naught after a year in the camp.) Another time, she came with two bread tickets. You see what diamonds can buy? Most of all, she showed great affection for the child still in diapers. (That's just a figure of speech. There are no diapers to be had.)

The baby was born three months ago. It is now four months since my wife got out of the camp. She was lucky not to have given birth there. That's all I needed!

Well, a few days later, Pola brought news of the meeting she had arranged for me with her brother. Do you get it? B. Cinejdek wanted to see me alone. He had a proposition for me, a jewel of a proposition, as Pola put it. Can you imagine the havoc B. Cinejdek's proposition wrought in our heads? The last few days before the meeting, my wife and I were in a feverish state. Plans blossomed beneath our skulls, such as . . . Well, I don't want to say them out loud. Quickly, we moved from small hopes to great ones. You can say what you like, but we artists do not want for fantasy.

Yes, I am an artist. Please don't hold it against me that I introduce myself without having been asked. But it's relevant, very relevant.

B. Cinejdek had become our obsession. Everything seemed possible, and then not only possible but real, because a millionaire had made an appointment with me. B. Cinejdek had a proposition for me, a jewel of a proposition. What else could it be but a contract? A contract for a commission, as they used to have in Paris before the war. A contract between a wealthy art lover and a painter or a draftsman or an engraver or a sculptor or just an illustrator. And the wealthy know what they are doing! Art works are always worth money, whereas money sometimes loses its worth, as nowadays.

Of course, it is for them, for the wealthy, that money no longer has any worth. For a Jewish artist, however, it still has some. No matter how worthless money has become in '43, for the likes of us it is even more precious than before the war. Just think of it: I have to pay thirty-seven francs per day for our one room. Thirty-seven francs every day! Can you imagine the golden opportunities we saw, the plans that raced through our heads? A few times we woke up drenched in sweat. You may laugh, but we sweated the way the rich do.

It's never easy to talk about the troubles you've been through. A year ago, they sent me to a camp, just me. They were still showing mercy. But what a terrible thing, when they later took my wife, six months pregnant, along with our three-year old daughter. Since obviously we weren't millionaires, and since we didn't have any good, devoted, loyal, or simply idealistic friends of the kind who sends to the unfortunate internees the customary weekly package filled with sausage, butter, bread, sugar or saccharine, we were soon in a state such that even the wildest cannibal would turn up his nose at us. It seems you can still see the effects of deprivation.

One fine day, as my wife was approaching delivery they released her together with our three-year-old. Later, I "released" myself and found her with two children. Is there any understanding nature's secrets? Jokes aside, it was no longer possible to live.

The "committee" gives us money, but how much does it give? Indeed, how much can it give, when today one hundred francs are worth two francs or three or perhaps eight? How am I supposed to know? Certainly, it's no business of mine. I am, after all, an artist. But even a cabinet-maker has to eat.

Still, it is a miracle that the "committee" gives. So how much can it give? It's easy to figure out. If it has a million in the till, it gives eight hundred francs. But if it has only two hundred thousand, it stops giving altogether.

Things were looking pretty bleak, when my wife's prewar acquaintance brought a ray of hope into our small room.

If you too were an artist, you might be able to appreciate how impatiently my wife and I awaited our jewel of a contract.

First, the day of the appointment came, then the hour. I was at the agreed-upon place a bit early and planned to wait as long as I possibly could. But *he* showed up at the very minute he was supposed to.

A well-dressed guy with his hair carefully parted on the side introduced himself in a pleasant voice: B. Cinejdek, Pola's brother.

After the introductions and other formalities, he invited me into a café, where he ordered a bottle of saccharine water. We sat at a small table and exchanged a few words at random when he suddenly stood up.

"Let's take a walk around town. We can't speak about serious matters here. In a café, a thousand eyes are watching you."

So after the bottle of saccharine soda was finished, we went out, and as we walked he questioned me about my life in the old country, in Paris, and here in G. It seemed as though he were planning to write an essay about me, a monograph! I have to admit that my life up to now has hardly been rich in bottles of champagne and even less so in heart-rending episodes. Nonetheless, I had made up my mind that he would purchase the contract from me very dearly, not for a mess of pottage. Signing the contract would cost that fledgling millionaire, and how! He'd pay through the nose. Then again, *he* was the one getting a good deal, since ultimately he'd be making money off everything I produce. You think you understand something about diamonds? Works of art are sometimes worth more than diamonds. Let's say I were to become famous. They'd write newspapers articles about me, print books about me, flock to my exhibitions, and downright come to blows at auctions over every one of my paintings. That's just fantasy? For a while, let's pretend it's reality, since things like that have indeed happened. What then? Well, B. Cinejdek would no longer be a millionaire but a billionaire. And here am I, a pauper and schnorrer who can't even treat his family to an afternoon at the movies, but who is going to turn the wartime bigshot B. Cinejdek into a billionaire. Me and my contract!

You've seen me around, you know me, so you've certainly figured out I am not one of those artists they call bohemians. I do not hold court among drunkards. Nor do I prey on girls who pose in the nude for painters and sculptors. When I walk into a café, people don't stand up and nudge each other with their elbows: "Look over there, it's Monsieur, or Docteur, What's-his-name." I'm just an ordinary Joe, like all of you. But while you sew, stitch, saw, hammer, glue, polish or file, I paint. That's all there is to it. So I needn't elaborate. I'll just mention one last time how my wife and I couldn't get the contract out of our heads

during the few days between the news of my appointment with Cinejdek and the actual meeting.

So we walked around town. B. Cinejdek would ask something and I
would answer. We still hadn't gotten to the point. We came to a street
corner where a color poster from the national lottery was hanging. B.
Cinejdek stood facing it. I had never noticed it before, never given it a
second glance. And even if I had, it wouldn't have mattered much. For
how many such posters do you think I have seen in my lifetime?

Now, however, when I recall that day, the first thing that springs to
mind is that poster, as though it were an evil omen, a symbol of doom
like the fiery handwriting on the wall in Belshazzar's night of terror.

Standing next to the poster from the national lottery, the swine
suddenly spoke up:

"How much do you want for your child?"

I can assure you that as soon as he spoke those words, I saw my
grandmother before my eyes, heard her voice ("May lightning strike
him!"), saw my mother and heard hers ("A bombshell!"). I looked at him
the way a clay golem gazes at a man possessed of knowledge but sees no
more than . . . an onion!

"For the little one," the swine went on. "I'd rather 'buy' the older
one, it's easier. But the little one is more practical."

"And the contract . . . ?" I asked, like a golem, hardly able to part
my lips.

With a smile on his, he took me by the arm and led me into an
elegant bar. No longer was he afraid of a thousand eyes! He laid out the
proposition to me in an ordinary, straightforward, businesslike
manner:

I should sell, hand over, lend, rent to him my little three-month-old
baby. . .

Just because he, B. Cinejdek, like every other Jew this summer, has
already been in a camp. . . . But he's a man with feelings. . . . Sure, if
you have gold, you can't resign yourself to staying in a camp. . . . Then
you had to be afraid of deportation. So he escaped and came with his
sister to G. But were you safe in G.? Probably not. . . . So he has a plan.
Since they don't send you back from Switzerland if you have a small
child, he could marry his sister and "borrow" a child. . . . "Borrow" a
child—God in heaven! (B. Cinejdek threw a sour glance more or less in
the direction of God.) Why is it wrong for him to borrow a child,
especially as he is ready to finance a trip to Switzerland for a poor
couple with two children and even to support them there for the dura-

tion of the war—on the sole condition that one of the children be "signed over" to him. He has already found a family who would "give" him two children, or three if he wanted. But it's a family with nine children. Add in two parents and that comes to eleven. Eleven people!

That's why he felt more "drawn" to me. . .

The whole time he bared his soul, I stood there like an idiot without the slightest thought in my head. I didn't notice the soles of my shoes burning beneath my feet. I didn't feel as though I were suspended between heaven and earth, or atop a snow-covered mountain, one step away from a deep, dark abyss.

Nothing happened. There was no need to call a doctor. I didn't pass out. I wasn't slapped on the face by some madman. But everything had turned black. Soon I felt as though a murderer were threatening me with a knife: "Your child or your life!"

Why did it seem that way? By nature, I am not a seer. I have never been the kind who worries about tomorrow. In that minute, however . . . What am I saying? In that split second, I saw the border clearly before me. We are on foot. Two couples. My wife is carrying the older child, and Pola Cinejdek, her own brother's wife, holds the other. All of us have gotten safely to the other side. We are brought before the guards. They ask us: "What are your names and what is your business?" They divide us up. The ones with the older child remain with them, and those with the infant are led away. Come next morning, the guards have changed, and new ones lead us away. Where? Listen, you'll be amazed: back to the border. We cry, we beg, we scream. The new guards, however, know nothing about a Cinejdek family with a baby. I wring my hands, but in my wife there has sprung up the lioness, the she-wolf, the leopardess, in a word: the Jewish mother. She roars: "Who will nurse the baby? 'Sister' Pola?" But guards are guards. They have pushed us back. Back over to "this side" of the border, where we will surely be caught, sent to an internment camp and, as though that were not enough, from there deported. . .

I don't know whether I simply imagined these things or actually saw them for a hundredth of a second before my eyes. But as you can tell, I didn't fall down and die. Nor did I rail at him and call him names. I just left the little wartime plutocrat sitting there, or rather standing there with his face to the poster for the five million franc lottery prize. And that was all.

That was all?

Yes, that was all.

Like a dumbstruck fool.

For when someone says to you. "Good morning," you answer, "Good day." And if someone says, "The devil take your father," you answer, "The devil take your mother."

And had it not been for the stark terror that came over me, all four of us would now be in safety. We wouldn't have to wake up with a start in the middle of the night, asking, "Did you hear the bell? Didn't you hear the bell?" And we wouldn't have to wonder, in the middle of the day, how to "keep body and soul together," as my grandmother would have said.

In short, we would all be living off the millionaire in Switzerland.

And maybe, just maybe, I would even have the contract. . .

—Translated by Alan Astro

WOLF WIEVIORKA

Too Bad He's a Frenchman*

This story, published in 1936, is translated from the Yiddish.

"If misfortune shall befall you," says a Jewish proverb, "it will come into your home on its own." That proverb, you will see, was coined with me in mind.

Let me introduce myself. My name is Neiberg. A cabinet-maker by trade, I have been living in Paris for fifteen years, and am a bachelor into the bargain.

I know full well that you aren't going to let the last part slip by. You will want to know why I haven't married, what I am waiting for, and the like. So let me tell you straight out that you aren't the first to come with such questions and objections. Matchmakers enough have beaten a path to my door, imploring me to let myself be made happy by them. But I have not been led astray. I took no fright, even when they warned me that, having reached my forties, I would probably never marry unless I did so now.

What do they mean by "now"?

Listen well. They have discovered I possess a noble pedigree, of which I had been totally unaware until quite recently. And that pedigree of mine has brought upon me the misfortune I want to tell you about.

My "pedigree" is that I am a Frenchman. Imagine me, of all things, as a "Frenchman"! In the entire fifteen years I have been in Paris, I have not eaten a single crayfish or any of the other creatures the French partake of with such relish. When I have so much as a glass of red wine with lunch, as I occasionally do, you should see the face I make. Now you know what kind of Frenchman I am. And I'm not ashamed to tell you another secret: even with the French language I am not on the friendliest of terms. Quite a Frenchman I am!

*"Er iz a frantsoyz, nebekh . . . " in W. Wewiorka [sic], *Gezamlte shriftn, ershter band: Mizrekh un mayrev* (Paris: W. Wewiorka Yubiley-Komitet, 1936), 139–47.

YFS 85, *Discourses of Jewish Identity in Twentieth-Century France,* ed. Alan Astro, © 1994 by Yale University.

113

What then were they going on about? About the fact that I am a naturalized French citizen. So all the laws and regulations and newspaper articles against foreigners do not apply to me. I had had the fortunate idea of filing for naturalization in the days when every foreigner could obtain French citizenship, provided he had been in the country for five years and had conducted himself properly.

Such was the "pedigree" the matchmakers had suddenly discovered in me. They tried to talk me into believing it was worth a fortune, more than a dowry. And when I saw so many acquaintances losing their work permits, when I saw their hopelessness and despair, it dawned on me that I indeed possessed something akin to noble birth. Still, I did not want to marry. It seemed to me that these times of crisis, insecurity, and fear of war were not conducive to marriage.

I would probably still be living in blissful bachelorhood, were not my "pedigree" to be my ruination.

Let me tell you my tale of woe.

At the time when the great turmoil started, when every foreign worker had to file an application with the Labor Ministry for a work permit, when there kept coming the response: "No! No! No!" two acquaintances of mine came up to my place and involved me in a conversation about how clever was he who had gotten naturalized while there was still time.

They counted me among the clever ones and showered me with compliments. It turned out I was not only clever, but good-hearted and kind. In short, they sweet-talked me so that by the time they got to the heart of the matter, they had me tied down and in their clutches. There was no way I could even think over what they asked of me.

And what was their request? It couldn't be more simple or straightforward.

Since I was a French citizen and a bachelor with no intention of marrying, and since the law states that the foreign-born wife of a Frenchman is eligible for French citizenship herself, they had a small request to make of me. They were sure I would not refuse, since after all they knew me to be a fine person with a good heart.

Following these introductory remarks, they explained what they wanted from me.

There was a little lady, a widow with two tiny children, whose application for a work permit had been denied. Her appeals had come to nought. Now only two options remained to her. Either she could marry a French citizen and thereby obtain, as a Frenchwoman, a work permit, or she could throw herself and her two children into the Seine. And they left it to me to decide which choice she should make! Of course, I would only have to see the woman for the "wedding" at City Hall. Afterwards, I would have no dealings with her and she none with me. And should I ever get it into my head to marry for real, that too would be no problem. I could simply divorce her and be done with the matter.

As I said to you: they heaped such flattery upon me that I didn't even try to resist.

Shortly after the aforementioned visit, I became the lawful husband of a woman of mannish appearance, who thanked me over and again for the favor I had done her. As she took leave, she assured me that meeting me had been a great pleasure. She hoped that if we ever saw each other again, she would be able to pay back one good turn with another.

Naturally, I explained to her that there was no need to thank me, for I had done no more than human decency required of me. I left my lawful "wife" with the firm intention of never seeing her again. Indeed, I soon forgot her. True, from time to time I recalled not so much my "wife" as the marriage, congratulating myself for having been a fine fellow, who had saved a widow from throwing herself and her two children into the Seine.

A month later, my "wife" honored me with a visit. She came one evening to explain that she felt very indebted to me for the good deed I had done. For that reason, she had come to find out how I was doing and how things were going. I thanked her and told her things were going just fine. She scolded me for keeping such an untidy home; you could immediately see, she said, that a man lived there alone. Then she voiced the philosophical notion that one must find a mate in life. In her opinion, it made no sense for a man to be by himself.

Judging from the way my "wife" had made herself comfortable, I realized she had no intention of leaving anytime soon. I took a look at the clock and said I had to get to an important meeting. I began to put on my coat. My "wife" noticed a button missing and offered to sew one on.

My "wife" tried to persuade me to skip that evening's meeting. When I assured her that was impossible, she asked me to honor her with a visit. She wanted her children to meet the man who had done them such a favor.

Why do I have to drag the story out? No doubt you have already understood that my "wife" managed to inch her way into my life but good. At first she came to "thank" me around twice a week. Seeing how gratitude was getting her nowhere, she began little by little to borrow money, since right now she was out of work. I lent her some and told her there was no problem, she could pay me back when she got work. The second time she asked, I made a face and gave her less than she wanted. The third time around, I said, "Sorry." By the fourth time, I had to accept the situation, like it or not, as my "better half" informed me that by law a man is required to support his wife. If I didn't like her enough to live with her, that was my business, but she would not give up her rights.

I don't have to go on about the scandal I raised, the cries I let out that made people come running. I needn't recount my appealing to her sense of justice, my asking her if this was the way to thank a man she didn't know from Adam for the good turn he had done her. It's not necessary to tell you all of that. You will believe me when I say that the whole time she smiled with a devilish smile, then asked how a man like myself, who could treat a woman so meanly, also had the nerve to speak about justice.

Can you believe that?

In short, every week I send support to my "wife." She has agreed to 100 francs a week, although she pointed out her generosity by saying the courts would have awarded her more. No longer does she visit me, but recently I got word that I should expect to increase my wife's payments, for I shall surely soon become a father.

Such is the bag of troubles that being French has brought upon me.

—Translated by Alan Astro

II. Cultural Contexts

SETH L. WOLITZ

Imagining the Jew in France: From 1945 to the Present

Imagining the Jew is a French intellectual pastime that dates back some two hundred years. On 27 September 1791, the National Assembly removed the humiliating legal restrictions placed upon the Jew under the ancien régime. It conferred full individual French citizenship on the Jew but also forcibly "emancipated" him from his *statut communitaire*, his status as a member of a juridically recognized distinct community. The Jewish people qua national grouping was thus dissolved by the National Assembly into one more legally tolerated religious association that in the course of natural assimilation might disappear.[1] As sociologist Annie Kriegel has noted:

> Emancipation was conceived in France from the very beginning in terms of the individual, in terms of the private person: the French Jew's relationship to France is as an individual, as a private citizen, the Jewish community as such is thinly woven, informal, and of an almost entirely private nature.[2]

This new sociopolitical contract seemed acceptable: release from the bondage of the ancien régime and from an outmoded identity and culture in exchange for the new freedoms guaranteed by the Declaration of the Rights of Man and the universalism implied in the new citizenship of the republic. The fusion of national citizenship and of

1. François Delpech, "L'Histoire des Juifs de France de 1780 à 1840" in Bernhard Blumenkranz and Albert Soboul, ed., *Les Juifs et la révolution française* (Toulouse: Privat, 1976), 10.
2. Annie Kriegel, "Postface" in Béatrice Philippe, *Etre juif dans la société française* (Paris: Montalba, 1979), 405–06.

YFS 85, *Discourses of Jewish Identity in Twentieth-Century France*, ed. Alan Astro, © 1994 by Yale University.

philosophical universalism became the distinguishing matrix of all friendly imaginings concerning the French Jew and his condition.

French citizenship entails an explicit legal and an implicit cultural adherence; universalism requires a philosophical adherence to the new Western principles of *liberté, égalité, fraternité* with their progressive, rationalistic ideals. These two often contradictory positions, French citizenship and philosophical universalism, were considered in Condorcetian terms as seamlessly fused. The subsequent history of France, however, has made this posture open to debate. Nevertheless, the original contract between the Jew and the French republic legitimized the individual aspiring to the *right* of passage through French citizenship into a world of universal reason. Conversely, surreptitiously, it expected a rapid abandonment of "particularistic" Jewish peoplehood and culture.

Thus, from 1791 to the present, with the exception of the Vichy years, the "French Jew" did not exist as a legal category of citizenship. The individual of Jewish origin exists merely as an ordinary French citizen, *un bon citoyen français*. Napoleon reinforced this legal perspective. French Jews in their vast majority pledged an oath of allegiance. As Frenchmen speak of *nos ancêtres les Gaulois*, they too bemusedly accepted the Gauls as their forebears. Such was the asking price for citizenship and normalization of their status de jure et de facto.

Unfortunately, legal fictions or imaginings rarely obtain in the de facto world. De facto normalization was hindered by anti-Semitism, whether deriving from religious differences, xenophobic atavisms, or theories inspired by Count Joseph Arthur de Gobineau, the nineteenth-century inventor of racism. In turn, the Dreyfus affair threw into question even the de jure status of French Jews as legitimate French citizens. It was the Dreyfus affair that really reopened the Jewish question.

La France juive by Edouard Drumont (1886) established the French anti-Semitic tenor of the twentieth century by denying the Jew his legitimacy in *la France réelle*, de facto France. Against this nonjuridical condemnation, the French Jew found himself helpless and threatened. Jean-François Lyotard, in his recent contribution to the Jewish question, *Heidegger et "les juifs,"* presents the condition of the European Jew in succinct terms:

> What is most real about real Jews is that Europe, at least, does not know what to do with them: Christians demand their conversion,

monarchs expel them, republics assimilate them, Nazis exterminate them.[3]

Inescapably, a sense of otherness and isolation results from the "placelessness" (non-lieu) in which the Jew is put by the anti-Semite (Heidegger et "les juifs," 13).

The responses of both French philosemites and French Jews until World War II were either defensive and apologetic or imbued with a Zionist perspective. Edmond Fleg né Flegenheimer (1874–1963) represents the former with his L'Anthologie juive (1923) and Pourquoi je suis juif (1928), and André Spire (1868–1966) with his Poèmes juifs (1919) represents the latter. The philosemites in literature, Jacques de Lacretelle (author of Silbermann [1922]) and the Tharaud brothers (Un Royaume de Dieu [1920]) defended Jewish sensibility and spirituality, although both Lacretelle and the Tharauds abandoned their philosemitism in the late thirties. Silence was the preferred modus operandi of French Jewry in the face of anti-Semitic slander. So long as their legal and juridical condition as French citizens was secure, French Jews until World War II chose to cope defensively with their detractors. The war changed even that strategy. Insofar as they were stripped of French citizenship and deported qua Jews, the trauma required explanation or interpretation. Jewish identity was reproblematized.

Jean-Paul Sartre's opuscule, Réflexions sur la question juive, appearing originally in 1946, changed the terrain of the discourse on the Jewish question in France.[4] Eschewing the quiddity of the Jewish being that served apologetics and religious revivalism, Sartre sought to question status: the existential, epistemological, and ontological condition of the Jewish man in his objective situation. By analyzing the Jew in a social realm, Sartre recognized Jews as victims of social aggression. His text, informed by the intention to be life-saving, immediate, and strictly practical, sought to understand the problem and propose a solution. Sartre limited his concern to the French Jew—"it is the problem of the French Jew that is our problem"—a specification too often overlooked by later critics (73). Moreover, as far as French Jews are concerned, our hindsight allows us to appreciate that Sartre's acute

3. Jean-François Lyotard, Heidegger and "the jews," trans. Andreas Michel and Mark S. Roberts (Minneapolis: University of Minnesota Press, 1990), 3, modified as per the original: Heidegger et "les juifs" (Paris: Galilée, 1988), 13.

4. Jean-Paul Sartre, Réflexions sur la question juive (Paris: Paul Morihien, 1946; reprt. Gallimard, 1954). An English version exists—Anti-Semite and Jew, trans. George J. Becker (New York: Grove, 1960)—but quotations here are directly rendered from the French original. Page numbers refer to the Gallimard edition.

speculations applied only to the academic and intellectual circles in Paris. They did not necessarily extend to Jews of the Marais quarter or those of Neuilly or Strasbourg.

Sartre's groundbreaking accomplishment was to emphasize the definition of the Jew from the aggressor's perspective that serves to drape the intended victim. He underscored that the anti-Semite functions in a distorted mental space in which the Jew embodies all the anti-Semite's fears, negativities and inadequacies. The Jew becomes the personification of absolute evil. He appears both physically and morally monstrous, has a crooked nose, economic proclivities like Shylock's, is sexually threatening, disloyal, etc. In short, he is a collage of stereotypical aggregates of the mediocre mind that is frightened by modernity and turns radically reactionary. The anti-Semite's definition of the Jew must be understood, for the anti-Semite is dangerous. When he obtains political power, he can and does physically eradicate the Jew as evil incarnate. Reason or apologetics are therefore useless defenses.

In dialectical fashion, Sartre then asks if the French Jew has, in fact, a presence in the social sphere with a definable self-projected identity. Sartre's critical eye discerns no uniqueness of identity, whether physiological, religious, or national, at least among contemporary French Jews. To the contrary, he witnesses only assimilationists functioning as historian Marc Bloch did, under the rubric of *civis Gallus sum*. (It is now known that sociologist Raymond Aron—at least the Aron of the 1930s—was Sartre's French Jewish model.) Sartre's observation of assimilationists leads to the most startling statement in the work: "The Jew is a man whom other men take to be a Jew: such is the simple truth. . . . It is the anti-Semite who creates the Jew" (84). Thus the French Jew does not exist juridically, nor does he exist as a self-willed presence; he is a "simulacrum," to use Baudrillard's term for an image without content.[5] At best, he is part of an "abstract historical community" that the West refuses to assimilate fully (80); instead, it creates the Jew in its negative image. The Jew is thus other to himself and to the Gentile. He walks with a mask placed on him by the Other, which he can never rip off. This increases his "inner dialectic" (*réflexivité*), as he seeks to root out his own undesirable Jewishness (115). Each French Jew shares with other French Jews only their undesirable *situation*, their psychosociological status or condition (81). What is authentically

5. Jean Baudrillard, *The Evil Demon of Images* (Sydney: The Power Institute of Fine Arts of the University of Sydney, 1988).

Jewish is their "shared condition" (*identité de situation*) leading to martyrdom (179).

Sartre then proposes as the solution to this dilemma not the inauthenticity of escape from a negative objective condition but the brave acceptance of its reality in order to revolt. However, revolt against the false image does not necessarily bring social amelioration, for as Sartre notes pessimistically, "the condition of the Jew is such that anything he does is turned against him" (175). The revolt can only be moral. By choosing to revolt, by recognizing one's objective condition, one assumes one's own identity, whether as a Frenchman of Jewish origin, a French Jew, or a Zionist. This self-definition is more desirable than passivity involved in the craven refusal to face the anti-Semite's postulates of Jewish maleficence. Ultimately, Sartre can only offer the classless society of the future socialist revolution to rid the Jew of his negative condition caused by the bourgeois class antagonisms that are the source of anti-Semitism. Following the collapse of most scientific socialist economies and regimes, we can only smile at Sartre's political solution.

Nevertheless, Sartre's opuscule of 1946 must be recognized as the basis of most intellectual debate in France concerning the Jew and his representation for the next forty years. Sartre established the existential approach to the Jewish question and focused upon the *social* issue of the Jew as the prime factor. By foregrounding the dyad—the Jew and his opponent, the anti-Semite—as the antipodes of the dilemma, Sartre forces both Jewish and Gentile French intellectuals to confront the Jewish question globally by avoiding isolated treatment of Judaism, the Jew, or the anti-Semite. After this small work, the Jew is no longer seen as sharing with other Jews a race or fate or faith. Rather, he is the phantom victim of the absolute tendency to exclude the Other. From Sartre's perspective, the entire Jewish question could have been obviated by gradual assimilation, had not anti-Semitism hindered the natural course of events.

Sartre was one of few French Gentiles who wrote sensitively about the continuing problems facing French Jewry after the war. This drew much praise from French Jewish critics, even as they broadened and refined some of his premises. Albert Memmi has written:

> Sartre's analysis in *Reflections on the Jewish Question* appears to me to contain more intuitions and insights than are found in tons of other publications.[6]

6. Albert Memmi, *Portrait d'un Juif* (Paris: Gallimard, 1962), 16.

As a French-speaking, Tunisian-born Jew, Memmi recognized that the end of Western imperialism and decolonization—the panacea demanded by socialists—did not resolve the Jewish question. This led him to publish *Portrait d'un Juif* in 1962 and *La Libération du Juif* in 1966.[7] In these works, Memmi uses his autobiographical experience—an insider's view—to test Sartre's analysis of the Jewish condition from the outside. He agrees with Sartre that "the Jew remains essentially an oppressed figure. That is how I have experienced my Jewish condition" (*Libération*, 14). However, he breaks with Sartre's notion that the Jew lacks distinctive characteristics, disregarding the fact that Sartre was describing a specific French Jewish milieu.

For Memmi, North African Jews are a colonized group, trapped in a provincial culture and an outmoded religion, but they possess an identity as part of the Jewish people. As a Sephardic Jew, he feels a commonality with Eastern European Jews. Indeed, he fully accepts Sartre's argument that there is a shared identity in the Jewish condition, but for him this identity is enhanced by being an ethnicity with a shared history of oppression and religious culture. It is religion that defines traditionally Jewish identity and peoplehood; both provide a Jewish specificity that is life-giving: the Jew "lives his Jewishness [*judéité*] in Judaism ['the totality of Jewish doctrines and Jewish institutions'] and in a perfectly positive milieu of social community [*judaïcité*]" (*Portrait*, 244; 17). But Memmi recognizes that the mellah or ghetto Jew is a disappearing type as the Jew encounters Westernization and modernity.

Memmi seeks a renewed Jewish culture in imitation of the renaissance of Third World nations. For Memmi, Sartre's phantom Jew must be given a renewed specificity, distinctive characteristics. What this new specificity might be remains unspecified. The oppressed Jew must seek national liberation as the essential ground for a cultural renovation. The State of Israel, for Memmi, best expresses this Jewish return to History (in the Hegelian sense), a regaining of geographic and cultural specificity with liberty of action or sovereignty. In this new condition, the secular culture in bud can finally emerge freed of its religious shackles. Memmi, therefore, skillfully fuses the existentialist analysis of the oppressed Jew with that of the situation of the colonized Jew. This is the dual condition of the Jew needing liberation from oppression and proffering a renewed cultural specificity to the phantom Jew of Sartre.

7. Memmi, *La Libération du Juif* (Paris: Gallimard, 1966).

Following Sartre, Memmi calls for the Jew to accept his situation, to refuse any consolation, and to act to change his objective condition. Memmi, however, does not expect socialism or the revolution to free the Jews from anti-Semitism; national sovereignty, nonetheless, will ease the burden. For the Jew in France, the existence of Israel provides psychological comfort and permits him as a French citizen to combat anti-Semitism and choose his own life-style, including participation in the growth and development of a positive French Jewish culture. Memmi, going beyond Sartre, seeks to assert his Jewish identity as a positivity:

> Jean-Paul Sartre, to whom I spoke of his book, *Reflections on the Jewish Question*, explained to me why he had believed that the Jew was almost uniquely a negativity: all his Jewish friends seemed Jewish in no other way. . . .
>
> I am convinced that if the eminent author were to rewrite his book today, he would develop the positive aspects more fully. It is within this generous but truncated perspective that one must place Sartre's conception, so popular in the post-war years, of the Jew as a pure vision of the Other. It was a friendly conception that sought to help and to save the Jews, but it is insufficient to account for the reality of Jewish existence. [*Portrait*, 241–42]

The philosopher Robert Misrahi, Memmi's contemporary, a Parisian-born Sephardic Jew whose family came from Istanbul, approaches Jewish identity from an assimilationist perspective in a detailed theoretical exposition, *La Condition réflexive de l'homme juif.*[8] This work, originally published by Sartre's press Les Temps Modernes, is distinctive in elaborating upon the dialectical or reflexive situation of the Jew that Sartre had noted earlier. Misrahi builds upon this perspective to reveal the Jew as a witness reflecting the exterior world and refracting it inwardly, as a self that is both reflector and reflection (*soi-même comme reflet et réflexion*) [46].

Therein lies Misrahi's defense of intellectual assimilation into the French substance. This assimilation corresponds to his entrance into universal as opposed to Jewish culture, which is either insubstantial or at best the stagnant and provincial culture of Jews like his parents. He has chosen the "French universe against the provincial" (*l'univers français contre le particulier*, 41), fully aware that an orthodox Jew would see this position as an abandonment. Misrahi makes no distinc-

8. Robert Misrahi, *La Condition réflexive de l'homme juif* (Paris: Julliard, 1963).

tion between universal culture and French culture; his perspective is based ultimately on the Condorcetian principles according to which reason and other ideals of the Enlightenment make the French republic a setting of universal culture. Therefore, he is as opposed to French right-wing nationalism as he is to Jewish orthodoxy. His France is the Universal Temple of Reason in Paris. The Jewish world, limited to particularistic community, is now superseded by France the Universal. This is the real emancipation and enlightenment that all Jews should desire.

Misrahi, in this sense, contributes to Sartre's basic view of the Jewish condition as a negativity. Indeed, he defines the modern Jewish condition in France as "a distinct figure without distinctive characteristics" (*une particularité sans détermination*) [151]. The Jew, following Sartre, is forced to face his Jewishness only when the anti-Semite threatens. In an act of authenticity, the Jew is then thrown back to an outmoded Jewish identity, now devoid of substance; he shares with other Jews merely an appellation and a situation. Modern Jewish identity is no more than a "dialectical nationality" created in defense against the anti-Semite (131). In its most complete form as a reactive nationalism, it is called Zionism. This distinct form of identity, a "dialectical" (*réflexive*) relationship, does create or reinforce the "consciousness of the Jew" and is valid against the mortal threat of anti-Semitism. Here Misrahi joins Sartre and Memmi in admitting that the life-threatening condition of the Jew is an inescapable fact.

The modern Jew, like himself, for whom "universal culture is the principal object of his research," demands unfortunately "a dialectical will (*volonté réflexive*) to assert himself against anti-Semitism," a hindrance to his assimilation into the universal (209). He must accept his negative "shared condition" (*identité de situation*) with all other Jews anywhere in the world, fully aware that their Jewishness is without content (211). The acceptance of his Jewish identity becomes an ethical principle. He affirms his "belonging to the Jewish collective" (*judaïcité*) as a "Jewish responsibility" and his Judaism as "a responsibility for the other Jews of the world as they are responsible for me" (231).

The existence of Israel fulfills Zionist ideals and offers a necessary solution to anti-Semitism by providing a haven for Jews. Its liberty and strength serve as a powerful dialectical response to anti-Semitism. Israel permits the Jew to be rid of a "Jewish" identity, for inside Israel Jews become ordinary men who can proceed to assimilate to the universal. What Misrahi implies, then, is that Israel's sovereignty and power provide the necessary security for the growth of enlightenment and universalism among Jews. Thus the French path to the universal should not be of necessity any faster or closer to universal than the Israeli path, since to choose to assimilate to the universal is, according to Misrahi, a subjective act that begins from some particularistic condition. Israel, therefore, must exist so that all persecuted or threatened Jews have a safe haven.

Misrahi, however, eschews any role for developing Hebrew culture as legitimate in itself, since in his perspective, universal culture is the only valid good. French culture seemingly bathes in this aura and thereby justifies Misrahi's presence in Paris, which is a site of universalism! Thus Israel is legitimized on the social plane, but held provincial on the cultural one. The Jew-in-the-world must remain in a dialectical situation between himself and other Jews and in a state of otherness or "friendly relations" between himself and the Gentiles:

> To be a Jew in the modern world and notably in France, one must reflect upon oneself as a Jew (se réfléchir à soi-même comme juif) and then act as one reflects upon oneself (comme on se réfléchit). [252]

Misrahi thus shares with Memmi the Sartrian notion that after an authentic consciousness-taking of one's situation as a Jew, one must act for one's own emancipation, for the sake of other Jews and all mankind:

> In a word, the Jew should always and wherever champion the universal against the particular and the shared identity of mankind against differentiations among men. [249]

In the diaspora, the French Jew plays the role of a "witness to the human condition" (257), an idea also found in Sartre. This means that the Jew is a minority figure in a world that has not yet arrived at universalism, a world that must, alas, include France:

> The diasporic Jew becomes seemingly the very incarnation of the negative dialectic (la réflexion d'opposition): the Jew is par excellence the man who thinks in opposition to himself. [248]

Jew as antithesis. Jew as the man who questions. From Misrahi's perspective, the Jew must be a man of the left, for the left is both rational and universalistic. In short, the Jew is in the reflexive condition or dialectical situation whence he began:

The Jew is the absolute Other in a society that has been unable to
bring about the absolutely identical, for equality among all men
[*l'identité avec tous les hommes*] is its primal project and absolute
end. [249]

Essentially, Misrahi has not proposed a change in the objective
condition of the Jew vis-à-vis the anti-Semite. However, he has sought
to reinterpret for the modern Jew his exposed position decanted of its
religious inspiration or messianic drive and has substituted for traditional Judaism the French rights of man: these are the new Ten Com-
mandments. In short, the Jew still remains on the front lines in the
adversarial encounter with the Gentile of the right wing, but now Jews
can make one with other universalists in seeking social justice. Thus
Misrahi reemphasizes the ultimate goal of Jewish assimilation into
the universal, yet maintains the Jew as an ethical authority—albeit
atheist—while one awaits the millenium. I wonder if this is anything
other than secularized repressed messianism.

Alain Finkielkraut, born in 1948, admits in *Le Juif imaginaire*
(1980) that Sartre's text, published two years before he was born, directly affected his vision of himself as a Jew:

How I liked Sartre! He told me that I was an authentic Jew, that I
assumed my condition and that it demanded courage, if not heroism,
to assert my membership within an accursed people.[9]

But for this Jew born after the war, acceptance of his Jewish identity
appears hardly courageous:

There was a large gap between what I believed to be so and the life I
actually led, which Sartre's magical prose covered. I was a secure
young Jew, nicely ensconced in the comfort of a revolt without any
danger. [16]

Finkielkraut argues that the postwar Jew in France lives in bad
faith, for the Jew as the oppressed figure in Sartre, Memmi, and Misrahi
belongs to the previous generation: "I inherited a suffering I had never
undergone; I kept the persecuted man's role but no longer underwent
the persecution" (12). To identify, as a Jew, with a people who had
intensely and unjustly suffered was exhilarating and provided one with
a sense of moral superiority and distinction. For the new generation,
Judaism does not fall under an "ethical or religious definition or the
Sartrian schema": it is merely suffering without suffering (22). These

9. Alain Finkielkraut, *Le Juif imaginaire* (Paris: Seuil, 1980), 16.

young Jews are the "imaginary Jews" of Finkielkraut's title (23). This does not mean that the anti-Semitic scourge is gone; now it is benign, after the great blood-letting. The French-born imaginary Jew can be a committed activist Jew (un Juif engagé) in the Sartrian sense, but that sense is without danger and therefore empty. In short, to use Sartre's term, he is inauthentic.

What can the French Jew born after World War II do to be an authentic Jew? Finkielkraut admits to a quandary. He knows that the Yiddish culture of his parents, Polish Jewish immigrants, was destroyed by genocide and turned into "folklore" (50). Yet it had been an authentic culture that fused modernity and Judaism, not some provincial, traditional Jewish culture of the kind dismissed by Misrahi and other assimilationists. Could it still serve as a model?

In France, survivors like Finkielkraut's parents simultaneously hastened their children's assimilation into French culture, yet insisted they maintain a historical identity as Jews, but "without content" (48). Finkielkraut thereby encounters Misrahi's definition of the modern Jew as "a distinct figure without distinctive characteristics" (une particularité sans détermination). The imaginary Jew hides the emptiness of this figure with the bravura of his supposedly Jewish activistic commitment (engagement) in good left-wing, atheistic, universalistic causes:

> As a Jew on the left, I asserted my Jewish identity in every one of my political choices . . . , but at the same time and for the same reason, I scorned Jewish culture. [212]

Unlike Sartre and Misrahi, Finkielkraut finds political engagement insufficient as a form of Jewish identity. Now closer to Memmi, Finkielkraut wants specificity, not particularité sans détermination or some universalism. He finds his politically committed Jewish self with its militant universalistic principles unfulfilling, for it lacks meaningful content. Jews like his parents were

> Jews on the inside and men on the outside . . . ; we are Jews on the outside, and on the inside we are men like all others, without any cultural specificity. [121]

Jewish otherness today merely consists in affirming an otherness without content. Finkielkraut goes on to accuse French Jews of his generation of another imaginary identity: acting as heroic Israelis in Paris:

> Without a community, without a belief, without a culture of their
> own, the Jews rescue their identity [by reading newspapers] daily and
> linking themselves [thus] to the collective of Israel. [160]

Jewish identity begins for Finkielkraut with the recognition of an
absence:

> Jewishness is what I lack, not what defines me. I call Jewish the part
> of me that does not resign itself to live in my own time, that
> cultivates the formidable supremacy of what has been over what is
> today. [51]

Starting from a point opposite from that of Memmi who lived an authentic life in the mellah of his childhood, Finkielkraut was born too
late to know the Jewish culture that would have been his: the Yiddish-
speaking world. He recognizes his difference and distance:

> Judaism is not natural to me. Between myself and the past there
> exists an insurmountable distance. The requirement of memory is
> born with the painful consciousness of the separation. [50]

It is this lack resonating so strongly that Lyotard will develop in his
Heidegger et "les juifs."

Finkielkraut conceives of the modern French Jew as a figure in
search of his Judaism: "the word 'Jew' designates the vacant place of a
past through which a clean sweep has been made" (176). He is reinvent-
ing the Jew and Judaism to fill the lack: "I value Judaism today because
it comes to me from the outside and brings me more than I contain"
(212). For Finkielkraut, the postwar French imaginary Jew revels in
pathetic narcissism, but authenticity begins with rejecting the left-
wing universalism and Jewish underdog political activism, preached
by Sartre and Misrahi but no longer valid. Now is the hour for the Jew in
a more pluralistic France to reconceive what was a distinct
particularity!

Thus what Misrahi and even Memmi in their haste for French
universality would consign to oblivion—the distinctiveness and positivity of their received Jewish cultural particularity—is what is reasserted by Finkielkraut. Two factors are involved in this change: 1)
Finkielkraut had Yiddish culture as his model, a modern Eastern European culture as opposed to the Sephardic folk cultures of Istanbul and
Tunis; 2) he is from a different historical generation.

Misrahi is similar to Finkielkraut in that they both belong to the
first generation in their families to be born in France, but Misrahi is

older. The Holocaust separates the mental spaces in which they function. Misrahi exposes French culture as his template to universality and his Jewishness as an ethical imperative until that happy day of universality. Finkielkraut, on the other hand, is a romantic tasting the bitterness of Lamartine's verse, "O temps, suspends ton vol" [O time, suspend thy flight!]. Born too late, he has turned his Jewish identity into a cult of memory. In an ironic sense, Finkielkraut is replaying the most classic Jewish scenario. As Talmudic Judaism sought to recover by memory Temple worship after the explusion from Palestine in the year 70 c.e., so Finkielkraut would rebuild secular Jewish life on an absence, a lack: the lost Jewish culture and community of pre-World War II. Jewish exile thus repeats itself not only spatially but temporally. Misrahi, the philosopher, would have no truck with such emotional needs. Memmi, more patient intellectually, could not subscribe to such an undertaking for himself because his experience in the mellah was too limiting, but he could appreciate this need to give content to Jewish identity.

Misrahi embraced the myths of the French republic. He believed that France was a unitary, universalist culture, or at least that it was supposed to be: this was an ideal carried over from before the war. Finkielkraut, born after the war, conceives of France more as a melting pot, which permits a greater variety of perspectives. Indeed, *la France indivisible* no longer really exists: "There are people for whom the terms 'French,' 'Catholic,' 'Western' no longer mean anything" (114, 118). Thus the Jew in France no longer needs to function according to some national universalistic ideal. Henceforth, all Frenchmen, Jewish or not, are trapped in everyday popular culture (*la culture du quotidien*), which is ultimately alienating. The Jew in France does have the option of rebuilding a meaningful identity beyond the empty category of the imaginary Jew. But Finkielkraut's new Jew, with his fluid parameters and content, is as much an invention as any conceived by Misrahi, Memmi, or Sartre.

What emerges from these postwar theoretical lucubrations is the desperate effort to create for modern France a Jew who can combat the anti-Semite, pass muster as a good French citizen and preserve his dignity qua human and Jew at the same time.

Sartre, to his credit, was the first to assert the importance for the Jew to accept the negative condition forced on him by anti-Semitism, in order to combat it. Sartre's error, which he later admitted, was that he had not realized that to be a Jew could have positive qualities.

Memmi established this point effectively and reinforced the Zionist ideal as the most positive response to both anti-Semitism and the need to renew Jewish cultural life. Misrahi, by defending the ideal of human assimilation to one worldwide fraternal universalism, decants the Jew of any particularism or negativity. He makes the Jew an antithetical figure who defends universal ideals until he disappears in the coming synthesis of universal humanity. Finkielkraut, from a later generation, requires the contemporary French Jew to stop performing for the Gentile. He must no longer pretend to be the oppressed hero with a splendid history of justice on his side, entirely unearned in his generation. Rather, he must recover the authentic inheritance of Jewish culture as a basis for building a new, meaningful, secular French Jewish existence.

Sartre, it is evident, opened the intellectual space for this French Jewish discourse based not on apologetics, faith, or essence, but rather on existential, phenomenological, and social realities. Ontology takes precedence over epistemology in these imaginings of the Jew. One deficiency is evident in Misrahi's dream of all mankind's assimilation to the universal: it is as much an ideal as the coming parousia. The only identity it leaves for the Jew is his present sorry condition as "a distinct figure without distinctive characteristics" (*une particularité sans détermination*). In turn, Memmi's and Finkielkraut's desire for a distinct figure *with* distinctive characteristics—*une particularité* avec *détermination*, one could say—remains unrealized. The Sartrian model and its existentialist elaborations appear no longer able to sustain the intellectual inquiry and emotional ferment of the contemporary generation, looking for a more personal spiritual identity.

Enters from off stage Emmanuel Lévinas, who fuses ontology and epistemology and offers an inside content for the modern Jew. Lévinas closes the Sartrian period of defining the Jew from his objective condition by returning to a renewable religious and philosophical tradition, positing *une particularité avec détermination*. His strong voice picks up the quiet counterpoint to the Sartrian existentialist position expressed earlier by the late professor from Strasbourg, André Neher.[10] Neher's writings helped revitalize academic Jewish studies, by providing fresh readings of Jewish ethical texts that relegitimized a modern French Jewish spiritual condition. Richard Marienstras in his collected articles, *Etre un peuple en diaspora*, also furthered a return to a tradi-

10. See, for example, André Neher, *L'Existence juive: Solitude et affrontements* (Paris: Seuil, 1962).

tional Jewish consciousness.[11] Marienstras, in fact, directly influenced Finkielkraut.

But it is Lévinas who has most strongly called for a return to the study of the living texts of traditional Judaism. Such has been the import of his Talmud sessions at the annual "Colloquia of French-speaking Jewish Intellectuals," which he helped establish in 1958.[12] Reading the traditional texts is hailed as the basis of an authentic Jewish identity, a determinative act of choice:

> It is not enough to take stock of what "we Jews" are and what we feel today. We would be running the risk of taking a compromised, alienated, forgotten, ill-adapted or even dead Judaism to be the essence of Judaism. We cannot be conscious of something in whatever way we wish! The other path is steep, but the only one to take: it brings us back to the source, the forgotten, ancient, difficult books, and plunges us into strict and laborious study. . . .
>
> Jewish identity is inscribed in these old documents. It cannot be annulled by simply ignoring these means of identification. . . . King Josiah ordered a kingdom to be established around an old lost book that was rediscovered by his clerks (The Book of the Torah in 622 B.C.E.). It is the perfect image of a life that delivers itself up to the texts. The myth of our Europe as being born of a similar inspiration was called the Renaissance.[13]

There is an ironic peripeteia in Lévinas's appeal to return to the very texts and practices from which the National Assembly in 1791 supposedly emancipated the Jews. The appeal has found fertile ground and signals renewed self-confidence among many French Jews, the consequence of which may be a new French Jewish intellectual modus vivendi. Fighting off the hidden cultural assimilationist appeal of Sartrian universalism, Lévinas recognizes it as an expression of Western hegemonic practice that needs to be confronted. A Jewish response is required:

> Jewish uniqueness awaits its philosophy. The servile imitation of European models no longer suffices. The search for references to

11. Richard Marienstras, Etre un peuple en diaspora (Paris: Maspero, 1975).

12. See, for example, Emmanuel Lévinas, "Qui est soi-même? Leçon talmudique" in Le "quant-à-soi": Données et débats: Actes du XXXe Colloque des intellectuels juifs de langue française: ed. Jean Halpérin and Georges Lévitte (Paris: Denoël, 1991), 219–29.

13. Lévinas, Difficult Freedom: Essays on Judaism, trans. Seán Hand (Baltimore: Johns Hopkins University Press, 1990), 52–53, modified as per the original: Difficile Liberté: Essais sur le judaïsme (Paris: Albin Michel, 1963), 76–77.

universality in our Biblical writings and in the texts of the Oral Law
still draws on the processes of assimilation. These texts, through
their two thousand-year-old commentaries, still have other things to
say.[14]

Lévinas is no cultural nationalist reactionary. Rather, his is the
voice of a renewed Jewish man, equivalent to the new voices in the
Third World beyond Westernization and decolonization:

We Jews who wish to remain as such know that our heritage is no
less humane than that of the West and is capable of integrating all
that our Occidental past has awakened amid our own possibilities.
[*L'Au-delà du verset,* 233]

Sartre paradoxically would have applauded this "revolt" as he admired
the Africans who reasserted their authenticity, but he expected it
would all lead back to rational—that is, Western—universalism devoid
of any origin. Memmi would be fascinated but discomforted by the
religious implications. Finkielkraut could also support Lévinas's intentions, albeit not to the point of being observant. Only Misrahi, the
cultural assimilationist to French universalism, would resist philo-
sophically. Shockingly, Lévinas returns to the Jew his quiddity, which
is Judaism, not his situation, the Sartrian base. The Jew, for Lévinas,
becomes authentic only by being shaped by Judaism, entering into the
dialectic with the traditional polysemic textual voices of Jewish
thought.

For the contemporary French Jew who is not trapped in everyday
popular culture, the two antipodes of the strongest intellectual, cultural, and emotional appeal in imagining the new Jewish identity are
Emmanuel Lévinas and the renewable religious philosophical tradition, and the secular existentialist choices of the Sartrian school. Not
since the Martin Buber-Franz Rosenzweig debates in Germany of the
1920s has there been anywhere, in the diaspora or in the land of Israel,
such intense intellectual debate as in France to define and imagine
the Jew.

14. Lévinas, *L'Au-delà du verset* (Paris: Minuit, 1982), 234.

ANNETTE WIEVIORKA

Jewish Identity in the First Accounts by Extermination Camp Survivors from France

The accounts published through 1948 by Jews who had been deported specifically as Jews from the internment camp in the Parisian suburb of Drancy to the extermination camp at Auschwitz are of particular interest to historians.[1] For the first time in the modern world, Jews were designated as such. This in effect undid all conversions, all mixed marriages and any level of assimilation. What the Dreyfus affair had failed to do was thus realized by the Nazi occupation and the Vichy government. To be a Jew became no longer a matter of one's free will, but merely a question of heredity; a Jew was now identified by the number of Jewish grandparents he or she had.[2] The individual could make what he or she wanted of this imposed designation, by accepting or rejecting it internally. Yet for the first time, it was possible to grasp what until then had remained intangible: the Jewish community hitherto uncircumscribable had become a community defined by fate; fate permeated its formerly vague contours, its complexity and its diversity. The first eyewitness accounts do more than describe the extermination process and the way it was perceived. They allow us to attempt to answer a series of questions, etched like a filigree within the stories themselves.

1. For a bibliography of the first accounts, see Annette Wieviorka, *Déportation et génocide: Entre la mémoire et l'oubli* (Paris: Plon, 1992). On the persecution of Jews in France, see notably Michael R. Marrus and Robert O. Paxton, *Vichy France and the Jews* (New York: Basic Books, 1981); Georges Wellers, *L'Etoile jaune à l'heure de Vichy* (Paris: Fayard, 1973); André Kaspi, *Les Juifs pendant l'Occupation* (Paris: Seuil, 1991).
2. For the Nazi definition of a Jew, see Raul Hilberg, *The Destruction of the European Jews*, rev. and definitive ed. (New York: Holmes & Meier, 1985), 65–80. For an analysis of the first anti-Semitic measures taken by Vichy, see Marrus and Paxton, 3–21.

YFS 85, *Discourses of Jewish Identity in Twentieth-Century France*, ed. Alan Astro,
© 1994 by Yale University.

How did various Jewish milieus react to the designation as Jews and to the ensuing persecution? Were they aware that behind the curtain of the world war, a war against the Jews—a genocide—was being waged? Was there any change in their relationship to France, in what might be called their French identity? How did they perceive their Jewish identity, be it rediscovered or imposed upon them? The first accounts, written immediately after the war before subsequent readings and pictures could clutter the survivors' memories, may help us answer these questions.

The first convoy left France for Auschwitz on 27 March 1942. Six more convoys would follow before the Vel' d'Hiv' roundup of 16 and 17 July of the same year.[3] Georges Wellers, who was arrested on 12 December 1941, imprisoned in Compiègne and then in Drancy, and who as the "spouse of an Aryan" (an official designation) avoided deportation until 30 June 1944, constitutes a privileged witness. According to him, the atmosphere in the detention rooms before deportation was serene and optimistic:

> At that time, most deportees had faith in their own physical and moral strength. They believed that Nazism would soon fall and that conditions for survival were assured in the future "labor camps" in Germany. They had little fear for the safety of their loved ones.[4]

The first convoys in the spring of 1942 established a particular ritual among the deportees. Upon leaving Drancy, they would sing the *Marseillaise*, followed by *Ce n'est qu'un au revoir mes frères* ("Until We Meet Again, My Brothers"). This ritual was identical to the one performed by non-Jewish deportees, such as the inmates leaving Compiègne. From the arrival of the arrestees of 16 July 1942 until July 1943 when the camp fell under exclusive German administration, the ritual at departure remained the same.

Where did the inmates imagine that the convoys were headed? In an infirmary, around September 1942, children came up with the word "Pichipoi," which was to be adopted by all deportees. Originally, it designated an imaginary place in Yiddish folklore and a popular children's rhyme. Made up from the Polish words *pich* ("drink") and *poi*

3. On 16–17 July 1942, French police rounded up 12,884 Jews in Paris. For five days, over 7,000 of the arrestees, including 4,000 children, were parked in the Vélodrome d'Hiver or "Vel' d'Hiv'," a Parisian sports arena. From there, almost all were sent to French internment camps and then murdered at Auschwitz.—*Trans.*

4. Georges Wellers, *De Drancy à Auschwitz* (Paris: Editions du Centre, 1946), 31. (All further references to Wellers are drawn from this work.)

("give the livestock water"), this fantastic hamlet came to stand for their last hope: "In the camp at Drancy, Pichipoi represented the unknown place where you were being sent, where things would be better and easier" (Wellers, 68).

André Schwarz-Bart writes in *The Last of the Just*:

> So it was that at Drancy a belief was current in a distant kingdom called Pichipoi, where the Jews, guided by the staves of their blond shepherds, would be permitted to graze industriously on the grass of a fresh start.[5]

The accounts written before the return of the survivors by those not deported show the latter to be unaware of the exact process and scale of extermination. In their work of synthesis, Darville and Wichené write that the children arriving at Drancy were thrown into the mud of the concentration camps, "veritable antechambers of death." It is in a note most likely added after the completion of the manuscript that the authors cite a report by Professor W. (doubtless Waitz) from the University of Strasbourg, recently repatriated from Auschwitz and Buchenwald. He states: "Almost all the deported children were burned in the ovens. The smallest ones were thrown in alive."[6] Thus Darville and Wichené, themselves imprisoned at Drancy, and so interested in the Jewish tragedy as to write one of the very first works on the subject, were unaware, even after Paris had already been liberated, of the fate of those who had not yet returned and who for the most part never would return. What can be expected, then, from the majority of French society?

Georges Wellers summarizes the perceptions that prevailed at the time:

> Until the end, no one in the camp really knew anything about the fate of the deportees. We knew that Radio London spoke of the horrors of gas chambers and other means of exterminating the Jews, but no one could believe it. We took these reports to be the exaggerations of English propaganda, and did not pay too much

5. André Schwarz-Bart, *The Last of the Just*, trans. Stephen Becker (New York: Atheneum, 1973), 351. The information in these paragraphs and some of the quotations come from Leizer Ran, "Tsu der biografye fun a folkslid," *Di goldene keyt*, 110–11 (1983), 211–18, which studies variants of this song through time and space. This article was translated from Yiddish into French by Aby Wieviorka: "Pourquoi 'Pitchipoï'? Biographie d'une chanson populaire," *Pardès* 16 (1992): 134–45.

6. Jacques Darville and Simon Wichené, *Drancy la Juive ou La Deuxième Inquisition* (Cachan, Seine: Breger, 1945).

attention to them. . . . No one would or could believe that the mass exterminations reported by British radio were actually going on. [71]

Wellers further specifies:

It was recognized that deportation was truly an exile, carried out under inhuman conditions, with forced labor and all manner of expected deprivations, but it was neither extermination nor forcible separation from loved ones. The length of the ordeal was considered the ultimate problem; one had to gain time. [114]

Available sources, rare as they might be, indicate that the deportees in fact did not know the destination of their convoys. It was only when they arrived in Auschwitz that they understood. The story they tell is always the same. Unfailingly, it was from deportees who had preceded them that they learned the fate of the men and women who arrived with them and climbed into the trucks headed for the gas chamber. According to eyewitness accounts, the process of extermination— selection upon arrival of the trains, further selection occurring periodically in the camp, the ultimate trip to the gas chamber—was never known before arrival at the camp. We have found no exception, not even among those claiming special knowledge before they were deported. This consistently repeated account, written by French deportees who did not know one another, lived in different places, and wrote their stories immediately upon their return, leads us to believe that all happened as we are told.

The image of the ovens spewing flames day and night becomes the symbol of extermination, much more so than the gas chamber, where death occurs inside the walls, without external traces, discernible only by those housed in neighboring barracks. There are accounts by deportees in the complex at Auschwitz and accounts by non-Jewish deportees in other camps that had no gas chambers—Buchenwald for example—or camps where the gas chamber was small and only operated for a few months, such as Ravensbrück. One of the elements uniting all these texts is the oven as a symbol.

With the arrival of Hungarian Jews at Auschwitz-Birkenau, extermination took on unprecedented proportions. The ovens burned day and night.[7] The numbers provided by the deportees are approximate and always exaggerated: 600,000, one million. How could anyone account for such a mass? The stench of burning flesh pervaded the camp.

7. Louise Alcan, *Sans Armes et sans bagages* (Limoges: Editions d'Art, 1947), 43.

Most deportees were acutely aware that Jews, and only Jews, were slated for systematic extermination, yet some accounts gloss over this fact.

In Julien Unger's work, *Le Sang et l'or*, the word "Jew" is virtually absent. Throughout Unger's account, the reader does not know whether the author is a Jew or not. In a chapter entitled "The Hungarian Massacre," he concludes:

> Thus were exterminated close to a million women and men who loved their country profoundly, who relished life and could have worked and lived in peace for a much longer time. But fascism had cast its bloodthirsty paw on their small land and had crushed it in its claws.[8]

Thus, in the account by Unger, who was a Jew deported from Drancy, the process and the extent of extermination is described in full, but the fact that the victims were Jews is completely erased.

Louise Alcan's work reflects a clear awareness that Jews were being exterminated, yet her postface, written in 1947 at the time of publication, stresses that 30,000 have returned from the camps. She makes no distinction there between concentration camps, to which members of the Resistance and hostages were deported, and the extermination camps to which Jews were sent. Yet of some 63,000 Resistants and hostages deported, 37,000 survived; of the 75,000 Jews deported from France, only 2,500 returned.

The perception of the Holocaust among those who were its victims was therefore belated, and in some cases incomplete. For the Jews of France, whether French for generations or immigrants, it was difficult and perhaps impossible to acknowledge that the French model of emancipation and integration, born of the Revolution and barely compromised by the Dreyfus affair, could have been rendered null and void by the Vichy government. They did not understand that they could be expelled de facto from the French nation, that their French citizenship meant nothing to the occupying forces, that they had become merely Jews to annihilate. The main difficulty in fully perceiving the Holocaust seems to stem from a deep, essential dilemma: the inability to grasp that they could belong to a Jewish collective, be it envisioned as a community, people, or nation.

8. Julien Unger, *Le Sang et l'or: Souvenirs de camps allemands* (Paris: Gallimard, 1946), 184.

The inmates expressed their intimate link to France by celebrating dates associated with French history, unlike the commemorations mentioned in survivors' accounts from Polish ghettos and camps, where references are to the Jewish calendar. As told by Julie Crémieux-Dunand, Drancy did not celebrate Passover, Rosh Hashanah, or Yom Kippur, but rather Bastille Day:

> Wednesday, 14 July [1943]. After roll call, lieutenant colonel Blum lets out a resounding "Attention!" The stair wardens remove their hats, all inmates remain motionless for a minute of silence to commemorate the national holiday and to commune in spirit with those fighting for the liberation of France.[9]

Louise Alcan describes the work site at Rajsko one year later: "All the Frenchwomen come together. We sing, and comrades from other countries join in. It's the festival of freedom" (52). She further notes that on 11 November of the same year, a minute of silence was observed, after which the deportees sang the *Marseillaise* (74). In this way, they celebrated the republic, France, the declaration of the rights of man, and victory over the Germans in the previous war.

At Drancy, Georges Wellers is struck by the attitude of the youth:

> The adolescents . . . held the fierce patriotism of their age group: the rare Germans we saw in the camp were considered monsters, the French inspectors and police who spoke with the Germans were ignominious traitors. Deportation frightened these young people mostly because it meant leaving France. The German Pichipoi was hostile and alarming, because it was German. [75]

This patriotism was expressed at Auschwitz as well. In the camps, the French were rarely privileged in the inmates' hierarchy, and were generally disliked and resented for their country's prewar and wartime policies: the betrayal of Czechoslovakia at Munich, the lack of expected military help to Poland after its invasion by the Wehrmacht. The fall of France in 1940 and the ensuant collaboration with the enemy further eroded any consideration for the French. In the world of the camps, where many nationalities coming into contact immediately reduced each other to immutable, blanket stereotypes, the French were reputed to be undisciplined, lazy, dirty, and incapable of adapting to group life.

9. Julie Crémieux-Dunand, *Le Relais des errants* (Paris: Desclée de Brower, 1945), 169–70.

Guy Kohen, twenty years old at the time, recounts: "I strongly defended my motherland in all circumstances, explaining as best I could that we had been the victims of traitors, and I was often beaten for not agreeing when others were besmirching my country."[10] Julien Unger, who immigrated from Poland as an adult, describes the reaction of a colonel to the generalized anti-French sentiment he considered unfounded. Having judged that silence was impossible in such a situation,

> the colonel, voicing the opinion of an overwhelming majority, remained unshakeable in his conviction that each of us had a duty to defend the honor of the true France wherever it was attacked. So it was agreed. [37]

Vichy and collaboration had not frayed the organic bond between France and its Jews. Georges Wellers speaks at length of his fellow inmate René Blum, younger brother of Léon Blum, head of the Popular Front government of 1936–37. Wellers and René Blum, who had become friends in the camp at Compiègne, encounter each other again at Drancy. Blum considers it essential to explain constantly that the Vichy government does not truly represent France. The task is often difficult and painful. At Blum's request, Wellers takes him to see the children arrested during the Vel' d'Hiv' roundup, who have been transferred to the internment camps at Pithiviers or Beaune-la-Rolande, where they are separated from their parents before being taken to Drancy. Wellers reports Blum's dialogue with a girl of twelve who shows him an article from the *Cri du Peuple*, the newspaper published by Jacques Doriot, one of the leading Parisian proponents of collaboration. The article denies that children have been separated from their parents.

> Blum quickly glanced through the paper and remarked to her, "You must know that this is a German paper, my child. You're French, aren't you?"
> "I don't want to be French anymore! The French are mean, they're so mean, I hate them! . . ."
> "You shouldn't say that," replied Blum gently. "You do know it's the Germans who are doing all this."
> The little girl broke in with the same vehemence: "That's not true! It isn't true! It was Frenchmen who came to our house. They

10. Guy Kohen, *Retour d'Auschwitz. Souvenirs du déporté 174.949* (Paris: no publ., 1946), 68.

looked for my little sister everywhere because Mom had hidden her. They found her when she started crying. Then they came to my school to get me. In Beaune-la-Rolande, it was French customs officials who held back my mother and my father and who took my sister and me away. And here, it's French gendarmes who guard us."

"My poor child, you're old enough to understand that all these French are bad French. They've sold themselves to the Germans and they've themselves become like Germans, worse than Germans. The true French are as revolted as you and I are. Only right now, there's nothing they can do."

"And why is there nothing they can do? They could have not gone after my sister. They could have left us with our parents. They are mean! Filthy!"

"You don't understand that these aren't real French people," Blum began again, gently and patiently. [144–45]

What text illustrates better than this dialogue the wounds tearing at French Jews? For a Jewish Frenchman like René Blum, nothing could be allowed to sully the image of France; France must remain good and generous.

In a novella *La Marche à l'étoile*, published underground in 1943, writer-essayist Vercors portrays how certain French Jews' trust was shattered.[11] The hero, Thomas Muritz, is overcome as a young child by a passion for "France, filled with radiance, generosity, intelligence, and justice" (23). At sixteen, he runs away from home, leaves his native Moravia, and makes it on foot to the land of his dreams. Naturalized, he marries a young woman born of the ancient French soil; one of his sons dies in the Great War. The narrator, who has lost sight of Muritz after the armistice of June 1940, runs into him one day in Paris. The old man is wearing a yellow star. The narrator speaks of "shameful" and "infamous" events for which Marshal Pétain bears responsibility: France's abandoning the province of Lorraine and handing over political refugees to the enemy (76). Muritz reacts with fury. These are lies playing into the hands of the Germans: "It isn't true. It isn't. It can't be true" (78). Interned at Drancy, Muritz is chosen as a hostage to be shot. The old man remains detached and serene, as he offers himself up in supreme sacrifice to his adopted fatherland. However, when he realizes that not Germans but Frenchmen have come to fetch him for execu-

11. Vercors, *La Marche à l'étoile* (Paris: Minuit, 1943). References in this article are to the 1945 reedition.

tion, the whole of his being collapses: "He began to strike his head with his fists in despair, to cry . . . and to sob" (90).

Longtime French natives and immigrants who had adopted the same system of values as Vercors's hero could hardly question that which formed the very core of their identity, for they had nothing to put in its stead. To remain whole in their own eyes, they had to continue to love France unreservedly. In the camps, they were first and foremost French. And when they returned home, everything fell back into place. "How beautiful is Lorraine, the land of my father," notes Louise Alcan on her way home. The train bringing back Julien Unger came to a stop: they were in France! Some men got off into the dark:

> Ah! To tread once more upon this cherished land, long dream of my exile.
> One man walks away from the others; he lies down on the ground, kisses this land of liberty, and the tears flow freely. [234]

These are the last words of Unger's account. Alcan tells of her arrival in Paris: "The eastern train-station. It is eight in the morning. A crowd has gathered beyond the fences. We are singing the *Marseillaise*. People watch us and cry" (118).

We find the same image of return in the account by Suzanne Birnbaum, repatriated to Lyons from Theresienstadt in early June 1945:

> At the moment when . . . our feet touch the soil of France, for the first time in seventeen months, we hear the *Marseillaise* being played. It is too much for us, too moving. We are returning from too far, our hearts explode, and we are led sobbing to the welcome center on the airfield.[12]

Birnbaum was arrested and turned over to the Germans by the French militia. This fact she erases. There is no resentment, no qualification of her identity as a Frenchwoman. This is reflected in the title of her account, *Une Française juive est revenue*—literally "a *Jewish French-woman* has come back," not "a *French Jewess* has come back."

As the *Marseillaise* had marked the departure, so it did the return. Life could go on in liberated France, no different from before. In March 1945, Henry Bulawko, longstanding militant in the Zionist-socialist youth movement Hashomer Hatsair, who would play a major role in

---

12. Suzanne Birnbaum, *Une Française juive est revenue* (Paris: Editions du Livre Français, 1946), 193.

several Jewish organizations upon his return, was staying at the re-grouping center for the French at Katowice, Poland, when he wrote the words to *Renaissance de la France*, to be sung to the tune of the *Chant du départ*:

> Brisant enfin ses fers,
> Notre France éternelle,
> Ayant connu un véritable enfer,
> A déployé à nouveau ses ailes.
> Le fier coq de la liberté
> A chanté le réveil de la patrie.
>
> *Refrain*
> Une République nouvelle
> Nous appelle à conquérir à nouveau
> Tout ce qui fit la France si belle: (*bis*)
> Sa Marseillaise et son drapeau.
>
> Breaking her chains at last,
> Our eternal France,
> Having truly tasted hell,
> Has unfurled her wings again.
> The proud rooster of liberty
> Sang as our country awakened.
>
> *Chorus*
> It is a new Republic
> Calling us to reclaim
> All that made France so beautiful: (*repeat*)
> Her Marseillaise and her banner.

Behind this identification with France there often—but not always—lies a sense of Jewish particularity, which some clearly want the Jews to give up should they feel the urge to cultivate it. Darville and Wichené's work is especially relevant in this respect. The conclusion of *Drancy la Juive*, published even before the deportees returned, sounds a widely heeded warning:

The Jews were turned by Hitler into scapegoats and public enemy number one. More than anyone else, they have paid their blood-soaked dues to barbarism. They were handed a sinister privilege, *and will not use it to cover themselves with the halo of martyrdom.* (emphasis added)

Maurice Martin du Gard, chronicler and literary critic, makes a similar remark in his journal:

> Jean-Jacques Bernard has returned in rather sorry shape from the concentration camp at Compiègne. Simone tells me he has declared, "We should nevertheless not go and present our bill!" One hopes for their sake that all his coreligionists will be as sensitive and wise.[13]

The suggestion of such writers is that the lot of the Jews during the war was part of a common tragedy. Their portion in it was perhaps greater, the difference quantitative rather than qualitative. Reintegrated into the bosom of the French homeland who would open her arms wide to foreigners, they should not seek to stand out by proclaiming their martyrdom. This type of analysis recurs in David Rousset's *L'Univers concentrationnaire*, considered to be the best study of the Nazi concentration-camp system. After describing Birkenau ("the great city of death"), the selection made upon arrival, the gas chamber, Rousset concludes: "Between these camps of destruction and the 'normal' camps, there is no *difference in nature*, but merely a *difference in degree*."[14] Likewise, in Vassili Grossman's *L'Enfer de Tréblinka*, published in 1946 by Artaud and also included in a large volume entitled *Années de guerre*, published by the Editions de Moscou in 1946, the author makes a point of always listing others, particularly Poles, along with the Jews in his recital of the victims of Treblinka.

The proud and zealous patriotism felt by certain French Jews prevented them, in their own opinion, from being part of a Jewish people or nation. No one better than Jean-Jacques Bernard describes French citizens of this sort, who found the label "Jew" ludicrously slapped onto them. Dignity did not permit them to avoid or refute this label, but they refused to internalize it. Bernard's book, *Le Camp de la mort lente: Compiègne 1941–42*, is dedicated to his comrades who disappeared into "the dungeons of the East." He has a single epitaph for all of them: "Killed in Action for France."[15] Those who like him were arrested in the early hours of 12 December 1941 accepted their ordeal "not out of any racial enthusiasm, but for love of France" (32).

13. Maurice Martin du Gard, *La Chronique de Vichy, 1940–44* (Paris: Flammarion, 1948), 348–49.

14. David Rousset, *L'Univers concentrationnaire* (Paris: Union Générale d'Editions, Collection 10/18, 1971 [orig. publ. 1946]), 51 (emphasis added).

15. Jean-Jacques Bernard, *Le Camp de la mort lente: Compiègne, 1941–42* (Paris: Albin Michel, 1944), 8. [An English version exists—*The Camp of Slow Death*, trans. Edward Owen Marsh (London: Gollancz, 1945)—but passages here are directly rendered from the French.—*Trans.*]

Such French people, long past the stage of assimilation according to Bernard, were shocked to find themselves confronted with Central and Eastern European Jews, "who had preserved in their hearts the sense of a Jewish community" (68). Bernard interprets the Germans' mixing some 700 French with 300 foreigners as a Machiavellian attempt to foster an embryonic Jewish society. This he could not accept at any cost. If he had to die in this tragedy, he did not want to be claimed as a victim by Judaism.[16] That some Jews should have gone out of their way to make him admit that he too was a Jew infuriated him. Yet neither Bernard nor others who display similar feelings were actually deported to death camps. In the survivors' accounts, when they describe Drancy or Auschwitz, the distinction between French Jew and foreign Jew has disappeared. Perhaps it paled before the amplitude of the tragedy.

While there were inmates who, like Bernard, fundamentally rejected a Jewish identity they had never felt, we also know from other eyewitness accounts that some Jews in French detention camps claimed their Jewishness. Georges Wellers compares the adolescents, all born in France, to the older Jews, especially the foreign ones:

> Many among them were confirmed believers, and they faithfully
> practiced their beliefs through the simple and humane rituals of
> Judaism. They were filled with resignation; they looked at the
> present and the future with a philosophical attitude steeped in
> fatalism, and with a certain bitter wisdom. Their background was
> often Polish, Rumanian, White Russian or Ukrainian; in their youth
> these people had witnessed or even been the victims of persecution.
> They saw anti-Semitism as a scourge that had to be endured with
> patience, as one endures an act of nature. Long and painful
> experience had accustomed them to mistrust all non-Jews, who, to
> their mind, were more or less anti-Semitic: the French were no
> worse than the Poles, and the Germans could not be much worse.
> They were all basically the same, vicious and hostile. . . . In the
> camp, these Jews remained faithful to their convictions and showed
> true greatness of spirit, sometimes in the most unexpected
> circumstances. [75]

Such old Jews, radically pessimistic, offered little that could appeal to youth. How could anybody identify with this twilight vision of

16. The idea is expressed in much the same terms in the testament left by the historian Marc Bloch, executed for his work in the Resistance: "A stranger to all credal dogmas, as to all pretended community of life and spirit based on race, I have, through life, felt that I was above all, and quite simply, a Frenchman" (*Strange Defeat*, trans. Gerard Hopkins [New York: Norton, 1968], 178).

Judaism? What response could be expected from the elderly to the obsessively piercing question repeated in all accounts: Why were people going after the Jews? Time and again, the question was phrased in almost identical terms. We still encounter it today.

All our writers deny the existence of a Semitic type. One glance at those held at Drancy or Compiègne made their diversity obvious. The idea that the opposite of "Jew" was "Aryan" seemed absurd; furthermore, the word "Aryan" usually is in quotation marks in the accounts. Rather, the writers see Jews as those whom others—the Germans— had designated as such. Did this label provoke any curiosity or discussion about the Jewish question among the inmates? For the vast majority, apparently not. As Georges Wellers writes:

> It is remarkable that the only factor that impelled anti-Semites to gather people inside the walls of Drancy—their belonging to the Jewish "race"—had barely any meaning for the inmates. . . . Drancy was a very poor school of Judaism. Spiritually, Judaism elicited few responses; biologically, it seemed an obviously senseless distinction when one looked upon the multiplicity of physical types, of mental outlooks, of habits and of tastes. . . . If one wished to prove the tenuousness of "Jewish" spirituality and the unfoundedness of racially motivated anti-Semitism, there was no better place to do so than Drancy. [84–85]

It does seem that Drancy and the camps in general fostered Christianity more than Judaism, that it was a far more important cultural presence than Judaism. Much reading went on at Drancy, notes Georges Wellers: "François Mauriac's *Life of Jesus* was passed from hand to hand. The *Thoughts* of Pascal were popular, as were works by Renan, but people were not very interested in the Holy Scriptures" (38–39).

Christmas was celebrated at Drancy as well as at Auschwitz. Unger devotes an entire chapter of his *Le Sang et l'or* to Christmas eve (93– 103). There was a Christmas tree: a few branches decorated with cotton batting from their blankets, with a little salt and crushed glass to simulate frost. A Saint Nicholas held in his right hand a bishop's crook finely braided out of aluminum wires. "Other comrades started working on the manger scenes" (94). All was there: the Wise Men and the Holy Virgin Mary, the heavenly angels and the Christ child, the lambs, donkeys, and oxen. But the most striking achievements were a large barbed-wire cross with a crucified Christ, and flowers in the colors of the French flag.

Thus the first opposite of "Jew" found in the accounts, "Aryan," is roundly rejected. The second one, "Christian," holds a definite appeal. It was during the persecutions that a Jewish teenager named Aron Lustiger converted to Catholicism. Today Monsignor Lustiger is archbishop of Paris. Marcel Bloch converted in the camps themselves; after the war, he would become the great aeronautics industrialist Marcel Dassault. In fact, the problem posed by conversions to Christianity would be a major concern of Jewish religious authorities after the Liberation.

Nevertheless, though only among a minority of the internees, a debate arose, especially at Drancy. Georges Wellers records the discussions regarding Jewry's future that took place among some thirty inmates, as the end of the war loomed; the debates were led by a physician named Lévy-Coblenz, who was eventually deported. Most believed that the "Jewish problem" would disappear along with Nazism; others thought that after 2,000 years anti-Semitism was not about to disappear, and that it was pointless to look for its causes. Rather, they held, it was necessary to assure the safety of the Jews, which meant creating a truly Jewish state of sufficiently large territory, sheltered from the harmful intentions of its neighbors. For some, these requisites could not be met by the Zionist proposal for a Jewish state in Palestine, too small to take in all Jews wishing to remain Jews, and afloat in a sea of Arab hostility. Some were for a Jewish state in the French colonies; those who opposed such an idea expressed faith in their French homeland, pointing to the ultimate resolution of the Dreyfus affair, which confirmed the decline of anti-Semitism in the nineteenth century. Also against the colonial proposal were those for whom a Jewish state could have no meaning outside of Palestine.

The Zionist project appears in Guy Kohen's account, not actually in the body of his text but indirectly through the remarks made by his father, Henry Kohen, at the beginning and the end of the volume. Before the war, the elder Kohen expended his energies trying to arrange a haven for Jews in French Guyana. In November 1941, he wrote to Pétain, suggesting once more that Jews be allowed to emigrate there. After the war, he asserted that only a Jewish state could resolve the Jewish question, and suggested that property of all kinds confiscated by the Germans be given to the Jewish community in Palestine. This would represent neither a gift nor reparations, but simple justice: merely partial restitution of what had once belonged to Jews and had been taken from them. Thus Henry Kohen sketched the first outline of

German reparations, a concept that would provoke heated debate in Israel and the diaspora at the beginning of the 1950s.

In the accounts by Jews deported from France we find two ideologies enduring at the very height of persecution. One concerns the emancipation effected by the French Revolution. Melded into a national community and tied to it by a sincere and powerful feeling of patriotism, these Jews denied even that the Vichy counter-revolution had in any way excised them from their nation. Their love of France remained intact. For some, the war that had just taken place was merely one in a series of Franco-German wars. Victory over a hereditary enemy returned France to them and them to France. To be a Jew had no national significance for them. None of their accounts called for any need to remain Jewish after and because of Auschwitz.

The other enduring ideology is communism. For the communists, Nazi anti-Semitism was not intrinsically specific; Nazism was merely one more variety of capitalism. Persecution was explained simply by the policy of "divide and conquer." Seen in this light, it affected not only Jews. Communist logic is taken to its extreme in the book by Pelagia Lewinska, especially in its preface: a denial, pure and simple, of the murderous reality of Nazi anti-Semitism. The author of the preface, Charles Eube, warns us: Nazi anti-Semitism was "hypocritical." It spared wealthy Jews:

> A Jew could become the supplier and protégé of the Gestapo when he proved as repulsive as they, and Madame Lewinska witnessed women inmates beating inmates at Auschwitz; in other words, Jewish women beating other Jewish women.[17]

Thus, in their accounts, the French Jews who had survived Auschwitz-Birkenau usually failed to grasp the full measure of what had just happened on Polish soil: a genocide, the destruction of a people. Their incomprehension is traceable essentially to the fact that they were not aware, or did not wish to be aware, of belonging to a people faced with a common destiny of extermination.

Fifty years later, the difference is striking. The memory of the Holocaust is present everywhere in France. Numerous survivors' accounts are now being published. Commemorative plaques and monuments proliferate. Demonstrations, survivors' marches, celebrations of *Yom*

17. Pelagia Lewinska, *Vingt mois à Auschwitz*, pref. Charles Eube (Paris: Nagel, 1945), 195.

ha-Shoah keep occurring.[18] A Presidential decree of February 1993 has made the anniversary of the Vel' d'Hiv roundup on 16 July into a "National Day Dedicated to the Memory of the Victims of Racist and Anti-Semitic Persecutions Committed Under the De Facto Authority Known as the 'Government of the French State' (1940–44)." What could have so deeply altered the Jews' understanding of their relationship to France?

The break came during the Six-Day War, which revealed and elicited new patterns of behavior among the Jews of France. They feared a new genocide in the form of the destruction of Israel, a crime called "State-cide" [*Etatcide*] by French sociologist Raymond Aron, who had until then never commented on his Jewish identity.[19] The Six-Day War also marked the rift between Jews and Communism in Poland, as it did among Jews in France generally and especially among those from Central and Eastern Europe. Furthermore—and France is the only country in which this was a consequence of the Six-Day War—it led Jews there to scuttle the belief that they could be fully assimilated. The impetus for the final disenchantment: de Gaulle's policies towards the Jewish state, and his press conference of 27 November 1967, in which he called the Jews "an elite people, self-assured and domineering."

Raymond Aron reacted in these terms:

> De Gaulle has knowingly and deliberately initiated a new phase of Jewish history and perhaps of anti-Semitism. Everything has once again become possible; everything is beginning again. Agreed, there is no threat of persecution, only of "ill-will." It is not the age of contempt, but the age of suspicion. [25]

With the dawning of this age of suspicion, many concurred with Aron's acknowledgment of a residual Jewish identity, difficult to define:

> However assimilated he is or reckons he is, the Jew keeps a feeling of solidarity both with his ancestors and with the other Jewish communities of the diaspora. Especially in our own day, after Hitler's persecutions, a Jew cannot flee from his destiny and ignore those who, in other places, have believed or do believe in the same God of Isaac and of Jacob, the God of his ancestors. [156]

18. *Yom ha-Shoah* (Hebrew): Holocaust Remembrance Day, observed either on the 27th day of the month of Nisan according to the Jewish calendar, or on 19 April.—*Trans.*

19. Raymond Aron, *De Gaulle, Israel and the Jews*, trans. John Sturrock (London: André Deutsch, 1969), 69. See also Aline Benain, "L'Itinéraire juif de Raymond Aron: Hasard, déchirement et dialectique d'appartenance," *Pardès* 11 (1990): 161–81.

This partial Jewish identity could come into conflict with one's French identity. To quote Aron again: "Since Hitler, I have known that France's interests would not always or necessarily coincide with those of the Jews or the Israelis" (64).

The Six-Day War pushed to the fore the exclusion of Jews under Vichy that had been consciously relegated to the background after World War II. It illustrated how Jewish memory could partake of the conflicts that pit the French against each other. This is particularly true ever since the terrorist attack on the synagogue in the rue Copernic, even though that attack has been attributed to Middle Eastern groups.[20] The memory of the dark years of occupation now forms an integral part of French political life.

This emergence of Jewish memory in France must be put into the context of the country's general situation as well. For the last twenty years France has been in the throes of a dual crisis, affecting both its national identity and the model, inherited from the Jacobin party of the revolutionary era, of a strong centralized republic destined to level all differences. The ideology of emancipation, which made Jews into French citizens of the Israelitic faith, is in retreat. A new model is in the making. The new sense of Jewish identity, especially for those born after the war and raised outside of Jewish tradition, is grounded in the Holocaust and in the reevaluation of France's part in it.

—Translated by Françoise Rosset

20. On Friday, 3 October 1980, during Sabbath eve services, a bomb exploded outside the Union Libérale Israélite in Paris, resulting in the deaths of three pedestrians. Four days later, some 300,000 people marched from the Place de la Nation to the Place de la République in condemnation of the attack.—*Trans.*

ARMAND VULLIET

Letters to Claude Lanzmann and to the *Grand Larousse**

41, boulevard Ney
75018 Paris

Mr. Claude Lanzmann
Editor of *Les Temps Modernes*

Dear Sir:

You will understand why I am sending you a copy of a letter which I have just sent to the editor of the *Grand Larousse Universel*.

I am not asking anything of you other than that you read it. Think what you will of it. I just thought it was important for it to reach you.

Sincerely yours,

A. Vulliet

c/o Montmartre Post Office
Quartier 218
19, rue Duc
75018 Paris

2 January 1993

The Editor of the
Grand Larousse Universel
Re: The entry "Shoah"

Dear Sir:

I have just read in the 1992 supplement to the encyclopedia *Grand Larousse Universel* the entry "Shoah,"[1] which I reproduce here:

---

*Armand Vulliet, "Lettres au *Grand Larousse* et à Claude Lanzmann," *Les Temps Modernes* 561 (April 1993): 57–66.

1. *Grand Larousse Universel*, Supplément 1992 (Paris: Larousse, 1992), 537, col. 1.

SHOAH: Hebrew word signifying "annihilation," used to designate the extermination by the Nazis of approximately five million Jews.

This term, which is often substituted for that of "Holocaust"—particularly in France since the film by Claude Lanzmann released under this title in 1985—recalls to Jewish memory and to universal memory an event whose unnameable and paroxysmal nature was expressed on different levels: the deliberate intent of one people to eliminate another for typically racist and ideological motives; the inscription of this crime in the context of the Western, Christian world without either culture or religion standing in its way; the central place accorded in Nazi ideology to the most malevolent form of anti-Judaism, aiming to debase, depersonalize, disfigure, destroy.

Because of this paroxysmal nature, the Shoah has always—but particularly since the 1980s—elicited contradictory reactions. On the one hand are attempts to trivialize the event by relativizing it, relating it by a process of "historical explanation" to others, none of which is unique. There have been numerous illustrations of this tendency in Germany. In France it has resulted in intolerable positions. Playing on the traumatized memory or silence of the survivors, on anti-Semitism, on a phantasmagoric "scientificality," on political or sociological resentments, "revisionists" or rather "negationists" have gone so far as to deny the Shoah. On the other hand, for many thinkers and writers (Adorno, Lévinas, Lyotard), the Shoah constitutes an event which marks a halt, which prohibits us from maintaining the same discourse, whether progressionist or nihilist, we would have used had it not occurred.

It is in the Jewish world, which it cut to the quick, that the Shoah has provoked the most profound and radical interrogations. However, because of its unique status, it is not only Judaism which it affects. Whether or not one shares a religious view of the world, it is not excessive to see in it an event of the same nature as the crucifixion of Jesus, on the very horizon of the history of humanity, in all its darkness and with all its enigmas. The Shoah, then, is not only a fracture at the heart of the West which throws the figures of its universality into question, but also a paradigmatic event for all men since it is the irruption of the radical evil which spares no one.

I offer you some comments:
—How, outside of any religious view of the world, can one compare the Shoah to the crucifixion of Jesus? Could you imagine a nonbeliever making such a comparison?

—How, not only outside of a religious view of the world, but outside of a specific religious conviction—Christianity—can one compare the Shoah to the crucifixion of Jesus? Could you imagine a Moslem or a Buddhist making such a comparison? Could you imagine it from a Jew?

—What is "an event of the same nature as the crucifixion of Jesus?" Given the context, this type of analogy leaves me perplexed. I don't get this "of the same nature as" at all.

—Thousands of people were crucified in antiquity. In what sense, outside of a specific religious conviction—Christianity—is the crucifixion of Jesus of particular importance? "Comparison is a legitimate historical exercise as long as it is well-founded, and to the extent that it does not lose sight of the singularity of every historical phenomenon."[2]

Until now, I have only seen mass murders compared to the Shoah—as seems to me to stand to reason: the elimination of the gypsies during the Second World War, for example, the Armenian genocide of 1915, the massacres perpetrated by the Khmer Rouge in the 1970s, Stalin's reign of terror. And I reiterate *compared to the Shoah*. I have never encountered the inverse procedure: *to compare the Shoah to. . . .* It is always the Shoah which is the point of departure for the comparison, it is from it that the comparison is made. It serves as a "paradigmatic" reference, as the author would say.

Still less have I seen it compared to an *individual* death. This is indeed the first time.

It suffices to recognize this, to realize that the author can find nothing better to convey the "unnameable and paroxysmal nature" of a mass extermination (and one such as humanity has never known!) than to put it on equal footing with the death of a single person, for one to say to oneself that there is something here which is not quite right, which sticks out, which cries out. Would it spontaneously occur to you, to anyone, to compare, with the aim of demonstrating its ignominy, the Armenian genocide of 1915 to the death of Socrates? The Ukrainian genocide of 1933 to the death of Jean Moulin? The massacre of an entire population in military reprisals to the murder of a neighbor? A massacre to the murder of so-and-so? If I may say so, doesn't a massacre suffice in itself? Is it necessary to compare it to the murder of

---

2. The article "Shoah" in the *Encyclopaedia Universalis* (Paris: Encyclopaedia Universalis, 1989), vol. 20, 997, col. 3.

a particular being in order to measure its infamy? Do some corpses count more than others?

—How can the death of Jesus be equivalent to a mass-murder outside a specific religious conviction: Christianity (Jesus as the man-of-pain taking the suffering of the world upon himself; in each suffering being, it is Jesus who suffers; the crucifixion of Jesus until the end of the world)?

—The author is not content—as though this posed no problem—with taking the death of a single person as the criterion for measuring the degree of abjection of the greatest extermination in history. He writes, in stupefying fashion, that "it is not excessive" to consider this murder of millions of Jews, which, as we know, was perpetrated in the most unspeakable manner, as more or less as grave and overwhelming ("of the same nature") as this death. I can see that one might feel some scruples about equating the murder of an individual with a genocide, but certainly not the reverse.

For this phrase to have meaning I am obliged to understand the following:

—Before the Shoah, the most important, the most traumatizing event of human history was the crucifixion of Jesus.

—After the Shoah, one can perhaps—with kid gloves on, with tongs, walking on hot coals, excusing oneself in advance—risk suggesting that, after all, why not, it is possible, it is not untenable that, in spite of everything, excuse me if I'm going too far, it's just a hypothesis, I'm not stating anything as a fact so don't put words in my mouth . . . the Shoah, hmm, well, "it is not excessive" to ask oneself whether ultimately, all things considered, without exaggeration, *mutatis mutandis* and vice versa—I've finished—might not be "an event of the same nature?"

—To whom is this discourse addressed? Before what auditorium is the orator speaking? What is he afraid of? To be reproached for his comparison, certainly, but by whom? Certainly not by non-Christians. Otherwise, he would have formulated his phrase the other way around: "It is not excessive to see in the crucifixion of Jesus an event of the same nature as the Shoah." For whom is this message intended?

—Or does the author mean that the Shoah has a redemptive value? Several million martyrs sacrificed themselves? To whom? For whom?

—The bibliography to the article mentions Dionys Mascolo's admirable book: *Autour d'un effort de mémoire: Sur une lettre de Robert Antelme*.[3] I shall quote from it:

> Robert remained bound his whole life—the same is true of us—to what he says in his letter. He brought us to the place from which he speaks, and we have never returned from it. . . . By means of his return, it is as though he had deported us to a Nazi camp with him, and as a result we found ourselves Judaized forever. And we also found ourselves bound together in our soul. [21–22]

As you see, the miraculous survivor of Buchenwald that Antelme is scarcely seems to have evoked for Mascolo the figure of the risen Jesus.

For in *L'Espèce humaine* (*The Human Race*) Antelme does speak of Jesus: once, without even naming him. He wrote (I apologize for the length of this quotation, but I cannot cut it):

> Good Friday. About seven o'clock, back from the factory, a few guys have gotten together and have sat down on the edges of two adjacent beds. Some are believers; some are not.
>
> But it's Good Friday. One man had accepted torture and death. A brother. They talked about him.
>
> One fellow had been able to get hold of an old Bible at Buchenwald. He reads a passage from the Gospel.
>
> The story of a man, just a man, the cross for a man, the story of one single man. He is able to speak, and the women who love him are there. He isn't disguised, he's handsome, in any case he has healthy flesh on his bones—he doesn't have lice, he's able to say new things and if he's mocked, at least it's because people are inclined to look upon him as if he were somebody.
>
> A story. A passion. In the distance, a cross. A faint cross, very far away. A beautiful story.
>
> K. died, and we didn't recognize him.
>
> Guys died saying: "The bastards, the shits. . . ."
>
> The little gypsies at Buchenwald, suffocated like rats.
>
> M.-L. A.—dead, the hair cut off her head, a skeleton.
>
> All the ashes upon the soil of Auschwitz.
>
> The guy's voice fades. A faint, slender story, a beautiful, derisory story.
>
> Another guy—he's a non-believer—speaks of this man's freedom.
>
> He had accepted, he says. In his cell in Fresnes, Jeanneton too had

3. Dionys Mascolo, *Autour d'un effort de mémoire: Sur une lettre de Robert Antelme* (Paris: Nadeau, 1987).

accepted. He told us: "I have the honor of announcing to you that I have been condemned to death."

And perhaps here too, there are a few who accept, understand, find that all this is *in order*.

The fine story of a superman, a story buried beneath tons of ashes from Auschwitz. He was allowed to have a story.

He spoke of love, and he was loved. The hair that wiped his feet, the nard, the disciple he loved. The wiped face. . . .

Here, the dead aren't given to their mothers, the mothers are killed along with them, their bread is eaten, and gold is yanked from their mouths to get more bread. They make soap from their bodies; or they make their skin into lamp shades for the SS bitches. No nail marks on the lamp shades, just artistic tatoos.

"Father, why hast thou. . . ."

Screams of children being suffocated. Silence of ashes spread across a plain.[4]

Mascolo notes in a sober and accurate way that this text dismisses the story of Jesus "as derisory, with a simply ironic gesture of boredom, more definitive than any invective" (87).

I cite Mascolo (and consequently Antelme) because he appears in the bibliography to the article. I could cite many writers in the same vein, but my aim is not to go through the literature of the camps. I am simply demonstrating by means of a concrete example, in this case the account of a deportee, that the comparison of the Shoah with the Passion is not self-evident, far from it.

To some, it would even appear as a major impropriety. I recall some recent facts:

The hailing of Auschwitz as the "Golgotha of the contemporary world" by a certain Mr. Karol Wojtyla, better known, no doubt, by the pseudonym John Paul II, his business title (or registered trademark), in June 1979, during the first papal visit ever made to that site; the canonization in 1981 of Maximilien Kolbe, a Polish Franciscan who died in Auschwitz and who had previously been a militant anti-Semite; the beatification on 1 May 1987 of Edith Stein, a German Jewish convert to Catholicism, who also died in Auschwitz; the establishment of a Carmelite convent and the erection of a cross within the camp's enclosure; the call for a "new evangelization" during the Pope's fourth visit to

4. Robert Antelme, *L'Espèce humaine* (Paris: Gallimard, 1978), 194–95; [orig. ed. Paris: Editions de la Cité Universelle, 1957]; English translation, *The Human Race* (Marlboro, VT: Marlboro University Press, 1992), 187–88.

Poland in June 1991. All of these facts have produced such a curious uproar that a number of bad spirits with a good sense of smell have sniffed out a suspicious odor, a kind of sulphurous emanation which is already quite familiar, its barbarous name hard to pronounce: Christianization, I believe.

That's it: the Christianization of the Shoah.

For after all—and I answer here the question that I asked earlier—if the author of this article politely excuses himself for daring to compare Hitler's genocide to the death by crucifixion of a man whose popularity runs high in our day with people who are running in circles, before what master is he soft-peddling, if not the great pensioner of the eternal city, the sworn watchdog of the one saving message, the uncompromising true prophet of the one and only triple winner? Apart from a scribbler in the pay of the supreme cassock, chief peddler, as everyone knows, of the Vatican fair and champion on all terrains of the voyage under the bull *urbi et orbi*, famous for pitching eternal life guaranteed *judenfrei*, who would state, without the slightest twinge of feeling about the extermination of the Jews, with incredible nonchalance and audacity (no reason is given: this is how it is, full stop), that for believers, whoever they may be, thus for Jews as well as for non-believers (?!) Jesus remains "on the horizon of [their] history?" He shines there at night like his colleagues Mars and Jupiter, I suppose, or like Saturn devouring his own young. During the Shoah, he doubtless couldn't be seen up there, because the smoke emanating from the crematoria obscured the view.

Who in France today, in 1992, possessing full and entire knowledge of the process of the destruction of the Jews, and since the release of Claude Lanzmann's film *Shoah* (which I regard as one of the major events of the last half-century, but who, really, has seen this film?), who other than the enmitred, gorged with the milk of the she-wolf, would lack the decency, have lost all shame, all sensitivity to the point that he no longer recognizes what is obvious: that to compare the Nazi genocide to the death of Jesus is to exterminate the Jews a second time, and this time to exterminate them for good? Under Hitler there were still Jews: dead, but Jews. With the enpoped there are only the dead, all members of the Christian people: the Jews never existed. Hitler exterminated the living Jews, the Church exterminates the dead. Jesus the alpha and the omega. The alpha: his death. The omega: the Shoah, or in other words, his death again, since the Shoah was not five to six million Jews who were annihilated, but Jesus crucified again and forever. It's the miracle of the little Jesuses. As Marek Edelman, survivor of the Warsaw ghetto, wrote at the time of the affair of the Carmelites at Auschwitz: "After all that I have lived through, I am forced once again to fight for the memory of my people so that they do not become a fragment in a Catholic martyrology."[5]

Two remarks in closing:

—I don't understand what the author means by a "radical evil which spares no one." Does he mean that all are guilty? Perpetrators as well as victims, Nazis as well as Jews, the children who entered the gas chambers as well as the SS who pushed them in, all of them acting together, all accomplices? Original sin in its raw form, in short, proved by $a + b$? I'm just asking.

—If Shoah = the crucifixion of Jesus, "the history of humanity" no longer contains either "darkness" or "enigmas." On the contrary. Everything is all too clear. And so what remains of the "unique character" of the Shoah?

If I am mistaken in my comprehension of the article, I make, in sackcloth and ashes, my humblest apologies to the author. If not, and if Larousse has indeed become a Christian publishing house, let it at least wear its true colors. For, as far as I know, its books are not sealed with the *imprimi potest*, the *nihil obstat* and the *imprimatur*. The unsuspecting individual who consults a wide-circulation reference work does not necessarily expect to read a catechism, a manual of apologetics, or an encyclopedia of Catholic, apostolic, and Roman theology.

Your most sincere and attentive reader,

Armand Vulliet
Postman
Montmartre Post Office
Paris, 18th arrondissement

P.S. A copy of this letter has been sent to Mr. Claude Lanzmann.

—Translated by Madeleine Dobie

5. Cited by Micheline and Nathan Weinstock, "Le Sens pervers du carmel d'Auschwitz," in *Pourquoi le carmel d'Auschwitz?* (Brussels: Editions de l'Université de Bruxelles, 1990), 29.

BERNARD SUCHECKY

The Carmelite Convent at Auschwitz: The Nature and Scope of a Failure*

This article was written in February 1993. On 5 July 1993, Bishop Tadeusz Rakoczy, whose diocese has jurisdiction over Osweicim (Auschwitz), announced the closure of the Carmelite convent on the site of the extermination camp.
—Special editor of this issue of Yale French Studies

Confronted with what is still too often, and with great complacency, called the "mystery of Auschwitz," Western thought, since 1945, has developed numerous lines of flight: historicization and localization taken to extremes; near-cosmic amplification; trivialization; outright denial; ideological discourse on memory or the rhetoric of "never again!" And last but not least, the cramming with religious meaning brutally demonstrated in the affair of the Carmelites of Auschwitz, and which, in its Wojtylian variant, manifests itself as a perverse subversion of the real: the catastrophe of Auschwitz transformed into a "victory won with Christ!"

In this last case what is in question is not merely a discourse gone adrift, but a social practice intent on political hegemony. But has this been recognized?

Today, with the removal of the Carmelite convent of Auschwitz, which a month ago was said to be imminent, postponed *sine die* for the umpteenth time, I have decided to take stock again.

In December 1986, I was the first on the site to observe the reality of what was then presented as a "project for the construction of a Carmelite convent at Auschwitz," and to collect curious declarations

*Bernard Suchecky, "Carmel d'Auschwitz: La Nature et l'ampleur d'un échec," *Les Temps Modernes* 561 (April 1993): 40–56.

YFS 85, *Discourses of Jewish Identity in Twentieth-Century France,* ed. Alan Astro,
© 1994 by Yale University.

from both the mother superior of the convent and the archbishop of Cracow.[1] Caught up in this complex story involving Poles, Jews, Auschwitz, the Church and various symbols, I had taken on a battle which I believed to be highly ethical rather than symbolic, religious, or political.

Nevertheless, I had experienced my first doubts in February 1987 in Geneva, where, before a Jewish delegation, four cardinals had just agreed to move the controversial convent to an information, education, meeting, and prayer center whose completion within two years was guaranteed.[2] At the end of this meeting, however, several participants told me: "We know very well that two years is too little. In five years, perhaps. But at least the principle of moving the Carmelites has been accepted, and that's what counts." The seeds of doubt were sown in my mind regarding an ostensibly secondary question: why are they preparing to default on the form if they're so sure about the content?

In any event, two years later, the Church had still done nothing which might have led one to believe that it would one day honor its agreements. Exploiting the vagueness of the Geneva document, the Church hierarchy gave the opposite impression of wanting to settle into an indefinitely provisional situation, putting its own temporal interests before its discourse of loving one's neighbor and defending human rights. It would have to be forced to keep its word. For their part, the Jewish leaders who had taken it upon themselves to negotiate at Geneva merely hid their wait-and-see policy under an occasional weak protest. Whether or not they understood the nature and value of what was at stake, they had just compromised themselves.

In the face of our unheroic capitulation of 22 February 1989, I felt that it was more urgent to reflect on what had happened to us than to sustain the illusion that a battle was still being waged. Wasn't the sole objective of what we had called the battle of the Carmelite convent the removal of an intrusive convent? But hadn't this initial goal been displaced, as the affair developed into a symptom? Into a symptom of what? Of what warning was this affair a sign?

1. I had been sent to Poland as the special envoy of *Regards*, a Jewish periodical published in Brussels, which played a central role in information and mobilization throughout this affair. But I was also charged with an official mission by the Consistoire central israélite of Belgium and the coordinating committee of Belgian Jewish organizations, the two main institutions of the Jewish community of that country.

2. In general for this article, see the documents collected by Michel Jarton, published under the title *Carmel d'Auschwitz: Les Pièces majeures du dossier*, supplement to *La Documentation catholique* 1991 (1 October 1989).

A SYMBOLIC FAILURE

By moving into Auschwitz, the Polish Church undoubtedly sought to install in the general consciousness categories intended to change the way of thinking, and not only about Auschwitz. "The convent of Auschwitz," wrote the Archbishop of Cracow, Cardinal Macharski, "symbolizes the Church's tasks regarding the heritage constituted by the former camp of Auschwitz-Birkenau."[3] What, then, were these tasks?

In the first available text on this subject—*Help to the Church in Distress* of October 1985—the Auschwitz convent was presented as "the sacred sign of the love, peace, and reconciliation which will testify to the victorious power of the cross of Jesus," and as a "spiritual fortress and the sign of the conversion of those of our countrymen who had gone astray." This first message was, however, rapidly tempered, no doubt to counteract the protests which it triggered from all quarters. From then on, only expiation, reconciliation, and "the love which is stronger than evil" would be emphasized in Poland. Yet even in this second form, the symbolic, reconciliatory action taken by the Polish Church at Auschwitz continued to fail. Like a graft that won't take, it simply couldn't succeed in etching itself into reality. Why?

Perhaps because forty years after Auschwitz had been the place of the most extreme negation of the Other, the Polish Church was about to repeat this fault, though only symbolically. When it spoke of the victims of Auschwitz, it was to strip them of their difference and even of their name, to assimilate them and group them into a mass of "anonymous martyrs," to reduce them to their suffering—but to a disembodied suffering, itself reduced to being the instrument of an ecclesiastical project: "suffering is the way of the Church." Incorporated into the symbolism of Christian martyrology, Auschwitz is transformed into a "symbol of the sacrifice accomplished with Christ."[4]

Disguised as "love," this Catholic discourse of indifferentiation leads to a double dissolution of the specificity of Auschwitz. On the one hand, it is as the universal church that the Polish Church renews at Auschwitz Christ's universal teaching of love. Alongside Maximilien Kolbe, said the Cardinal Archbishop of Cracow, Karol Wojtyla, millions

---

3. Cardinal F. Macharski, "Nel campo di sterminio un convento segno piu forte del male," *Osservatore Romano*, 20 February 1986.
4. Cf., the many texts collected in Karol Wojtyla [John Paul II], *Maximilien Kolbe: Patron de notre siècle difficile* (Paris: Lethielleux, 1982).

of "anonymous" martyrs "gave" their lives at Auschwitz: "But humanity was saved; from their ashes, we are all restored to life." Auschwitz, the Cardinal Archbishop of Cracow, Franciszek Macharski, later said, "could well become a new crossing of the Red Sea, paving the way for a New Covenant for the whole of humanity."[5] The historical Auschwitz, the rout of humanity, is thus transfigured into an Auschwitz of Love, reassuring but hypnotic.[6] On the other hand, it is as guarantor of a Polish identity whose inner core is necessarily Catholicism that the Polish Church speaks and acts in this way at Auschwitz. It thus reinscribes the site in the local tradition of Polish "national messianism," magnifying the suffering of the messiah-nation while erasing the diversity of the victims' identities, the diversity of the crimes committed at Auschwitz and consequently, that of the inherent logic of these crimes. By acting in this way, the Polish Church is behaving in a way no different from that of the Communist authorities; like them, it has shamelessly ideologized Auschwitz and used it to its own religious and political ends.

Once installed in this place of the dead, in which the human does not reside, the Polish Church refused to hear the living who reproached it for its errors and its contradictions. Failing to open onto anything beyond itself, reproducing itself at every turn in the affair, without others, without any real Other, the symbolic act of the Polish Church turned into the angry simulation of a penitence and a reconciliation which never actually came to pass. Locked inside the stubborn repetition of this failure, it ended up abandoning its "repentance" and its "reconciliation," and allowed its anger and resentment to explode. Nothing remained of the love which had previously been professed except a blind rage which spread throughout the social body. The "elder brothers," whom in the great synagogue in Rome in April 1986 one claimed to love, were reduced in Czestochowa, in August 1989, to a pitifully anti-Semitic caricature.[7]

Things had come full circle; the symbolic convent once again embraced the triumphal mission which it had initially been assigned: that of testifying to "the victorious power of Christ's cross."

5. Cardinal F. Macharski, "A Polish Response to Nostra Aetate," *Christian-Jewish Relations* 18/4 (December 1985): 4–5.
6. For this aspect of the affair, see, in particular, my "La Christianisation de la Shoah," *Esprit* 5/150 (May 1989): 98–114.
7. Cf., Cardinal Glemp's speech at the pilgrimage to the Black Madonna at Jasna Gora, 26 August 1989.

The Poles did, in fact, have something else to say. But they spoke timidly, because they weren't yet confident that the historical upheavals which were taking place, particularly during the summer of 1989, would allow them to take their leave of the Church. "How can we take a stand?" asked Wladyslaw Frasiniuk, president of Solidarity for the Wroclaw area, and an almost legendary figure in the history of the union. "The Church has always supported us in difficult times, and we might need it tomorrow."[8] In the end, this Judeophile Polish party—Catholic intellectuals belonging to the liberal wing of Solidarity dissidents who broke with the Communist party in the 1960s, certain members of the clergy—rallied to the objectives defined early on by an eminent section of the French Catholic hierarchy.

CONSENSUS AT ANY PRICE

For it was the Archbishop of Lyons, Cardinal Decourtray, who would finally lay the foundations for a Judeo-Catholic consensus likely to lead to a solution that would be "acceptable to all parties." Auschwitz, he said in December 1985, "is first and foremost the symbol of the Shoah, in other words, of the attempted total extermination of the Jews. Such an ordeal has conferred on the Jewish people a particular dignity, which belongs to it alone."[9] The action of the Auschwitz Carmelites, however noble and sincere their motivations, strikes a blow at this dignity; it wounds the Jews who have already suffered enough. Moreover, it imperils the precious improvements made in Judeo-Catholic relations since Vatican II. The controversial convent must therefore be moved, while ensuring that the Catholic Church doesn't "lose face" in the process.

Here was a radical change in perspective, since the focus of this discourse seemed to be not the mission of the Church, but the catastrophe of Auschwitz and the suffering of the Jewish people. However, by keeping the controversy within the religious domain and by demanding compassion for the Jews, perceived as *victims* rather than as citizens within their rights, this discourse masked the question of the Church's historical responsibility regarding both the advent of Nazism, and, further back in history, the promulgation of an anti-Jewish sentiment which became firmly entrenched over the course of the centuries. It also masked the political and juridical nature of the con-

8. *Libération*, 2–3 September 1989.
9. Interview broadcast on Radio France, 6 December 1985.

flict surrounding the Carmelite convent. The entire Catholic Church (and not just that of Poland) should have been questioned about its project for a second evangelization of Europe and about the nonchalance with which it got out of respecting the convention of international law which, notably, prohibited it from transforming the Theatergebäude of Auschwitz I into a convent.[10]

The aftermath is well-known. The consensus was formally sanctioned during negotiations which took place in Geneva in July 1986 (Geneva I) and February 1987 (Geneva II). The Jewish negotiators should have had nothing to negotiate there other than the muffling of Jewish protests, their silence over Birkenau and Sobibor (where there had been churches since 1983), and over the general movement which had led the Church to appropriate the sites of the Shoah. But they went even further, endorsing the construction of a Catholic center in which the Carmelites would be rehoused. The Church, already assured that it would retain its positions at Birkenau and Sobibor, found itself given the opportunity to reinforce its politico-religious hold on Auschwitz and to capitalize on it in the campaign for the Christian re-foundation of Europe promoted by the Vatican.

When, in the course of the tumultuous summer of 1989,[11] this consensus was threatened with ruin by the fits of temper—whether involuntary or deliberate—of Cardinal Macharski and the primate of Poland, it was saved by the resolve of the Western cardinals who had been its instigators. Should we be surprised at this, or rather consider that they had a clearer perspective on the broader interests of the Church and the acceleration of history to the East than their Polish homologues? The latter continued to drag their feet, blinded by their narrow national-messianism, and it was finally the Vatican that obliged them to set their clock forward by involving Cardinal Willebrands, president of the Vatican commission for religious relations with Jews. His public declaration of 19 September 1989,[12] seen as the expression of the personal opinion of the Polish pope, was as ambiguous and vague as the earlier official texts to which it referred. But Rome had spoken, and it was claimed that the case was "closed." As a

10. Cf., the 1972 UNESCO charter on the protection of the world's natural and cultural patrimony and the list of its sites. The camps of Auschwitz-Birkenau were placed on this list at the request of the Polish government in 1978.

11. The tumult was triggered on 14 July by the intrusion into the convent garden by six American Jews led by Rabbi Avi Weiss. Cf., La Documentation catholique, 40.

12. La Documentation catholique, insert.

result, the Jews were restored to their debarment in the role of inconsolable victims, earnestly asked to understand, to be silent and wait.

A POLITICAL DEFEAT

"The Jews have lost the battle of the Carmelite convent," declared Claude Lanzmann, one of the few personalities who did not join his voice to the general celebration of the consensus, a few days before Cardinal Willebrand's statement: "Even if the Carmelites withdraw, the Jews will still have lost: the mean Jews will have chased off a few innocent nuns who had no ill intentions. There shouldn't have been negotiations, there should have been protests. Today, the Jewish negotiators have been cheated before the entire world. They have no means of obtaining the departure of the Carmelites."[13]

In fact, three and a half years later, where exactly are we? We have accepted the presence of the churches at Birkenau and Sobibor. The center we accepted at Geneva II is completed and already employs forty-odd people. It was supposed to be Catholic, it is more likely to be ecumenical or even Judeo-Christian since, retreating once again, the Jewish negotiators of Geneva have announced Jewish participation in its activities. There is even some question of building a rabbinical school, a yeshiva, nearby: it is being seriously considered in Israel. The new convent, in which the occupants of the present controversial one are supposed to be rehoused, is practically finished and inhabitable—but still not inhabited. Lastly, following the mission confided in October 1989 to a Polish government commission, an international commission is attempting to rethink the museum system of Auschwitz-Birkenau so as to introduce a little more historical truth, a little more pedagogy, and a little more spirituality. (But of what kind? Judeo-Christian? Is Auschwitz going to be ideologized yet again?)

In short, should we agree with Théo Klein that "for the first time in its history, the Church has negotiated with the Jews and actually conceded something to them"?[14] Or rather, should we consider that it turned an initially delicate situation to its own advantage in order to pursue its goal of winning ascendancy in the best conditions for itself? Doesn't the center built opposite Auschwitz I testify to the fact that the Church has succeeded in constituting a religious front whose voca-

13. *L'Evénement du jeudi* 253 (7–13 September 1989): 54.
14. Théo Klein has devoted a whole work to the defense of this viewpoint: *L'Affaire du carmel d'Auschwitz* (Paris: Jacques Bertoin, 1991).

tion could be the implementation of the program outlined by Cardinal Macharski in December 1986 in *Christian-Jewish Relations*? "Faith in the God of Abraham and Moses, of the Patriarchs and the Prophets, the God in whom Christians recognize the God of Christ, will protect humanity against a new paroxysm of lethal madness far more effectively than ideologies" (Macharski, 4–5). As an Auschwitz survivor now living in Brussels said to me, "We didn't want a convent, and we're going to get a cathedral." With our consent! So what does the projected removal of the squatters of the Theatergebäude of Auschwitz I matter?

What has happened to us to bring us to this juncture?

By denouncing as we did the presence of a Carmelite convent in Auschwitz, we expressed, among ourselves and to non-Jews, our refusal of Catholic indifferentiation: Auschwitz should remain "empty," preserved from all appropriations, from all prefabricated meanings. Nevertheless, we made some serious mistakes which must be recognized and examined.

The first was not to distinguish—at least not clearly enough—the religious from the political. I was myself involved in fostering this confusion. By blowing the shofar, the ritual ram's horn, in front of the Carmelite convent of Auschwitz during a demonstration organized by the European Union of Jewish Students on 23 July 1989, I unavoidably created a religious image which, though it distorted our motives and our objectives, was immediately seized upon by the television crews that were present. Whatever the pertinence of the symbol of the shofar in such circumstances, and the political value of the statement made to the journalists who were observing us, it neglected the fact that "the mass-media hide by exhibiting and neutralize by dramatizing."[15]

The center of gravity of this affair, however, lay less at the intersection of memory and theology, where it has generally been placed, than at that of ethics and politics. Beneath the symbolic forms, the religious figures or metaphysical categories that were brought into play, lurked essential issues, such as responsibility or the relationship to the Other.

This question of the Other did not arise in the abstract, but within an international juridical and political framework, notably as defined

---

15. Edouard Delruelle, "Oubli et communication de masse: Quelques mécanismes de neutralisation de l'innomable," *Bulletin trimestriel de la Fondation Auschwitz* 34 (October-December 1992): 57. On the demonstration of 23 July 1989, see my account in *La Documentation catholique*, op. cit., 41, and an independent Polish version: Pawel Smolenski (Thomas Jerz) in *Kultura* 10 (1989), translated and published under the title "Un dimanche à Auschwitz," *L'Arche* 394 (April 1990).

by the UNESCO agreement signed by states including ours. And in fact, we failed to call on them. On 15 June 1986, that is, during the period immediately preceding Geneva I, Georges Wellers, honorary research director at the Centre National de la Recherche Scientifique and president of the association of former prisoners of the camp Auschwitz III (Buna-Monowitz), wrote:

> The States which co-signed the UNESCO Convention regarding the protection of the world's cultural and natural heritage have the "duty" to intervene in order that the protected heritage be conserved in its original state.
>
> It follows that the problem of the Auschwitz convent should naturally be settled between, on the one hand, the Polish government, and on the other, the co-signatory governments of countries whose nationals were detained in, or died in Auschwitz-Birkenau. The countries directly involved in this problem are: Austria, Belgium, Czechoslovakia, France, East and West Germany, Greece, Holland, Hungary, Italy, Norway, Russia, Yugoslavia.
>
> It is thus not natural for there to be a disturbing confrontation between Jewish communities and the hierarchy of the Catholic Church of Poland, which are in no way qualified to deal with a flagrant violation of the international convention concerning "the conservation and protection of the universal heritage," namely the radical transformation of the Theatergebäude . . . into a Carmelite convent.
>
> It is not their concern, it is the concern of the co-signatory governments. The representatives of the Jewish communities should alert their governments![16]

But at the time that these lines were written, it was already too late to change the course of the affair. All efforts were directed towards a confrontation between the Church and Jewish institutions rather than towards a questioning of rights, democracy, pluralism, and responsibility.

Our second mistake stems from the discourse on memory which we have pursued. It was rapidly reduced to a caricature—"Don't put a cross through my memory!"—incapable of taking into account circumstances and their changes, of interpreting events and of situating them in a broader context, of bringing the debate onto a terrain other than that of relations between the Church hierarchy and the Jewish organizations. It was incapable of making us anything but *victims* or

16. Georges Wellers, letter to Léon Masliah, director of the French monthly *Information juive*.

heirs, painfully delicate, the dead and the survivors; incapable, finally, of taking into account the suffering of others in Auschwitz in anything more than an inadequate form: "Of course," we said, "there were Gypsies, Poles, Soviets in Auschwitz"—we don't really like to mention homosexuals—"but. . . ." And everything was in this *but*.

Did this discourse, above all else, serve to meet a deficiency in contemporary Jewish thought, a lack which is no longer filled by national ideologies, secularism or even Jewish religion? Did it also serve to mask divisions within the Jewish community? Was it not, above all, the discourse of a fictional "we"?

Moreover, by proclaiming "Don't put a cross through my memory!" weren't we wrong about the memory in need of protection? Wasn't the memory threatened by the Church primarily that of the non-Jewish world, in other words that of the historical consciousness of our societies?

Our third mistake was to have negotiated. It was the most limited option, and necessarily entailed the self-limitation of Jewish demands. To this end, we proclaimed that "Auschwitz is the supreme symbol of the Shoah." In so doing, we fabricated or reaffirmed, without any critical spirit, a symbol which embraced neither the whole reality of the Shoah nor that of the Christianization of the sites of the Shoah. Why? Perhaps because in restricting our demands we sought to limit the potential violence of the confrontation with the Church, whose power we overestimated: the phantasmal vision of an all-powerful Church, inherited from another age. Perhaps because we have "preferred" to remain *victims*, in other words, to infantilize ourselves, rather than to take responsibility.

Responsibility? For what should Jews take responsibility? Not for the Shoah, of course, but for our destiny and our identity since the Shoah. Are we condemned to organize our interior geography around a "capital of pain"? Is our duty to be the "silence-bearers" or "absence-bearers for six million of our brothers" of which Ady Steg spoke at Geneva II? Burying these dead who are not yet quite dead in us, and who make us not quite living—is that not the *sine qua non* for us to stop behaving as *victims*, for us to get back on the path of history?

"NICHT VERANTWORTLICH"

The Judeo-Catholic consensus to which I referred above was built around the French, and later on, the Belgian, Catholic hierarchies; and probably with the support of a significant section of the Roman curia.

On a ground which they chose: that of the suffering and religious profession of Jews after Auschwitz, viewed within the context of Judeo-Christian relations since Vatican II.

But if this consensus has proved effective, it is because the whole social universe called for it. There was undoubtedly a general consensus, shared and expressed by the media, political figures and structures, international institutions (UNESCO in particular), and an intelligentsia which is generally quicker to show its capacity for critical thought. Faced with a conflict which it took to be a religious controversy, this intelligentsia chose to remain a spectator, only entering the fray in summer 1989 when everything had already been played out.

It seems to me that the basis for this consensus can be expressed as follows: "Given what Auschwitz represents *for the Jews*, let's avoid making them suffer any more." But wasn't a significant denial at work here, a means of avoiding the question: "What does Auschwitz represent *for us non-Jews*?"

This denial leads me to extend the scope of my observations and reflections. Various other controversies exploded during the one regarding the Carmelite convent at Auschwitz, all of which had Auschwitz in the background. I recall to memory: the outcry provoked in the United States over President Reagan's visit to the German military cemetery at Bitburg; the revelations concerning the past of the former Secretary-General of the U.N., Kurt Waldheim; the beatification of Edith Stein; the trial of Ivan Demjanjuk in Jerusalem and that of Klaus Barbie in Lyons; the Touvier, Papon and Bousquet affairs; and the beginnings of a controversy surrounding "Vichy France and the Republic" on the occasion of the 50th anniversary of the Vel' d'Hiv' roundup of Parisian Jews. And during this same period, numerous university colloquia, scholarly books, and remarkable films contributed to raising, a little more, the veil cast over a period which our societies remember with difficulty, not to say bad grace.

In all of these controversies, colloquia, books, and films, the same questions and the same confrontations re-emerged: memory and forgetting, the work of mourning and the need to assume guilt and responsibility, with a double question at the root: even today, what do we do with these crimes *and* what do they do to us?

All of these affairs very quickly went beyond the domains of memory and history, in which they originated, to fuel, in the political arena, some very contemporary passions. Debates arose, sometimes very crude, sometimes still-born, concerning the juridical structures of democracy, rights, and even the essence of the Republic. As a result, we have seen clashes between, on the one hand, ethical imperatives (notably a morality based on responsibility) and, on the other, electoral contingencies, the *Realpolitik* of states and institutions, and national or international consensuses that are to be preserved.

Responsibility? Many reactions have taken the path of denial: "The German dead to whom I shall pay homage in Bitburg," said President Reagan, "were not who you say they were," were not, in other words, SS members. Or they were just Waffen-SS. "You've got the wrong Ivan," Demjanjuk responded in Jerusalem. "I wasn't where you say I was"— not at Treblinka, as accused, in fact, but at Sobibor. Was that more innocent? "I wasn't where you say I was," was also the claim of Kurt Waldheim, who later confessed: "All right, I was there, but I didn't do what you say I did." "Edith Stein didn't die for the reasons you're invoking," said the priests preparing to beatify her. "Vichy was not what you say it was," judged the French magistrates who released Paul Touvier. Or: "Vichy wasn't the Republic."

Aren't all of these denials echoes of the Carmelites' denial: "We don't have the intentions you're attributing to us. Anyway, the dead of Auschwitz aren't those you say they were. Those people died elsewhere, in Birkenau!" In short, it is as if the plea *nicht schuldig*—I am not guilty" which Adolf Eichmann entered before his Israeli judges some twenty-five years ago, were today echoed in a *"nicht verantwortlich*—I am not responsible, I don't have to answer for that," proclaimed by whole segments of our societies.

A GAME WITH THE DEAD

In sum, the period of the affair of the Carmelite convent of Auschwitz will, for me, have been one of difficult awakenings in which we suddenly realize that we have run away. We ran away, for example, whenever, in a literary or philosophical mode, we maintained that it is the genocide itself which eludes our thought, that is ungraspable, unattainable. It is a hole, we have said, an emptiness, something senseless, a sacred, inexpressible mystery. Or, to cite Emmanuel Lévinas: "The Shoah exceeds the dimensions of thought, its memory cannot enter the dimensions of consciousness and adopt forms. . . . "[17] As a result, we have, unsurprisingly, remained unable to name this event: genocide,

17. Emmanuel Lévinas, *Information juive*, October 1989.

Holocaust, Shoah, Auschwitz? The names succeed each other, float and slide over the event just as the event itself seems to slide over history without anchoring itself, without becoming inscribed in it. An imaginary and convenient evasion which, in the real order of things, is not that of the object, but of the subject: it is not the genocide which escapes us, but we who seek to avoid the hard duty of facing up to it.

Whether by lulling ourselves with optimistic illusions or by enclosing ourselves within a supposedly interminable mourning, we have fled before the need to face the reality and amplitude of a failure. Of a double failure, in fact, since, having been unable to stand in the way of Nazism and its genocidal outburst, our societies have since been unable to reflect on their failure, to draw lessons from it and incorporate them into their *political* behavior. At the very most they covered their impotence with a veil provided by the inconsistent rhetoric of "never again."

In short, any excuse is good enough for us to dodge, to escape what we doubtless fear to learn about ourselves, our societies, or our failures. Everything, even the most unexpected things, can sometimes reveal themselves to be the most suspect. Take for example *fetichism*. Thus, in 1971, on the occasion of the beatification of Maximilien Kolbe, Cardinal Wojtyla gave the Bishops of countries whose nationals had died in Auschwitz, urns containing dust from Auschwitz-Birkenau, presented as the symbolic remains of Maximilien Kolbe. Today, these urns can be found in the cathedrals of our European capitals. In 1983, Cardinal Macharski went one step further by offering the Archbishop of Vienna, Cardinal Franz König, an urn containing ashes taken from the crematoria of Auschwitz-Birkenau. It was a game with the dead, and in particular, our dead, which the priests are unfortunately not the only ones to play. In August 1989, with negotiations over the Carmelite affair in full swing, a Polish journalist revealed that the soil of Birkenau had become the object of a profitable traffic: credulous Poles were buying it by the kilo. Returning home, they put it through a sieve in the hope of finding some of the "Jews' gold"! Also in August 1989—but this passed unnoticed—a delegation from the United States government Holocaust Memorial Council purchased from the Polish government "Holocaust artifacts" preserved in the Auschwitz museum: suitcases, clothes and prostheses, in order to display them in the future Holocaust Memorial in Washington. Quite recently, this same council bought from the Polish government a barracks from Birkenau to be reassembled in the said memorial. So as not to be outdone, the Simon

Wiesenthal Center in Los Angeles did the same with a barracks from Majdanek!

So what is the significance of the battle—lost or won—of the Auschwitz convent in the face of these other manifestations of thoughtlessness? With Auschwitz hasn't something essential been irremediably affected in man? Was Theodor Adorno really wrong when he suggested that in the wake of Auschwitz we are "on a rubbish heap that has made even reflection on one's own damaged state useless"?[18]

—Translated by Madeleine Dobie

18. Theodor W. Adorno, *Notes to Literature*, vol. 1, trans. Shierry Weber Nicholsen (New York: Columbia University Press, 1991), 244.

MEYER JAÏS

Report on Jewish Culture*
(Excerpt)

What has Judaism, which gave the world the Bible, which produced the Talmud, which shone with particular brilliance during the Middle Ages—think, for example, of the place occupied by a Maimonides in the medieval intellectual world—what has Judaism given the world since the emancipation of the Jews?[1] Of course we have had no shortage of Jewish geniuses. There is perhaps not a single branch of human knowledge which hasn't been distinguished by one of our people. We have had scholars, writers, first-rate metaphysicians, and we have made an enormous contribution to the progress of intelligence. But in the specific domain of spiritual life, do you know of a single Jewish author whose intrinsically Jewish work has in any way altered the course of universal thought? Is there a single work whose inspiration has been drawn from the purest sources of Judaism, which has been nourished by its substance, and which has left on its Jewish or non-Jewish reader an imprint comparable to that left, for example, by the work of a Pascal? Is there a work which could bring us today to imitate Louis Gillet, who wrote in a letter to Romain Rolland: "At 15 I read Pascal: none of your objections to Christianity has any power over me."

Because Judaism has suffered since its emancipation from an almost total sterility, how could a genius like Bergson have considered it

*Meyer Jaïs, "Rapport sur la culture juive," presented to the Assises du Judaïsme Français in 1948, reprinted in *Pardès* 14 (1991): 94–100.

1. Emancipation refers to the granting of full rights as citizens to Jews. In France, this occurred at the time of the Revolution. [All notes to this piece are by the special editor.]

YFS 85, *Discourses of Jewish Identity in Twentieth-Century France,* ed. Alan Astro, © 1994 by Yale University.

worthy of nourishing his thought? Thus, in his book on *Les deux sources de la morale et de la religion*, he devotes only two pages to it, and these are only in order to declare it inferior to Christianity which he judges to be the perfect religion, or, in his vocabulary, the active mysticism *par excellence*. You can easily imagine the effect on both Jewish and non-Jewish minds of the opinion of one of humanity's most powerful thinkers, and one whose judgment derives added legitimacy from the fact that its author was born a Jew.

I only realized the degree to which this case represents something not only serious but also humiliating for us when, attending a course given at the Collège de France this year by Professor Baruzi, I heard this great specialist of mystical life state, without any hesitation, that he wasn't at all convinced that Bergson had correctly interpreted the facts when he claimed that for the Christian mystic, action is the end and indeed the crowning achievement of contemplation, since this perfectly expresses the position most characteristic of Judaism. What, I ask you, could be sadder than to see a Jew, and one of such eminence, contest what is ours and attribute it to others who, more conscious and more protective of their originality, reject it out of hand?

If only there had been someone, either here or elsewhere, to inform Bergson, to provide him with the principles of appreciation which were unavailable to him, and to obtain, if only regarding this one point, the necessary rectification. The complete inadequacy which we have displayed has exposed to all eyes our miserable poverty.

As a result of the elimination of Jewish culture, Judaism has lacked true theologians, original philosophers who, steeped in our civilization and nourished by its substance, could have compared its ideas with those of Western civilization and maintained a Jewish soul, a specifically Jewish spirit. With this kind of synthesis, the new generation could have discovered a means of remaining faithful to its past, of fully adhering to the tenets of our faith while effectively participating in the movement of universal thought, as Saadia and Maimonides did for the men of their time. But the many talented scholars, men of letters, and orators of the nineteenth century were not adequate to such a task. We needed minds powerful enough not merely to adapt Jewish thought to a particular philosophy which happened to be in vogue, as Hermann Cohen did in Germany, but to rethink, in accordance with Judaism, the entire metaphysical and moral reflection of the West. The result of such an effort would have served not only Israel, but also the whole world, which could have profited from it.

The fact that it was not attempted can of course never be sufficiently regretted. Within Judaism, it has resulted in this inferiority complex which affects us all, whether or not we choose to admit it, and which explains many defections. This complex is already manifest in the Jewish student. Foundering among comrades whose religious education has filled them with prejudices towards him, he bitterly notes that the solution which the professor proposes to such and such a problem can be supported or refuted by a parallel, specifically Christian solution in which his fellows take great pride, while Judaism sheds no light for him. This complex exists in the vast majority of our intellectuals whose reactions are ordinarily as follows. Either they find complete satisfaction in an extraordinarily intense intellectual activity, and feel nothing but disdain for all religions, Judaism included, since they consider it the product of a primitive mentality and accuse it of lying at the origin of all errors and divisions—whence, let it be said in passing, the accusation of being a source of disintegration, which is often leveled at us by adversaries who, moreover, are far from being our moral equals, and whose superficial piety generally consists in speaking a certain language and assuming a studiously affected pose. Or, on the contrary, they feel themselves pushed towards the problems of inner life by a real need—for one must make allowances for snobbery—but they approach all its problems with a mind so Christianized that they judge Judaism *a priori* incapable of satisfying their mystical aspirations, condemn it without knowing it, deplore the fact that they were born into it, and turn away from it, even if they don't go as far as conversion.

In both cases the approaches—however diverse—lead to the same outcome: Jews flee from themselves, they deny themselves as Jews and if they continue to feel different from others it is in an entirely negative sense. They retain a semblance of identity, not so much by what they affirm as by what they deny. They are other than the others without being themselves. Jean-Paul Sartre gives an admirable description of this condition in his *Réflexions sur la question juive*. They belong to what he calls the category of inauthentic Jews. One should thus not be surprised when, in converting, they have the illusion, not of abandoning Judaism, but, on the contrary, of rediscovering it, as Jean-Jacques Bernard, for example, has maintained.

Finally, this complex exists even among those who attempt to defend Judaism. I'm not simply referring to an author like Marcel Brunschwig who entitled his book *Le vrai visage d'Israël*, and who had the audacity to pen this phrase on page 16: "It is this Judaism—which, over time has evolved towards universal monotheism, profound spirituality, and a higher moral ideal—which paved the way for Christianity. And one can understand how the great philosopher Henri Bergson could write in his will that he saw Catholicism as the culmination of Judaism." Or consider Julien Benda who, in the first issue of the collection *Alef*, took it upon himself to devote a whole article to the relationship between justice and charity in Judaism, a subject about which he knows absolutely nothing. And how can one hold it against them when the official representatives of Judaism have censored themselves for so long? Overscrupulous and unwilling to antagonize the majority whose tolerance, as we know, is not unlimited, they failed to emphasize what distinguishes us, from the perspective of dogma as well as that of ethics. Instead they limited their efforts to demonstrating that what exists in Christianity can already be found among us. They avoided responding to the diverse accusations with which Christian literature is teeming, and fell back on a moral teaching whose equivalent could be found almost anywhere. Claudel's impression of American rabbis, could, I believe, be applied to the whole of Western Judaism: "When I lived in America, I sometimes came across sermons by rabbis in the newspapers. It was the same disgusting humanitarian drivel that flows unceasingly from Protestant books. How did the gold become tarnished? How was its prodigious color changed? It is sad when a son of Israel can no longer distinguish himself from a Baptist or a Methodist."

Our material situation has also suffered from this depersonalization. Was it not established that God sent us to the four corners of the world for the glory of our religion and the good of humanity? And, as Greece, when conquered by Rome, overcame it in turn through the superiority of its culture, we should have jealously protected the purity of our message and offered the world the whole wealth of our moral and religious experience without abandoning even the smallest scrap of it. And while strengthening ourselves through contact with alien cultures, we should have made our personal contribution to them. Whereas the very opposite occurred. We are often accused of being parasites. For once, this reproach is perhaps not completely unfounded. Spiritually speaking we cannot have the impression that we have decisively influenced the moral evolution of humanity. We have paid very dearly for it. In recent times, it has cost us six million martyrs. We have been the principal victims of the collapse of civilization, and this is doubtless because we were not without involvement in the causes of this atrocious drama. In the world's determination to persecute and annihilate us, one might think that it dimly feels, in betraying us, that we have betrayed it, since we have not fulfilled the role God assigned to us, and in view of which He set us apart from other men. The author of *The Anatomy of Peace*, inspecting the different causes which provoked the recent crisis in moral consciousness, devotes a whole chapter to the weakening of spiritual families among which he includes Judaism.[2] For my part, I am ready to recognize that this accusation is well-founded, but I would add that if the other faiths seem, as such, to have shared the responsibility for this bloody tragedy—I refer you to Jules Isaac's book[3]—Judaism itself is only at fault in that it lacked the men who could guarantee that its teaching would have sufficient influence. There can indeed be no doubt that, given its way of posing and solving the different problems of the relationships of God with humanity, of man with his neighbor, between peoples, of religion and life, of the spiritual and the temporal, of justice and charity, of universalism and particularism, Judaism, were it better diffused and better known, would provide humanity with the means of emerging from the impasse in which it has been caught for twenty centuries, and of making decisive progress.

If this analysis of the situation is correct, the only conclusion which can be drawn from our exposé is the following: everything possible must be done to ensure that Jews regain consciousness of their Judaism. The most obvious means of achieving this would be the establishment, on as wide a scale as possible, of private schools for Jewish primary, secondary, and higher education, where, in a dialogue with a very extensive general culture, our youth could acquire a true Jewish culture. There is no more urgent or more important task for the leaders responsible for the future of Judaism. The Ecole Maïmonide is already in existence and even if one doesn't share all the views of its admirable director, whose sincerity and courage inspire the most profound respect, one cannot but rejoice in the precious results which it has already obtained. But a single school is not enough. We need a whole network of similar establishments which cannot, we know, be built overnight, but which must be at least partially realized by next year.

2. Emery Reves, "The Failure of Religion," in *The Anatomy of Peace* 8th ed. (New York: Harper and Brothers, 1946), 76–87.

3. Jules Isaac, *Jésus et Israël* (Paris: Albin Michel, 1948); *Jesus and Israel*, trans. Sally Gran (New York: Holt, Rinehart and Winston, 1971).

That is why I propose to you, for the next school year, the reopening of the Talmud Torah on the premises of the rabbinical school and the opening of a Jewish high school with elementary classes on the premises of the rue Claude Bernard.

I will say only one word in response to those who are not full partisans of the generalized institution of a private, Jewish educational system. I will not mention that such schools exist in America, in Belgium, and elsewhere. I will not recall the considerable efforts of both Catholics and Protestants to maintain, in France and elsewhere, their private educational systems. I will not inform them that in Alsace-Lorraine, almost up to the time of the war, each community had its own primary schools and that this did not affect either their mutual understanding or their common loyalty to their country. I will simply insist on the following point. It is in the interest of Judaism, as of the whole world, that we be ourselves, completely and proudly, because it is in this way, and in this way alone, that we will best be able to serve others. It is in this way that we will be able to recover ourselves, recapture ourselves, and regain our identity and our dignity; and it is in this way that we will be able to command the sympathy and respect of our co-citizens. In his discourse on assimilation, Chief Rabbi David Haguenau had already forcefully maintained that: "Honor, the undying principle at the heart of every Frenchman, objects to anyone who attempts to protect himself by flight, and is pitiless towards any such attempt. There is a name for the amorphous beings who seek, at any price, to be absorbed into the mass, shrugging off the weight of their ancestry; they are called 'rootless' [déracinés]."

Since, by God's will, we are separated from the world, though in the world and for the world, just as the scholar is isolated from the crowd—not because he isn't interested in it, but on the contrary, to improve its lot—let us be ourselves. An ill-conceived assimilation has deprived us of almost all of our creative energy without, however, guaranteeing our material security. Our contributions are only credited on an individual basis, and then only if we go as far as complete fusion, in other words, conversion. Assimilation must therefore give way to self-consciousness, to pride, to the joy of being what we are, which cannot be obtained without a true Jewish culture.

The unforgettable Maurice Vexler had already embarked on this path; he had the great merit of correctly posing the Jewish question, and would have solved it had World War I not brought a premature end to his life; it is the path taken by Edmond Fleg, and you know the magnificent and original literary creation to which it led him. It is this task that would have been fulfilled by our much regretted philosopher, Jacob Gordin, who was suddenly taken from us, but who has left behind him enthusiastic disciples who will continue his work; and it is also, I believe, the direction of the admirable class of seminarians which our Master, the Chief Rabbi Liber, collected around him immediately after the Liberation, and from whom we may expect great things. In fact, it would certainly not be an exaggeration to say that it is the only path of salvation available to our Judaism at this decisive turning-point in its history, if it hopes to resume its triumphant march.

Indeed, we are forced to recognize that religion is unfortunately no longer the tie binding all Jews indiscriminately. Nor is Jewish nationalism, since only yesterday you witnessed here the debates it can provoke. However, there is a ground on which all those who draw on the authority of Judaism can agree, a ground which can supply this mystique of Union of which President Meiss spoke to us so eloquently yesterday, with its most solid foundation, and it is that of Jewish culture. If, as is too often forgotten, Israel is a religion, if it is a people, yet more than a people, it is because in reality Judaism is a civilization, and thus essentially a culture.

—Translated by Madeleine Dobie

DAVID J. JACOBSON

Jews for Genius: The Unholy Disorders of Maurice Sachs

"The Germans have the most delightful way of opening their hearts
to you, but I, alas! am unable to profit by it."
—Maurice Sachs, Hamburg, 1943

In the recent spate of historical studies and newly edited diaries and
autobiographical writings of some of France's most notorious anti-
Semitic writers and artists between the world wars, there appear a
perplexing, though by no means unexpected, number of Jewish friends,
associates, wives, mistresses. Cracks of various sizes in what had
seemed safely solid monoliths of racial hatred grow, for instance, with
anecdotes of Drieu la Rochelle's attempt to save his Jewish ex-wife and
her children from deportation at Drancy; of the fascist Maurice Bar-
dèche's early penchant for "unpretty Jewish girls" and his later marriage
to the "hook-nosed" sister of his political cohort Brasillach; of the
collaborationist sculptor Maillol's effort to prevent, through the help of
Hitler's favorite sculptor, the Paris-based Arno Breker, his Jewish
model's deportation to Auschwitz—if only for the sake of his work.[1]

The lives, letters, and journals of other, generally less heinous figures reveal a related discrepancy: an oscillation between sporadic out-
bursts against suddenly generalized Jews and an almost effusive philo-
Semitism reserved for individual ones. In the private writings of Jean
Cocteau, for example, this tendency has become especially clear with
the recent publication of both his wartime diaries and of Henri
Raczymow's exhaustive biography of Cocteau's one-time admirer and
eventual foe, Maurice Sachs.[2] The rapturous description in the diaries

1. On Aristide Maillol, for example, see Michèle C. Cone, *Artists Under Vichy: A
Case of Prejudice and Persecution* (Princeton, N.J.: Princeton University Press, 1992),
161; on Cocteau's relation to Breker, see Francis Steegmuller, *Cocteau: A Biography*
(Boston: David R. Godine, 1986), 440.
2. Jean Cocteau, *Journal, 1942–1945*, ed. Jean Touzot (Paris: Gallimard, 1989);
Henri Raczymow, *Maurice Sachs, ou Les travaux forcés de la frivolité* (Paris: Gallimard,
1988).

YFS 85, *Discourses of Jewish Identity in Twentieth-Century France*, ed. Alan Astro,
© 1994 by Yale University.

of long-time friend Simone Benda "en juive sublime" is but one case of a racial typology absorbed by the author decades before the "sublime" sufferings of the Occupation, part of a repertoire of fin de siècle exoticism. The abiding picturesqueness of Cocteau's Jewish friends, and particularly of this witty actress, suggests how aptly the ubiquitous figure of Sheherazade, staving off her execution by the amusement her storytelling offers, suited the arts in France in the first decade of the century. Cocteau's rage at the histrionic excesses of his very young friend Sachs, on the other hand, demonstrates how easily, even in the *années folles* of the 1920s, the fine line between entertainment and exhibitionism—which Cocteau himself overstepped more than most artists of his time—could be drawn to mark an offending Jew as an upstart. The offense for which Sachs is probably best known, his ambiguous collusion with the Nazis in Germany, was rehearsed in much earlier assumptions of racial "passing." Regarding himself first of all as a half-Jew by willfully assuming that the father who abandoned him in childhood was a gentile (apparently he was not), the nineteen-year-old Sachs presumed to do what fashionable Parisians were supposed to do in 1925: embrace the Church. The present essay will in fact center on the sordid scene of Sachs's breach of priestly vows and the rancor it unleashes in a friend and mentor who had hitherto been inexplicably charmed by him. For Cocteau's ironic indignation at Sachs's "exhibitionism" neatly illustrates the secret complicity or "fraternal rivalry" between Jewish "showing off" and the esthetic demands of a period that at least one cultural history has called "the age of astonishment."[3]

Notorious for his posthumous memoirs *Le Sabbat* and *La Chasse à courre* (translated as *Witches' Sabbath* and *The Hunt*) Maurice Sachs (1906–1945) had hoped to be notorious in his lifetime for novels and plays that were either never completed or, if published, not successful.[4] The disorder that characterizes his autobiography also undermined his fitful later attempts at fiction. Sachs's initial dismay, however, at being relegated to memoir writing gave way to elation by the time he applied his skills of observation to outright spying on fellow Frenchmen for the

---

3. So Jack Anderson titles his chapter on the Russian Ballet, which begins with reference to Cocteau, in his *Ballet and Modern Dance* (Princeton: Princeton Book Company, 1986).

4. Maurice Sachs, *Le Sabbat* (Paris: Corrêa, 1946) and *La Chasse à courre* (Paris: Gallimard, 1949); translations will be from *Witches' Sabbath and The Hunt*, trans. Richard Howard (New York: Ballantine, 1966).

Hamburg Gestapo, in a period he complacently describes in a letter as "one of the most curious *chapters* of my life" (quoted in Raczymow, 430; emphasis added). In the end the twin influences he boasted of, the literature of the parvenu-adventurer (Casanova, the characters Rastignac and Julien Sorel) and the aphoristic style of the French moralist tradition converged finally in his "Stendhalian" bliss of writing in prison. Despite his dramatic ambitions, Sachs's nearly successful attempts to write for the famous actor Pierre Fresnay and others paled beside the personal scandals he staged for a Paris elite for some twenty years. From the time of his teens, the physically unappealing yet highly seductive Sachs, whom Cocteau has depicted in his memoirs stuffing his pockets with toilet paper he pretended was money, followed an essentially theatrical calling, an endless getting into character. Sachs has hastily been labelled "the Jean Genet of the twenties," but the resemblance is superficial, based on their shared combination of homosexuality, thieving, black marketeering, and later fascination with Nazi Germany.[5] What divides them is Sachs's inherent want of formal mastery, his avowed sentimentality, contrition, longing for a vanished and indifferent mother, and his bourgeois snobbery. His attainments beyond the memoirs involved securing establishment positions: sitting on the editorial boards of the *Nouvelle Revue française* and Gallimard, selling important art, creating private libraries for more advanced *arrivistes*. In this longing to penetrate enshrined institutions, he shows affiliation with the Cocteau described by Sartre as "a man who had spent his whole life seeking a tribunal simply to corrupt it."[6]

Vowing absurdly and continually to himself to "have genius," Sachs may have meant nothing more by the term than the scant celebrity he managed to attain by the time of the Occupation. The memoirist who states in *Witches' Sabbath* that "the book of my youth could bear as a subtitle: In Search of the Legendary" (39) can boast, by the end of *The Hunt*: "No matter how shameful my life had been, I had also become a personage of note, with my own legend, in the eyes of some young men" (357). Sachs's closest maternal relatives had similarly pursued "legends," though not their own, spending or marrying their way toward famous artists: his major inheritance from the financially and

---

5. For the comparison to Genet, see, for example, Arthur Gold and Robert Fizdale's biography of Misia Sert, *Misia* (New York: Random House, 1980), 216.

6. Quoted in Frederick Brown, *An Impersonation of Angels: A Biography of Jean Cocteau* (New York: Viking, 1968), 339.

emotionally unstable Sachs family was a link, however tenuous, to the remnant social circles of Bizet, Anatole France, and Proust (his grandmother Alice had wed the composer's dissolute son Jacques Bizet, and thus become the daughter-in-law of Geneviève Straus, a notable salon figure and intimate friend of Proust's). As the family also lost substantial amounts of money in fraud, extravagance, and mismanagement, the cultivated but indigent young Sachs would turn for income to art dealing, art criticism, and at times art theft. Commerce seemed a very temporary expedient: yet in chastising himself for resembling "a little Jewish merchant" as he presses unwanted devotion on his first idol, André Gide, Sachs fails to acknowledge his striking temperamental similarity to a real-life merchant, his grandfather Georges Sachs, a charming and importunate friend and devotee of Anatole France, his era's candidate for literary immortality. Grandfather and grandson were united by a mania for grandiose projects, Georges's for Anatole France, Maurice's, alas, for his own never-reached "future works"; yet some of the secretarial duties Cocteau allowed his young friend in the early 1920s suggest similar promotional leanings.

In *Witches' Sabbath*, Sachs defines himself historically as a member of an "adoring generation," as opposed to the critical and captious one that would succeed it. True as this may be in part, it obscures the depressing repetitions of family traits he otherwise acknowledges in his memoir, which is burdened with a strong sense of hereditary curse, and opens with a maxim attributed to Wilde: "Hereditary is the only god we can name." Georges Sachs had used his wealth from a thriving jeweler's trade to back the founding of his friend Jaurès's newspaper *L'Humanité*. Penniless, his grandson charmed his way to close friendship with Cocteau and Max Jacob, acquaintance with Gide, the philosopher Maritain, and writers associated with the *Nouvelle Revue française*. Those not won over were often revolted by him, at times along classic anti-Semitic lines; thus the title question of novelist Marcel Jouhandeau's 1936 article for *Action française*, "How I Became an Anti-Semite," can be answered by the single name of Sachs. His flattery and servility, and his "short memory" in the face of insults, made him the author's quintessential Jew, "enemy of the interior," adversary of the French soul; and during the Occupation, Sachs, an open, even unctuous admirer of Jouhandeau's novels, answered the abuse by exaggerating his obsequiousness: later, during the Occupation, he "laid at the feet" of the author's wife black market "merchandise" accompanying a letter to her. It is Jouhandeau himself, however, who records that letter and the meeting that led to it, at which Sachs "had the naïveté to think his old enemy did not recognize him behind a new black beard" (quoted in Raczymow, 386). Feebly identifying himself in his Occupation memoir *The Hunt* as "Jewish on my mother's side" (since maternity determined racial identity), the adventurer Sachs went out of his way to call attention to himself, seeking official recognition as an author and proposing literary projects to blond German attachés of the *Cahiers franco-allemands* who met his brazenness with "inexplicable" aversion. It was Sachs's insistence on France's "loss of standards" during a discussion with Jouhandeau that first roused the latter's hatred. Well into the war Sachs would play Frencher than the 'true' French, getting himself thrown out of the Comédie Française for loudly jeering a performance of *Phèdre* he considered mediocre.

Meanwhile, in 1923, at the start of Sachs's literary apprenticeship, the photo on his wall of the "god" Gide came down the moment a young friend informed him the older writer was "finished" and "there's only Cocteau"—whom Sachs soon met and won over.

It was not long after, in 1925, late in the postwar religious revival, that Cocteau, approaching his mid-thirties and bereaved by the death of his protégé Raymond Radiguet, was converted, or won back, to his native religion, by Maritain. The incongruousness of this conversion is evidenced by the "medicinal" motif that dominates it: persuaded by his spiritual guide to renounce his opium habit in a Paris detoxification clinic, Cocteau had also to be cajoled, rather blasphemously, by his long-converted Jewish friend Max Jacob to "take the Host like an aspirin tablet."

Soon after this startling turn, Sachs wrote to Cocteau to ask for "permission" to "follow in his path," making it clear that, although he claimed Jacob had equally inspired his sudden craving for baptism, the real communion he sought in his new Catholicism was with Cocteau himself. Sachs's main experience of religion, he claimed, had been exclusion from Sunday mass at boarding school with the other boys who made up its ten-percent quota of Jews, most of them wealthy, religiously trained Sephardim from whom he was in turn socially excluded by his "freethinking" background.

But whether he now sought redemption or discipline, or just attention by outdoing his mentor in the one way he could, Sachs quickly capped his baptism under Maritain's guidance with the decision to take holy orders. Cocteau later maintained that Sachs, precociously self-supporting and dissolute despite the legal guardianship of his grandmother, entered a Parisian seminary to dodge creditors. The surprise his novitiate caused is clear from a young friend's greeting on his return to secular life: "When we heard that you were in the *Seminary* we thought it was a new night club, and we asked for the address so we could come and have dinner with you" (*Witches' Sabbath*, 104).

To his credit, perhaps, the foppish Sachs endured over a half-year of scholastic theology, minimal hygiene, and increasingly ineffective hairshirts. As summer approached, his worldly maternal grandmother, Alice Bizet, arranged the vacation he was still allowed before taking his vows, apparently unaware that the southern destination she had chosen for both of them for its quiet had just become a favorite resort of the very sort of Parisians from whom he had supposedly parted company. Joking to him about the designer "cassock"-dress she too had once worn, she was probably also unaware how closely Maurice, who had chosen to wear his robes prematurely, shared her crossover tastes:

> The black was becoming, and made me look slender. . . . And when
> the reader recalls that even as a child I dreamed of being a girl, it
> is easy to imagine what strange and dissimulated dissatisfactions
> . . . were suddenly gratified when with both hands, like a young
> woman, I gradually raised the skirts of my robe to climb the stairs.
> [*Witches' Sabbath*, 109]

This would prove to be less disturbing, however, than the way Sachs soon chose to end his spiritual travesty.

Witches' Sabbath refutes stories that on the beach at Juan-les-Pins Sachs stripped, or stripteased, out of his priest's robes to reveal a pink bathing suit. If the denial is true, then at least he avoided the temptation to pay homage to his friend Max Jacob's image of "penitents in pink tights" (*Les Pénitents en maillots roses*, the title of a 1925 poetry volume)—leaving the greater temptation of successfully courting a fifteen- or sixteen-year-old American boy, whose outraged mother threatened Sachs with prison and denounced him to the local bishop. Cocteau, vacationing nearby at Villefranche and outraged that Sachs dared to present the boy to him, ordered Sachs to return immediately to Paris, where he of course faced seminary expulsion (an event not crushing enough to prevent his quick return to the resort, a fact the memoirs don't report).

Whereas Sachs's grandmother supposedly had no inkling of these events, but returned unquestioningly with him to Paris, Cocteau's mother soon asked her son to account for the alarming rumors she was hearing in Paris about his young friend's conduct. Sachs, who in 1923 had vanished with his mother to England for two years, after saving her from suicide and the law when she committed a major financial fraud, doted on the dignified Madame Cocteau, and her son records that the waifish Maurice was their constant guest. Although interpreters of Cocteau's life fail to credit his brief conversion to maternal influence, Cocteau for all his celebrated vices still lived with a highly devout mother who attended mass daily. Perhaps, then, to defuse the implications of these rumors for his own sake, or to pose for her as a kind of defender of the faith, Cocteau twisted facts to represent Sachs's young conquest as an enemy of Catholicism determined to discredit "a priest"—one whose only goal in the encounter had been "artistic education" and "conversion" (quoted in Raczymow, 135).

Sachs doted on the kindly but reserved Madame Cocteau, but how did she view him? Did pious mother and 'decadent' son share a private anti-Semitism, one he relied on the better to strengthen his ties with her, as in the following passage that comes after his explanation of Sachs's conduct?

> Maurice is a chameleon. He has a mania for mimicry. [*Il a la maladie du mimétisme.*] Set him down on white, and he turns white. Unfortunately the beach of Juan-les-Pins is rather motley-colored. Maurice imitates, and always will imitate, with that Jewish need to impress the world and 'stand out' when he thinks he's on even footing [*ce besoin juif d'épater le monde et de 'camper' en se croyant stable*]. Where he fools himself, and really irks me, is in writing "we" instead of "I" and in pretending that our experiences [*nos aventures*] are similar. . . . [quoted in Raczymow, 135]

A stunning self-contradiction arises in Cocteau, the arch-showman and enchanter venting disdain for self-display. As for Sachs's adaptability (a euphemism or corollary of what was often called Jewish "rootlessness"), no one, and Sachs least of all, could deny the accuracy of the reproach, especially on this occasion. In *Witches' Sabbath* he admits to having adapted to seminary life "too quickly, and too superficially" (108). Yet a certain residue of resentment still clings to Cocteau's mixed metaphor of a self-camouflaging creature voluntarily calling attention to itself, threatened and threatening by not knowing its place.

In the season before the premiere of his spectacular play *Orphée*, the preface to which defines poetry as an "exhibitionnisme suprême," it is remarkable to find Cocteau denouncing the "need to impress" or "astonish" as "Jewish." Cocteau's entire career to this point had hinged on "astonishing"—and incidentally, in its first stages at least, on astonishing a few highly influential Jewish artists, stars in an undeniably rather shallow tradition of virtuosity that the young Cocteau did his best to perpetuate.

Well before Diaghilev's well-known order to him to "Astonish me!", Cocteau, a pampered and precocious adolescent who tried charming famous friends by dancing for them on restaurant tabletops, passed muster by first impressing the poet-editor Catulle Mendès with his verse, which he also recited on invitation at the salon of Sarah Bernhardt (as an annotation to Cocteau's journals puts it, "Sarah Bernhardt l'invita à s'exhiber [sic] un soir devant le cercle de ses amis"). The "Jewishness" of these artists is secondary: Bernhardt, baptized, attended a convent school; and Mendès, a Wagner-worshiping anti-Dreyfusard of Sephardic descent, is said to have cautioned his fellow Jew and poet Gustave Kahn: "We Semites are marvelous assimilators, but expect nothing original of us" (quoted in Brown, 26). What matters more is the extent to which Cocteau himself assumed the poetic and personal manner of cultural arbiters like Mendès, whom he described as the "all-important" editor of his youth.[7] Cocteau, moreover, claimed to have been rescued from the "taint" of his family's eclecticism by Mendès, among others; yet as biographer Frederick Brown points out, Mendès's tawdry bric-a-brac esthetic was itself the height of eclecticism, and remained permanently impressed on Cocteau's decorative style, be it scenic or domestic.

Even more significant, however, given Cocteau's "chameleon" metaphor, is the fact that the same biographer, who makes no mention of the above letter by Cocteau to his mother, should, after examples of the young poet's systematic imitation of older writers, describe him as "taking on the color of whatever review published him" (Brown, 26). Having met him around 1911, the socialite Elisabeth de Gramont also described Cocteau as "imitating everyone, even people whom he hadn't met, or the deceased" (quoted in Brown, 67). As for the venerated older artists who befriended him, Cocteau would pay homage by flaunting signature elements of their works before them: writing to Gide he signs himself "Nathanaël" (the young dedicatee of *Les Nourri-*

7. See Cocteau's chapter on Mendès in *Journal d'un inconnu*, translated in the compilation: Jean Cocteau, *My Contemporaries*, ed. and trans. Mary Crosland (Philadelphia: Chilton Book Company, 1968), 6–13.

tures terrestres); for Picasso he dresses as a harlequin; for Proust he uses a gesture peculiar to the character Saint-Loup, etc.: flattery, but an insinuating sort that, to borrow the terms of his letter home, aggressively says "we."

Like Proust, Jacob, and other writers of the day (and inevitably, also like Sachs), Cocteau excelled in often cruel impersonations of friends. At the same time, the Cocteau whom Brown and other chroniclers portray breaks down almost organ by organ into a patchwork of behavioral quotations: the hand motions of Proust's friend Robert de Montesquiou, often considered the model for Charlus; Countess Anna de Nouailles's handwriting (soon indistinguishable from her admirer's); and so on. In this sense Sachs's infamous (and contested) later forgery of a note from Cocteau to his mother, authorizing his removal of most of the contents of Cocteau's room, is mimicry of mimicry, a lamely literal version of his master's own earlier history of "thefts," echoed too in Cocteau's coy (Gidian) disclaimer that his homosexual confession *Le Livre blanc* is an anonymous "found manuscript": "I am . . . still tempted to lay my name thereto, theft tempting our fingers to seize an object gilded by the peril and gratuity of the act . . . " (quoted in Brown, 282).

Sachs has been viewed in relation to Cocteau as a parasite "starving by slow degrees once he had been expelled from his victim" (quoted in Brown, 247). But when Sachs finally turned against his former idol in *Witches' Sabbath*, he depicted Cocteau as himself a parasite, imitating and vulgarizing innovations of true artistic pioneers. One reason for this sheer vindictiveness was the fact that Cocteau laid a sort of curse on his friend, assuring him he could be anything he wanted but a writer, the thing he of course wanted most to be (as recounted in the "Introduction by the French Publisher" to *The Hunt*, 262). Unaware that Sachs, though lacking formal power, was endowed with considerable descriptive and aphoristic prowess, and that he was preparing a memoir whose scathing portrait of him would significantly sway his postwar reputation, Cocteau seemed to value him as a kind of (stereotypically Jewish?) promoter and entrepreneur.

Yet it must be acknowledged that, far from abandoning Sachs, Cocteau remained a friend, helping him, for instance, to organize one of the few projects he would realize—the short-lived imprint "La Collection Maurice Sachs," begun in 1928 and characteristically conceived as a library of Christian edification, featuring a reprint of Léon Bloy's *Le Salut par les Juifs*, drawings by Max Jacob "on the Death and Sufferings of Jesus, Son of God," and Cocteau's *Le Mystère laïc*. But typically, too, the pattern would be broken with Cocteau's controversial *White Book*, which no denial of authorship could save from the suspicions of Cocteau's spiritual creditors, starting with Maritain. Sachs's venture might well have been intended as a way to save face after his fall from the priesthood, a proof that his motive for converting had not been to copy every motion his mentor made. Similarly, in 1924, Sachs, acting as a secretary to Cocteau, had chosen to decorate a bookstore's window display of various Cocteau manuscripts by mounting them within a replica of his famously chic bedroom: one more raid on "the interior," perhaps, but also an act of renunciation, a show of willingness to share and evangelize his "god."

Having literally prayed in early youth to the image of Cocteau, Sachs, in *Witches' Sabbath*, would compare the influence or spell Cocteau cast on Sachs's generation to the one the Ballets Russes designer Leon Bakst had cast on Cocteau's. The comparison is instructive in relation to the latter's remarks on the "Jewish need": Bakst, born Rosenberg, chose an ethnically unidentifiable, un-Russian-sounding pseudonym, and set the tone in France for the "motley-colored" exoticism with which Cocteau would imbue his more picturesque Jewish friends. Several of the mostly East European Jews settling in Montparnasse when Cocteau first scouted it for his Right Bank social set became friends and artistic peers. As a catalogue essay on the Circle of Montparnasse rather benignly observes:

> Cocteau's entry into the artistic life of Montparnasse more or less coincided with that of the foreign Jewish artists, and it may be for that reason that he seems to have given them and their heritage rather more thought than the average Frenchman.[8]

Of less concern than his thought, however, are Cocteau's more formulaic responses: for instance, the "huge Jewish melancholy" he attributes to his friend Max Jacob, in a tribute Sachs uses as the epigraph of his own abrasive Jacob portrait in *Witches' Sabbath*. For the hugeness of Jacob's melancholy was on exhibition scale, so to speak; and surely it was in part this standard of "hugeness" that encouraged Sachs's bad behavior in 1926. Sachs's vow to "have genius" derived from several sources, among them the common devaluation of the term; an evolu-

---

8. Kenneth E. Silver, "Jewish Artists in Paris, 1905–1945," in Kenneth E. Silver and Romy Golan, eds., *The Circle of Montparnasse: Jewish Artists in France, 1905–1945* (New York: The Jewish Museum and Universe Books, 1985), 22.

tionary view that demanded his advance beyond his grandfather's mere taste for literature; and the emerging expectation phenomena like the "circle of Montparnasse" roused that, as one gentile put it, "there is a renaissance of spirit in the people of Israel, an evolution from the critical to the creative temper."[9] Cocteau's final gesture, incidentally, in his portrait of Sachs in *Journal d'un inconnu*, of welcoming him into his private "pantheon," besides resembling the act of clemency an operatic king might show his would-be assassin, further illustrates the recklessly hyperbolic level praise assumed in Sachs's day.

It is instructive in this regard to consider the tone Sachs adopts toward Cocteau's "sublime Jewess," Simone Casimir-Perrier, born Benda, and known on the stage ca. 1905 as "Madame Simone." She had been instrumental in gaining Cocteau early acceptance, above all by introducing him to her close friend the poet-countess Anna de Noailles. Frederick Brown describes Simone as "a petite, beautiful, and highly literate Jewess" (50). In Sachs's *The Hunt*, however, she appears in somewhat less flattering terms, aged of course but also mentioned merely in passing for some favor she can do Maurice as an old friend of his grandmother's. Yet he does pause in his narration to quote a quip of hers from the turn of the century that still had resonance for Sachs at the time of memoir-writing: "Everybody's bored, but the Jews are the only ones who know they're bored" (263).

As Brown explains, Simone's talent, much like Colette's, emerged suddenly out of an unhappy marriage: she allegedly turned to the stage to spite the actor-husband who waited until their wedding night to inform her he'd married her for her money. Far from citing her beauty or "sublimity," Sachs writes: "She had a lively conversational talent, sensitivity, a fierce, untamed quality in her acting, and almost a touch of genius, together with the suggestion of a hump on her back." (*The Hunt*, 263).

How sadly, in its final position, that hump seems to reflect the burden of Madame Simone's racial prescience, also recalling Sachs's own sense of physical disadvantage as an overweight, balding, never-handsome homosexual, of possessing less than genius, of narrowly surviving by his wits. At the outset of an Occupation memoir that devolves into a paean to Nazi Germany, Sachs's account of two decades of "forced labor in the camp of frivolity" closely bears out Hannah

---

9. Quoted in René Gimpel, *Diary of an Art Dealer*, trans. John Rosenberg (New York: Farrar, Straus and Giroux, 1966), 349.

Arendt's sketch of high society's "exception Jews" in post-Dreyfus France:

> Concentration on an artificially complicated inner life helped Jews
> to respond to the unreasonable demands of society, to be strange and
> exciting, to develop a certain immediacy of self-expression and
> presentation which were originally the attributes of the actor and the
> virtuoso, people whom society has always half denied and half
> admired.[10]

Either because he himself failed to qualify as picturesque or because he secretly understood the deformations it exacted of those who were, Sachs, first introduced to Max Jacob through Cocteau, confuted the portrait of Jacob as a big-hearted, Rouault-like clown. With his first allusion to "Max Jacob, whom the devil had converted around 1913," Sachs sets the tone for his ambivalent friendship with the one writer convinced of his literary promise, counting on him to produce "a great popular novel" (quoted in Raczymow, 146). It is Jacob whose "double nature"—"more double than anyone and yet so simple in each of his characters"—first prompts Sachs's image of the *sabbat*, a term denoting both the hubbub of a witches' sabbath and the repose of the Judeo-Christian sabbath. At the start of *Le Sabbat* Sachs boasts of having been born on a Sunday, "jour de paresse"; the *sabbat* in its other meaning could refer to the ultimately threatening frenzy of the *années folles*, climaxing in a persecutory *chasse à courre*, not merely to the riotousness of his friends' lives and styles. Jacob alarms him with a "loquacious and chaotic pen" fueled by a "warped soul" that rivals Sachs's own disorder. It is the chapter of *Witches' Sabbath* devoted to Jacob that briefly and rather furtively contains Sachs's account of the Juan-les-Pins fiasco, through which Jacob became a valued friend, having "foreseen" Sachs's debacle by virtue of his own unruliness (122). While Jacob's comic character necessarily remains indelible here, Sachs does not fail to note his "persecution mania," his alternately tender and venomous voices, his confusion of friends and foes, his repentance over his impulsive generosity. The disorder they share bars Jacob, in Sachs's view, from true poetic greatness. In addition, perhaps Sachs's attention to Jacob's hedging of spontaneous affections reflects his own insecurity as a convert, and that mixture of sentimentality and cynicism Sachs attributes in his own temper to the major lesson of his childhood, learned through abandonment by family and homosexual

10. Hannah Arendt, *The Origins of Totalitarianism*, new ed. (New York: Harcourt Brace Jovanovich, 1979), 67.

schoolmates alike—"that one can be ashamed of loving" (*Witches' Sabbath*, 28).

At times, for the lay brother Max Jacob, that embarrassed loving would extend to Church and Christendom. As late as the year of Sachs's conversion, an editorial colleague of Maritain's wrote—at a time when Jacob actually lived in dire poverty—of "his clawlike Jew's fingers, used to counting gold and handling precious objects" (quoted in Raczymow, 95). Still, Jacob was a zealous proselytizer who typically wrote of "a Jew, that is, a future Catholic."[11] Sachs depicts him singing liturgy at the top of his lungs wildly off-key, yet remarks that his casuistical spirit (which one encounters in parodic form in much of his prose poetry) kept him from any true "Christian rigor" (*Witches' Sabbath*, 124). The point, incidentally, invalidates the simpleminded dichotomy of Christian heart and Jewish head which Jacob tried to embrace: "Les juifs sont des hommes de l'esprit; j'ai besoin d'hommes du coeur" ["Jews are men of the mind; I need men of the heart."] (quoted in Andreu, 97).

Vaguely royalist in pose, and antidemocratic despite the crucial influence on his work of "popular" poetry and religious expression, Jacob defended the Jews as "le peuple le plus aristo du monde" ["the most aristocratic people in the world"] (quoted in Andreu, 153). Though vowed to poverty, he did indeed "handle precious objects" whenever possible; Sachs was to adopt a similar dandyism and a far deeper contempt for the French lower classes, particularly when forced to work among them in labor camp during his first months in Hamburg in late 1942.

When lashing out at Jews as "enemies of the interior," critics like Jouhandeau overlook the allure of Catholicism's "externality" of observance and confession. If the faith was debased to a costume drama through Sachs's cassock-farce, Jacob, for all his convert's zeal, allowed his professions of faith to verge on exquisite camp. His well-known accounts of epiphanies were sartorial spectacles—as was only right, perhaps, for the son of an embroiderer-tailor. Christ illuminates Max's room like a model on the runway: "What beauty, what elegance and gentleness in Him! Look at his shoulders and the way he holds himself. He's wearing a dress [*une robe*] of yellow silk with blue ornaments. He turns around and I see his calm radiant face. . . ."[12]

And despite the hints of self-hatred in his Christian fervor, Jacob

11. Pierre Andreu, *Vie et mort de Max Jacob* (Paris: La Table Ronde, 1982), 59.

12. Jacob, "La Révélation," in *Mid-Century French Poets*, ed. and trans. Wallace Fowlie (New York: Grove, 1955), 40.

obliquely acknowledges his ancestry and its forced uprootings in the 1922 "Art poétique," contemporary with Sachs's first spasms of hero worship: "Man is a venerating animal. He venerates as easily as he purges himself. When they take away from him the gods of his fathers, he looks for others abroad. The nineteenth century invented the worship of genius" (Jacob, 36). Jacob's father, however, like all his family, was an atheist, and the gods of Sachs's fathers were dying artist-gods.

Sachs began the 1930s as an art dealer in New York, became a radio and lecture-circuit political commentator on subjects he knew next to nothing about, converted to Protestantism on wedding an influential pastor's daughter whom he soon abandoned for a young man he met in Los Angeles, with whom he returned to France, where he would attempt to be a novelist, art dealer and critic, essayist, playwright, actor, translator of British dramas, editor, and finally black marketeer. The "great advantage of travel," he wrote, is "not only that you leave behind your friends, but also the image that those friends form of you" (quoted in Raczymow, 184). Having formed himself so exclusively on the images of his supposed friends, Sachs fled them in panic; but to "conquer" New York he proceeded to imitate in a vacuum their every mannerism and tic.

Likewise, his unfathomable flight into a bare existence in Germany, in November 1942, began with a crisis over a lost trunk: a hoard of silk shirts, English-style suits, walking-sticks, books by Jews as well as Aryans, demonstrating either his utter naïveté or the defiance of political reality the entire venture would suggest.

During the Occupation, in fact, Sachs had briefly adopted an orphaned German-Jewish boy—who proved, however, not to possess the genius Sachs felt a son of his should have—and worked on a "novel of ideas" about the Jewish choice of assimilation or Zionism. Though he survived at this point by defining himself as at most half-Jewish, it is hard to read his German "honeymoon"—his term—as chiefly a denial of his origins. Nonetheless it did represent, according to *The Hunt*, a chance for the "expiation" of his former weaknesses (368). Just as the ultramundane Paris wastrel had once rhapsodized on his worship of nature, so the thwarted dandy was haunted in his last years by the thought of a more denuded life: most directly, through confinement, deprivation, and the peaceful severing of body and soul it could grant him; but, more distantly, in flashes, through the ascetic example of Soutine's art.

In his German idyll Sachs experiences an "enchantment" with German character that does not appear to have been a mere feint for the censors or labor-camp authorities: he seems rather to have gained considerable freedom of expression with his promotion from labor-camp crane operator to Gestapo spy (on the French and the German Resistance members: lest Sachs's Casanovan self-fashioning seem a victimless crime, note that at the very least he was responsible for the arrests and deaths of local members of a major Resistance group, the "White Rose"). Sachs exploited the chance to pretend women correspondents in France had been his lovers, yet also writes candidly to other friends of new homosexual loves in Germany.

Sachs had, by the way, done his military service in Germany after seminary expulsion, and allegedly been chosen as boyfriend, despite his protests of homosexuality, by an overpowering German woman working near his base. The Germany of his "honeymoon," however, is practically devoid of women. His "enchantment" at the country's "perfect naturalness of manner among all the various classes," its "virility without vanity," etc., has French analogues (ignored by Sachs) in the Baron de Charlus's rooting for the German troops of World War I, or Cocteau's wartime tribute to Arno Breker's Aryan warrior figures. The Germanic typology, of course, has roots in classic anti-Semitic tracts of the late nineteenth century, such as Edouard Drumont's *La France juive*.

In Sachs, however, the counterpart to Drumont's "enthusiastic, heroic, chivalrous, frank, trusting" Aryan is no longer the "mercenary, greedy, scheming, clever, cunning" Jew,[13] but the venal Frenchman, or more precisely, Frenchwoman, who "still bestows her love only in exchange for her own security" (*The Hunt*, 394). Accordingly, it is in the German section of *The Hunt* that Sachs rails against the harmfulness of prolonged maternal influence (an easy enough target for a man abandoned by a mother who had also been abandoned by hers), the hardened materialism of women, and the "modern myth" of the female companion.

Thus Sachs's confession of expiating his weaknesses through Germany's "incomparable human virtues" blurs misogyny and Jewishness (not to speak of homosexuality) as much as did Otto Weininger's 1903 classic of "Jewish self-hatred," *Sex and Character*.[14] Yet Sachs's

13. Quoted in Seth L. Wolitz, *The Proustian Community* (New York: New York University Press, 1971), 150.

14. Otto Weininger, *Geschlecht und Charakter* (Vienna: Wilhelm Braumüller, 1903); *Sex and Character* (New York: G. P. Putnam and Sons, 1906). On Weininger, see Sander L. Gilman, *Jewish Self-Hatred* (Baltimore: Johns Hopkins University, 1986).

diatribes against weak, calculating Woman once again echo his earlier attacks on Cocteau, who succumbs to "those almost hysterical fits of despair to which actors and women are most subject"; who mistakes "for the impulses of the heart his tormenting and anguished, feverish, feminine desire to possess everything" (*Witches' Sabbath*, 77, 76). Naturally, in the next breath Sachs confesses to similar greed, though without drawing parallels: "I wanted to own everything, do everything" (80).

In similarly self-accusatory criticism, Sachs, limited to writing from life, chides Cocteau for having neglected his craft as he "turned his efforts on life itself" (*Witches' Sabbath*, 74). In his later memoirs, Cocteau would perversely describe Sachs as "occupied by me the way France was occupied by Germany."[15] Yet during the actual Occupation his disciple discovered a "hearty" climate in Hamburg that was a systematic antidote to what he had long viewed as Cocteau's usurpation of "heart" as a personal symbol: "the heart, an eternal password Cocteau used so often. . . . I must say that I have rarely met a man who had less heart than Jean Cocteau. . . . He burned as ice burns, without giving warmth" (76). In consolation for his years of French beguilement, Sachs rediscovers his own unhardened "heart" in the happy captivity of the labor camp, noting: "Everything about me has grown tougher but my heart" (quoted in Raczymow, 430). But earlier, during his black-marketeering days in occupied Paris, he had shown an appalling capacity to cite the German "heart" against himself: " 'One should keep a cool head and a warm heart,' Goebbels had said. In those days, I had a heart of ice where my fellow traffickers were concerned, and my head was on fire" (*The Hunt*, 319).

Yet to penetrate to the warm heart of the Reich, in the few hours of leisure he is granted at first, he must have recourse to the old sartorial tools of seduction:

> Life is made worthwhile by the thought that I shall be living among them [the Germans] in a month. And to think that all this might perhaps have happened as soon as I arrived if only I'd had a decent suit of clothes to wear! [*The Hunt*, 384]

And no sooner has Sachs voiced this embarrassment over his wardrobe to the genie-like new friend "among them" than that friend immediately provides a new suit, though not without the assurance that, "in

15. Cocteau, *Le Passé défini*, vol. 2 (Paris: Gallimard, 1985); quoted from *Past Tense*, vol. 2, trans. Richard Howard (San Diego: Harcourt Brace Jovanovich, 1988), 322.

Germany we pay no attention to such things; it's only the heart that counts."

"Je suis bien payé, rhabillé de neuf et bien considéré," writes Sachs to a French friend after his advancement to informer (quoted in Raczymow, 430). "Re-dressed" in the regard his Gestapo colleagues show him, the archindividualist poses as willing spectator of the Decline of the West, the yielding of the Individual to the Species; and as at the end of *Witches' Sabbath*, his second memoir concludes with a juvenile fantasy of ending his days in the carnal paradise of a mythic Orient. But the euphoria of these days is caused by more than the vast weight loss his normally fat body undergoes through food rationing: by what he describes as the joy of body and soul going their separate ways, a "disembodiedness" he had experienced in the asceticism of the seminary. Achieving this lightness is easy, he claims, merely "a matter of having a good doctor"; and Germany, it seems, has become that good doctor for Sachs.

The duel of flesh and spirit is also fought in Sachs's grandiose lists of "future works," containing both an "Eloge du corps" ("Praise of the Body") and a "Monsieur Klo" (roughly, "Mister W.C."), a picaresque alter ego, presumably, for the homosexual exploits Sachs promised French friends he would recount. In face of the contrary blisses of dress and bodilessness, the scatalogical name, meant perhaps to identify his source of contacts, sums up a lifetime of unprepossessingness, recalling the scene from school days when Maurice observed a poor woman from a train giving birth to a child by the roadside, "comme une merde." "What a problem escaping from the mass!" reads one huge understatement to his French publisher dated March 1943 (*The Hunt*, 259). Utter expendability had been the fate of Georges Sachs too: "When Georges Sachs died, Anatole France offered him this splendid funeral oration: 'It's a pity! He took up so much room' ("il était meublant") (*Witches' Sabbath*, 14, translation modified).

Shedding weight, body, possessions, convinced he can shed his Western identity, the "enemy of the interior" still brags of "the little Ministry of the Interior I run at the camp" (quoted in Raczymow, 422). He longs both for mobility in Hamburg and the captivity required for him to record its fruits. Nero-like amid the city's ruin, Sachs serenely chronicles his reading of two French collaborationists' history of the cinema, by the light of Allied bombings.

Yet beyond the fancy-dress, Arabian Nights Orient that still beckoned through German mortification, beyond the "Oriental languor"

he had attributed both to Cocteau and to himself, he retains the consciousness of a "great Oriental ardor" ("la grande flamme orientale")
his escapades do not quell. News of the death in France of Chaim
Soutine reaches Sachs in burned-out Hamburg. Soutine's turbulent
canvases, often wrought in one sitting, had roused Sachs's extremist
rejection of "intellectualistic" modern painters from Balthus to Picasso. In the fiercely shy Soutine, said to have first reached Paris by
freight train, Sachs glimpses the "hereditary fever" of the Jews, a fever
much different from his own chillier strain, yet moving him to write in
1932:

> There is no such thing as a Semitic painter (a great one, I mean) . . .
> yet his work contains all the passion of the great chosen people: their
> distress, their finesse, their rage to destroy, but also their love of the
> human and the tenderness that goes with it, and the deep
> perspicacity that makes the Jewish eye so penetrating. . . . Israel: the
> lucky misfortune, the misfortune that's worked out. . . . [quoted in
> Raczymow, 192]

Sachs's own piercing eye, his own destructive rage, had ceased, by
the end of his days in France, to take in more than a few random images
of Jewish distress. An elegant doctor come to treat Sachs's septicemia,
affluent clients he fleeces in their panic to escape the Germans, a trio of
wretched Polish tailors sharing a southbound train with him, are the
Jews in his Occupation journals.

Yet the chameleon Sachs himself, set on brown, did not quite pass
unremarked. His independence isolated him from his mostly homosexual fellow spies, who still refer to him at times as "the Jew" (quoted
in Raczymow, 439). Though willing to turn in other resistance workers,
he refused, for example, to hand over a Jesuit priest. In the end, the
signs of privilege and protection he did not renounce when finally
imprisoned among anti-Nazi subversives gave him away as an informer; he died—if we accept Raczymow's emendation of several more
gruesome accounts—exhausted on a long prisoners' march out of the
city.

If Soutine, the poor "Oriental" Jew, brought a pang to Sachs's
Sunday-sabbath complacency, he also offered a contemporary analogue
to the *Tableau des moeurs de ce temps* Sachs first conceived as proof of
his link to the French moralist tradition.[16] This assemblage of "characters" (in the literary genre sense) from all strata of society, as a "tab-

16. Sachs, *Tableau des moeurs de ce temps* (Paris: Gallimard, 1954).

leau," recalls the impulsive and incisive portraiture of a Soutine reliant on the single sitting; "the luminosity of putrescence" one critic describes in his paintings of animal carcasses might broadly apply to Sachs's disjointed "tableau" of his era.[17]

As for Sachs's German-Jewish origins, his flight to Hamburg, the birthplace of his maternal grandmother and other relatives known in childhood, can be said to stand as the symbolic erasure of at least a century of German-Jewish longing for Paris. The immigration that longing induced spawned a culture that culminated precisely in a high art of mimicry, stylistically assimilationist, yet endowed with considerable satirical force. The two modern Jews who, in Nietzsche's eyes, "approached genius"—Heine and Offenbach—were both naturalized Parisians; and when (vindictively) contrasting the latter artist with Wagner, Nietzsche defined his operettas "as French music with the spirit of Voltaire," as works of genius "if one understands by artistic genius the great freedom under the law, divine frivolity, facility in the hardest things."[18]

Sachs, the self-professed *moraliste* whom Raczymow rightly labels "Manichean" (unfortunately, his biography stints on an assessment of the often stunning character sketches in *Tableau des moeurs de ce temps*), spoke of wit in France dying with Musset, but failed to consider its continuation in artists of roughly his own racial background. The grim *moraliste* character sketch we might make of Sachs today would depict a young Jew inventing a classical French literary ancestry in a changeling fantasy that eludes a German-Jewish genealogy still pertinent in its terms of near-genius, frivolity, mimicry, boredom, buffoonery.

It was this lineage that the philosopher and cultural critic Siegfried Kracauer, a new German refugee in Paris, began to trace in 1935, in a biography of Offenbach commissioned by the publisher Grasset (who would soon be writing capitulatory prefaces to "la puissance créatrice du Führer").[19] Sachs, an avid follower of developments in publishing and intellectual circles, apparently took no notice of the transient German-Jewish writers whose plight and whose ruminations on Franco-German history might have given him pause before his night ride in quest of the German Elf-King.

17. George Heard Hamilton, *Painting and Sculpture in Europe 1880–1940* (Harmondsworth, England: Pelican, 1967), 431.

18. See aphorisms 832 to 835, Friedrich Nietzsche, *The Will to Power*, trans. Walter Kaufmann (New York: Random House, 1967), 439.

19. Quoted in an annotation to Cocteau, *Journal 1942–1945*, 378.

Offenbach's promise to the Parisian public of a "mutual insurance society for the combating of boredom" in no way detracted from the mordancy of his caricature of a society itself operetta-like, "living in a dream world, obstinately refusing to wake up and face reality."[20] For all the scorn he would predictably heap on Offenbach's shallow, Jewish "cosmopolitan" music, even Wagner in later years conceded to it something of a Mozartean lightness and clarity—and Jean Cocteau inadvertently perhaps repeated the Mozart analogy in the 1950s, marveling at the deftness of *La Belle Hélène*, a work Proust's Saint-Loup was ashamed to have his father prefer to Wagner. Moreover, it is reported that shortly before his death in the camp at Drancy, Max Jacob would sing, quite out of tune, of course, for the morale of his fellow inmates, no longer Catholic liturgy, but, with a fellow captive who shared his taste for nineteenth-century operetta, "*Le Petit Faust* et autres airs d'Offenbach" (Andreu, 289).

As for the composer himself, Offenbach became the quintessential representative of early Parisian boulevard culture, a "man of the crowd" who feared nothing more than quiet and solitude. Generously introduced into the city's salons by his aristocratic compatriot Flotow, it was as a cello prodigy "denaturing" that most "soulful" of instruments that the adolescent émigré first astonished with his "genius for imitation" (the two terms are not antithetical here). And if we close with a seemingly incongruous evocation of Offenbach, it is because a remark Kracauer quotes might serve as an apt epitaph for the age of Franco-Jewish assimilation that embraces Maurice Sachs's "forced labors" as well: "A woman music-lover once said of him that he played every conceivable instrument except his own."[21]

---

20. David Frisby, *Fragments of Modernity: Theories of Modernity in the Work of Simmel, Kracauer, and Benjamin* (Cambridge, Mass.: Massachusetts Institute of Technology, 1986), 179. On Kracauer's Offenbach project, see also Michel Espagne, "Siegfried Kracauer et Paris," *Pardès* 14 (1991): 146–71.

21. Siegfried Kracauer, *Orpheus in Paris*, trans. Gwenda David and Eric Mosbacher (New York: Knopf, 1938), 79.

GÉRARD HADDAD

Judaism in the Life and Work of Jacques Lacan: A Preliminary Study

Lacan's works resound with his anger at self-proclaimed "orthodox Freudians." According to Lacan, these guardians of the Temple distinguish themselves principally by their misunderstanding of the true Freudian orientation and by their neglect of certain fundamental concepts of psychoanalysis.

Yet while Lacan denounced the misfortunes of Freudianism, the same fate lay in store for his own thought. Even in his lifetime, and despite the boisterous and stifling adulation which surrounded him, Lacan encountered the same ignorance, the same distortion of his thought. After his death, this betrayal by the disciples worsened. Several of his closest students openly rejected his teachings, while most others preferred to keep them under wraps.

Actually, within the history of ideas and the transmission of doctrines, this may be a kind of universal law, one which is echoed in the Gospels themselves. When Jesus addresses Peter, the disciple who will carry on his work, does he not say, "This very night, before the cock crows, you will have denied me three times" (Matthew 26–34)? The law of the disciple intrinsically entails misunderstanding, distortion of the master's thought and the rejection of his most salient points. If the faithful transmission of a doctrine ideally should be concerned as much with impasses and unresolved questions as with overstepping obstacles, then conversely, so that the doctrine may act as the foundation on which an institution can be built, it must immediately suture those questions which trouble it and which confer upon it both its value as truth and its perilous instability.

YFS 85, *Discourses of Jewish Identity in Twentieth-Century France*, ed. Alan Astro, © 1994 by Yale University.

Lacan created his works in an atmosphere of constant debate, as much with his contemporaries (anthropologists, linguists, logicians, writers) as with the great Ancients. His debate with Freud was, of course, his greatest concern; but he also debated with philosophers, mostly with Plato, Aristotle, Kant, Hegel and Heidegger; with theologians Augustinian and Thomistic; as well as with great writers past and present— Shakespeare, Molière, Joyce, Duras, etc.

What student today could correctly articulate those issues in Plato and Aristotle, for example, which puzzled Lacan and gave him pause?

One factor that sheds light on the notion of the disciples' misunderstanding of the master is the apparently marginal yet essential question of Lacan's relationship to Judaism. Actually this question constitutes one of the unrecognized axes of his thought, one which he worked and reworked throughout his lifetime, apparently in a minor way—not because it was not important, but rather because intellectual circumstances did not welcome it. The intellectual atmosphere from the 1950s to the 1970s, the period during which Lacan's teaching developed, was in no way geared toward this interest. The proliferation of works on Judaism did not begin until the early 1980s, and this passion owes much to Lacan, to his influence, which extended beyond the closed circle of his students. His own interest seemed to most encouragement enough to return to a field lain fallow, barely cultivated by a few traditionalist groups. Despite all this, the passages in his work which address this question are sufficiently consistent to bear witness to his interest.

To deny this element of Lacan's thought is to distort the perspective of his work, its true stakes. And yet his "official" students maintain this denial, this blind spot. For them, the Jewish question is not significant within the context of Lacanian studies. My own study, a preliminary one, will attempt at least to show that the question should be asked. It will include bits of personal testimony with little claim to academic worth. Without my own analysis as a patient of Lacan's, this aspect of his work would no doubt have escaped me. I was in analysis with him from September 1968 to July 1981. During this period of thirteen years, without a doubt the most formative ones of my life, I arrived each day at his office at 5, rue de Lille. From 1974 on, the year in which I began my thesis in medicine, he encouraged and supported me in my efforts to raise the question of a Freudian reading of Judaism. After this long period of visits, I could testify that his habit of adorning his seminars with Hebrew letters (next to Chinese ideograms) certainly derived from a serious knowledge of Hebrew texts.[1]

By a strange and unfortunate anomaly, the study of Jacques Lacan's biography is difficult. In France, a country fond of biographies—each year numerous volumes on the personalities who have left their mark on French intellectual life appear—to this day none has been written about Lacan. His life remains shrouded in mystery, a result of the family's veto. The unbelievable atmosphere of clandestine conflicts, cabals, and power struggles, which today still divide the Lacanians, merely reinforces this veto.

Lacan was born in 1901 to a Catholic family. His brother was a monk, and he received a solid religious upbringing himself. His familiarity with the writings of Saint Augustine, Saint Thomas Aquinas, and the great mystics (Saint Theresa of Avila, Saint John of the Cross, Master Eckardt) attests to this fact. It seems from certain bits of evidence that in the thirties, the same period during which he had his decisive encounter with psychoanalysis, Lacan also discovered Judaism in the course of a true spiritual crisis. How did this encounter occur? Apparently, it was the result of his reading *Israël et l'humanité* by Elie Benamozegh, published at the very beginning of the century, thanks to the devotion of Aimé Pallière, a defrocked Catholic seminarian who became so attached to Judaism that he almost converted.[2] Lacan seems throughout his life to have been profoundly influenced by this book of Kabbalistic inspiration, written in a fine philosophical prose. He drew from it some of his own formulations. What proof can we offer to support such a statement? There are two testimonials, one public, the other private.

On certain Fridays, Lacan would stage at the Hôpital Psychiatrique

1. For typographical reasons, these Hebrew letters are often omitted from the duplicated transcriptions of the seminars. They are more symptomatically omitted from the version edited by Jacques-Alain Miller and published by Editions du Seuil. Nevertheless, cf., Seminar XVII, *L'Envers de la psychanalyse* (Paris: Seuil, 1991), 133. Numerous "pirate" editions do include these Hebrew annotations, specifically the reproduced text of the seminar on *L'Angoisse* held at the Bibliothèque Nationale de Paris (Paris: Editions du Piranha, 1982), 2 vols. The transcription of the single session of the seminar on "Les Noms-du-Père" (20 November 1963) appeared in the *Bulletin de l'Association Freudienne* 12/13 (April/June 1985).

2. Elie Benamozegh, *Israël et l'humanité* (Paris: Ernest Leroux, 1914), or abridged (Paris: Albin Michel, 1961); Aimé Pallière, *Le Sanctuaire inconnu* (Paris: Rieder, 1926), or in a new edition (Paris: Minuit, 1950).

de Sainte-Anne what he called his "presentation of patients." After an in-depth dialogue with a hospitalized individual which might last more than an hour, he would offer a few thoughts to the audience which he allowed to attend those sessions. Several of these presentations left a lasting impression on the participants.[3]

Thus, in 1974, a young man about thirty years old was admitted for examination. His parents, both Jewish, had met in a concentration camp after it had been liberated by an allied army before they returned to France. They came to love each other under tragic conditions, and exchanged the strange vow that they would never tell their children of their Jewish background. Because of it they had suffered too much and so wished to break the chain of suffering. Thirty years later, their son, who had been conceived in the camp, was presented to Lacan. He had fallen prey to a "mystical" delirium centered specifically on this Judaism. Lacan, in the ensuing exchange, made two very important remarks.

After escorting his patient out of the room, he returned, clearly moved, and repeated several times, "He read it! He read it!" What had this patient read? Benamozegh's book! Lacan, then more than 70 years old, voiced the high regard he had for this work, which, according to him, was "the best introduction to the Kabbalah," and invited his audience to read it. Moreover, in regard to the parents' oath never to acknowledge or transmit their Judaism, he said, "This is what I call a foreclosure [*forclusion*] of the Name-of-the-Father [*Nom-du-Père*]." It was one of the rare occasions when his audience received a concrete example of this fundamental concept of his teaching on psychosis.

Towards the end of my analysis by Lacan, I was seized by a new interest in Benamozegh and Pallière and decided to study them. I had been familiar with these authors since adolescence, and their books had played a decisive role in my spiritual development. The case presentation which I had recently witnessed renewed my interest in these authors and I began a nearly exhaustive reading of their works. Exceptionally, Lacan gave me his approval on the project.

In the thirties, Lacan married a Jewish woman, Sylvia Maklès, who, for suspicious reasons, was referred to by the family name of her first husband, Georges Bataille. The story goes that at the beginning of the

3. Unfortunately, there is no exhaustive inventory of these "presentations of patients." The event I describe here was organized by Dr. Marcel Czermack.

German occupation of Paris, Lacan presented himself at the prefecture of police and succeeded in obtaining his wife's dossier, spiriting it away under the noses of the bureaucrats. Thus Sylvia was spared the persecutions which soon would befall Parisian Jews.[4]

From their marriage a girl was born, in the midst of the war, and she was given a Hebrew name, Judith—a great imprudence at the time. The girl's destiny seems to bear the mark of her father's desire. She linked her life to two Jewish intellectuals, first to the brilliant anthropologist of Tunisian origin, Lucien Sebbag,[5] who committed suicide; then to the philosopher, Jacques-Alain Miller, who would become the executor of Lacan's will and the controversial editor of his seminars.

Lacan frequented many Jewish intellectuals. His colleagues, other analysts, were for the most part Jewish, like Sacha Nacht who, before becoming his inflexible adversary, was a very close friend. There were also Roman Jakobson and Claude Lévi-Strauss, brilliant representatives of the structuralist human sciences, which Lacan considered to be refined versions of psychoanalysis. Doubtless all these Jews were profoundly assimilated. He acknowledged at the end of his life (as did Aimé Pallière) that his sympathies for Judaism and Jews were not repaid. This remark was the result of many painful disappointments: his expulsion from the International Psychoanalytical Association (I.P.A.) and his fallout with Lévi-Strauss. In one of his last lectures, while recounting the story of Joseph sold by his brothers, he cried, "The Jews know what a brother is good for, to be sold into slavery in Egypt." For the audience at this lecture, of which I was a member, there was no doubt that Lacan clearly identified with Joseph.

My limited knowledge prevents me from further exploring the role of Judaism in Lacan's life. In any case, it is ultimately secondary to his writings, and it is the study of these writings with which I am most concerned here.

There is not a single seminar by Lacan which does not contain more or less consistent explorations of Judaism, Freud's Jewish identity, and the history of the Jewish people. The texts which deal with the principal

4. This episode is recounted in Catherine Clément, *The Lives and Legends of Jacques Lacan*, trans. Arthur Goldhammer (New York: Columbia University Press, 1983), 19.

5. Sebbag is the author of *Marxisme et structuralisme*, 2nd ed. (Paris: Payot, 1969). We are indebted to him for his important work on the Pueblo Native Americans of New Mexico.

notions of Lacanian doctrine, the "object 'a'" and the *Nom-du-Père*, are obviously very significant.

First, the "object 'a'": toward the end of his life, I heard Lacan publicly and humbly acknowledge never having added anything to Freud's thought, with the possible exception of his elaboration of the "object 'a.'" Lacan developed this concept from Freudian theories of the "lost object," then still called a "drive-object" [*objet pulsionnel*] or a "part-object" [*objet partiel*].[6] Freud had recognized the existence of two part-objects and suspected that of a third. The two fundamental lost objects were the maternal teat and the fecal staff. Through the study of voyeuro-exhibitionist perversion, Freud sensed, but without clearly articulating it, the existence of a third drive, which Lacan later called the scopic drive [*pulsion scopique*], in which the role of the lost object harks back to the gaze of the Other.[7]

This step took on considerable importance, for this object, unlike the two previous ones, derives from no biological function, either nursing or excremental. Psychoanalysis thus found itself stripped of its pseudobiological or medical straightjacket by which certain of its practitioners, indeed some of the most eminent, had sought to restrain it. In other words, psychoanalysis, by introducing the object of the gaze, reveals that it has no link whatsoever with the natural sciences. It establishes itself firmly on the side of culture, that is, within human specificity.

Lacan goes even further by proposing a fourth drive-object which Freud almost never mentions, despite the importance of this object in psychotic hallucinations: the voice. With this notion of an invocative drive [*pulsion invoquante*], Lacan completes the catalogue of drives and their objects which, according to him, are four in number. Thus within the parenthesis which encompasses the breast, the feces, the gaze, and the voice, the "object 'a'"—the cause of desire—is constituted.

Let us turn to the 1963 seminar on *l'Angoisse*, the very moment in Lacan's teaching at which this concept emerges.[8] One discovers that it is precisely in a moment of reflection on Judaism that Lacan produced his "object 'a.'" First he discusses circumcision and critiques the ac-

6. Cf., Sigmund Freud, *Project for a Scientific Psychology* in *The Standard Edition of the Psychological Works of Sigmund Freud* (London: Hogarth, 1966), vol. 1, and *Three Essays on Sexuality*, vol. 7.

7. Lacan develops the notion of a *pulsion scopique* most clearly in his Seminar XI, *Les quatre concepts fondamentaux de la psychanalyse* (Paris: Seuil, 1973), chapters 6 and 14.

8. See, for example, in the "Piranha" version, the session of 22 May 1963.

cepted interpretation of an equivalency between it and castration. In a reference to Nunberg, Lacan holds that the foreskin represents a female equivalent from which the male subject distances himself and that its removal is equivalent to the fall of the "object 'a.'" Then, in one of the last sessions of the seminar, Lacan comments on Reik's article on the shofar.[9] It is precisely here, in this commentary, that the voice-object emerges. The sound of the shofar is the voice of the imaginary father, of the ram sacrificed by Abraham in place of his son Isaac.

The following year, Lacan planned to develop these questions and to clarify his idea of the *Nom-du-Père*. Then came his exclusion from the I.P.A., which led to several consequences for him, some quite serious for the development of psychoanalysis.[10] He first decided to suspend his seminar, although he had already given its first session: an extended meditation on Judaism, or, more precisely, on Isaac, with commentaries drawn from Jewish tradition, from the Talmud and Rashi.

The great theoretical project of the seminar, barely begun, on the *Noms-du-Père* seems to have been a reexamination of the fundamental concept of psychoanalysis, the Oedipus complex. According to Lacan, all new theoretical advancements—particularly in relation to the question of psychosis—depend on this reexamination. Moreover, this strategy—as is clear from rereading the single session of the 1964 seminar—implies an investigation of Judaism, which Freud carefully and neurotically bypassed. The "excommunication" of Lacan interrupted this project.

The second consequence of the I.P.A.'s exclusion was that Lacan founded his own school, the Ecole Freudienne de Paris (E.F.P.). The school was three years in the making. Its organization was set out in a text of some twenty pages known by the title "Proposition du 9 octobre 1967." This text defines the principles which organize the school and institutes the *passe*, or the procedure by which the title *Analyste de l'Ecole* (which replaces the I.P.A.'s title of *didacticien*) is attained. The failure of the project outlined in this text led Lacan to dissolve the E.F.P. in 1980. An examination of this extremely dense text is particularly important to an understanding of the history of the Lacanian movement. The "Proposition" exists in two different versions, which

9. Theodor Reik, "Das Ritual: Psychoanalytische Studien" in *Imago* (Leipzig, Vienna, Zurich: Internationaler Psychoanalytischer Verlag, 1928), book 11, ch. 4.

10. See "L'Excommunication" in Jacques-Alain Miller, ed., *Supplément* to *Ornicar: Bulletin périodique du Champ Freudien* 8 (1977).

present important differences of formulation. These differences clarify the place of Judaism in Lacanian doctrine.

We know that Lacan's teaching, from beginning to end, is based on the distinction—often repeated, even harped on—between three categories[11]: the Imaginary, an extension of the visual image of the body; the Symbolic (of language or of the signifier); and the Real defined as impossible (to represent, to manipulate): I.S.R.—or R.S.I., the title of one of his last emblematic seminars. They are strange letters, the first three in the name Israel. A gratuitous speculation? We shall see! These letters were surely on his mind, for he writes in the first version of the "Proposition":

> The solidarity of these three principal functions which we have just traced finds its point of intersection in the existence of the Jews—which does not surprise us, since we know the importance of their presence in the psychoanalytic movement. It is impossible to unburden oneself of the consecutive segregation of this ethnic group through Marx's considerations, through Sartre's even less so. This is why, especially why, the religion of the Jews must be questioned within our hearts [*mise en question dans notre sein*].[12]

This enigmatic paragraph disappears from the second version. Yet it calls for commentary. First we must consider the identification of the "point of intersection [of the] three principal functions" with "the existence of the Jews." Later, particularly in the seminar "R.S.I.," which is largely concerned with the Borromean knot, Lacan identifies the intersection of the three circles of the knot, a representation of his three categories, with the "object 'a,'" the object-cause of desire but also the place and function of the psychoanalyst in the cure. For Lacan, then, the Jewish people occupy the same space as the "object 'a,'" which also explains the following phrase in the paragraph: "Which does not surprise us, since we know the importance of their presence in the psychoanalytic movement."[13]

11. Lacan held a conference in 1949 on these three categories, well before he began his seminars in 1953. He develops them further with his theory of the Borromean knot, the first elements of which are laid out in Seminar XX, *Encore* (Paris: Seuil, 1975), then again in Seminar XXI, *Les Non-dupes errent* (1973–74) and R.S.I. (1974–75), both of which are unpublished.

12. "Proposition du 9 octobre 1967" [first version], *Analytica* (Paris: Ornicar, 1978), 23. The second version appeared in *Scilicet* 1 (1968) and is reprinted in subsequent annual bulletins of the E.F.P. [Unless otherwise noted all translations of Lacan are my own.—Trans.]

13. In his theory of the Borromean knot, Lacan identifies the intersection of the

Another point on which Lacan does not vary concerns the importance which he lends to the practice of textual interpretation in the
training of psychoanalysts, to the "textual knowledge" he demands of
them. We find an emphatic affirmation of this in one of his central
writings, "L'Instance de la lettre dans l'inconscient."[14] The knowledge
of the psychoanalyst consists first of all in his ability to read (listen to)
his patient's discourse, and to read Freud's texts as well as the great
works of world literature.

Where then can one learn this art, this rhetoric? Lacan answers:
"Here is the area in which we determine whom to admit to study. It is
he from whom the sophist and the talmudist, the peddler of stories and
the bard, have drawn their strength, which at every moment we recover, more or less clumsily, for our own use" ("Proposition du 9
octobre 1967," second version).

A few years later Lacan returned at length to this brief allusion to
the art of reading the Talmud, in a long interview on Belgian radio.[15] We
find here an emphatic encomium of the Midrash, the art of reading
which constitutes the principal intellectual activity of the Jewish people. At the extreme, psychoanalysis is assimilated to the Midrash, but a
secularized Midrash, torn from its original purpose, the study of sacred
texts, so that it might be applied to the discourse of ordinary
analysands.[16]

This leaves us with the rather emphatic last sentence of our quotation: "This is why, especially why, the religion of the Jews must be
questioned within our hearts."

What does this mean, this "questioning within our hearts" of the
religion of the Jews? Does this expression not seem strange? Why does
the "Proposition" not, by the same token, invite us to "question Christians within our hearts?"

---

three circles of the knot as the "object 'a.'" See, for example, the seminar *R.S.I.*, the
session of 10 December 1974, published in *Ornicar* 2 (1975): 95. Moreover, Lacan suggests the identification of the Jewish people with the "object 'a'" or with the notion of
"remnant" [*reste*] basing himself on the word of the Prophet Isaiah, *sh'erit* [remnant],
quoted in Hebrew in the seminar on *L'Angoisse*, 8 May 1963.

14. Lacan, *Ecrits* (Paris: Seuil, 1966), 493–528; text translated as "The Agency of the
Letter in the Unconscious" in *Ecrits: A Selection*, trans. Alan Sheridan (New York:
Norton, 1977), 147–78.

15. Lacan, "Radiophonie" in *Scilicet* 2/3 (Paris: Seuil, 1970): 80–81.

16. See Gérard Haddad, *L'Enfant illégitime: Sources talmudiques de la psychanalyse*, first edition (Paris: Hachette, 1981) or 2nd edition (Paris: Point Hors Ligne, 1990),
15–28 and 261 to the end.

It can be understood as an invitation to "de-Judaize" psycho-analysis. But the many Jews at the head of its institution had always advocated a strict secularism and affirmed antipathy for their Jewish background—an antipathy which caused many strange symptoms! Thus, when Anne Berman translated Freud's *Moses and Monotheism* into French, she edited out part of the first sentence: "To deny a people of the man whom it praises as the greatest of its sons is not a deed to be undertaken light-heartedly, *especially by one belonging to that people.*" The italicized portion of the sentence is missing from her trans-lation.[17] Would Lacan then suppose that, although denied, the struc-tures of the synagogue still had considerable influence at the heart of psychoanalysis? This is the logical interpretation of the first lesson of Seminar XI, *Les quatre concepts fondamentaux de la psychanalyse,* which immediately followed Lacan's break with the I.P.A. In this text, Lacan compares his lot to that of the excommunicated Spinoza, who is left without the possibility of recourse to the institution of the "syna-gogue," explicitly mentioned. In this case he uses the Hebrew words, *kherem* and *shamatta* (*Les quatre concepts,* 9).

Here we come to one of the most important (although misun-derstood) aspects of Lacanian thought. For Lacan, the Oedipus com-plex, on the one hand, is the central principle of psychoanalytic theory. Without it, Freudianism becomes mere paranoid ravings: "Remove Oedipus, and psychoanalysis in its fullest extent becomes entirely subject to the discourse of President Schreber," writes Lacan in the "Proposition du 9 octobre 1967" (second version, 27). But at the same time, "Oedipus poses a problem," a break in theoretical development, with the idealization of the father (cf., Seminar XVII, 97, and the "Pro-position du 9 octobre 1967"). This break derives from the neurosis of Freud himself, who, in his analysis, evaded his intimate relationship with Judaism. This Judaism eventually comes to represent both the hidden motive behind the birth of psychoanalysis and its dead-end, figured by the concept of the ideal father. According to Lacan, some-thing lies beyond this concept. But in fact this perspective can only be revealed by a questioning of Judaism.

The expression *en question,* which is found so frequently in Lacan's writing, perhaps has another meaning, one which does not necessarily weaken the first. He entitles an important text of the *Ecrits,* "Du sujet

17. Freud, *Moïse et le monothéisme,* trans. Anne Berman (Paris: Gallimard, 1948). The English translation is from *Moses and Monotheism,* trans. Katherine Jones (New York: Vintage, 1967), 3.

enfin en question." In this case, he is doubtless questioning the nature of the subject of the unconscious, he is interested in this essential concept, a direct consequence of the concept of the signifier. But Lacan also notes "subjective destitution" as a criterion of so-called training analysis. We thus may consider a structure, either in order to reinforce it or to destroy it.

Here we touch on one of the principal difficulties in an understanding of Lacan's texts, one which we will identify, for lack of a better term, as ambivalence. Of course Lacan wanted us to consider Judaism, to study it actively. He also of course wished for a "de-Judaization" of psychoanalysis, just as he wished more generally to attack the heavy religiosity which reigns there. But instead of this theoretical initiative, Lacan obtained completely different results with his school between 1967 and 1980. He found there a dramatic deepening of "religious fervor." The questioning of Judaism came to be understood as an unbearable hostility towards Judaism.

The project of finding a way out of the dead-end which psychoanalysis constructed in the "ideal father" or "dead father" proves to be an illusion. None of his students would make it through this bottleneck, this "gully," for the simple reason that not one of them truly understood the project. Those who might have had an inkling, in spite of everything, were quickly brought to their senses by the little clique of "students" who held the keys to the academy.

Faced with such a collapse, Lacan had the presence of mind to admit defeat. On a theoretical level, he did an about-face and retreated into the accepted Freudian camp. "I have added nothing to Freud," he repeated at the end of his life. As for the question of the father, he declared to me one day in 1978, "all is there," meaning that there was nothing beyond that concept. On an institutional level, he had decided to dissolve the perverse church which his discourse had spawned. This decision is a painful intellectual tragedy, but also a human one. Many of those who followed him were overcome by it.

The "Proposition du 9 octobre 1967" contains another important component of Lacan's relationship with Judaism, one which concerns the recent history of the Jewish people, namely the Holocaust. In veiled terms, this text was really a bomb launched at the I.P.A., an accusing finger pointed at the psychoanalytic institution's skeleton in the closet which was actively suppressed, untouchable. Strangely, it would remain so even for Lacan's own students.

Let us turn to the first version of the "Proposition." Lacan here denounces the I.P.A. analysts' waning interest in the Oedipus complex:

> The marginalization of the Oedipal dialectic continues to become more and more pronounced, both in theory and in practice.
>
> Now, this exclusion has a corresponding effect in the real, one which is concealed in dark shadows. It is the correlative accession of the universalization of the subject proceeding from science, of the fundamental phenomenon whose eruption was shown by the concentration camp [*c'est l'avènement corrélatif de l'universalisation du sujet procédant de la science, du phénomène fondamental dont le camp de concentration a montré l'éruption*].
> ["Proposition," second version, 22]

The second version of the "Proposition" is even clearer. Lacan repeats the three famous categories here, which he also calls "facticities": the Symbolic, discussed through the Oedipal question; the Imaginary, which is also that of the psychoanalytic institution; and, finally, the Real, the category which he had insistently promoted. What is the Real in our time?

> The third facticity, a real one, too real, real enough that the Real is more prudish in promoting it than is language, is what makes it possible for us to speak the words *concentration camp*, something on which, it seems to me, our thinkers, wavering between humanism and terror, have not concentrated long enough. Suffice it to say that what we have seen emerging from it, to our horror, represents a reaction of precursors to what will go on developing as a consequence of the reshaping of social groups by science.
> ["Proposition," second version, 29]

Let us add to the citation by recalling the conclusion of the Seminar of 1964–65 on *Les quatre concepts fondamentaux de la psychanalyse*:

> There is something profoundly masked in the critique of the history that we have experienced. This, re-enacting the most monstrous and supposedly superseded forms of the holocaust, is the drama of Nazism.
>
> I would hold that no meaning given to history, based on Hegelian-Marxist premises, is capable of accounting for this resurgence—which only goes to show that the offering to obscure gods of an object of sacrifice is something to which few subjects can resist succumbing, as if under some monstrous spell.
>
> Ignorance, indifference, an averting of the eyes may explain

beneath what veil this mystery still remains hidden. But for whoever is capable of turning a courageous gaze towards this phenomenon— and again there are certainly few who would not succumb to the fascination of the sacrifice in itself—the sacrifice signifies that, in the object of our desires, we try to find the evidence for the presence of desire of this Other that I call here *the dark God*.[18]

These texts, for those who wish to meditate on them, are of considerable import: the emergence of the concentration camp phenomenon as a consequence of the exclusion of the "Oedipal dialectic," of the decline of the paternal signifier, the Real identified as the Holocaust and the recent history of the Jewish people.

Lacan then turns to examine the history of the I.P.A. during the "dark years," as they were called. Let us quote from the first version of the "Proposition":

The rise of a world organized by all kinds of segregation is what psychoanalysis has shown itself to be attuned to, by not allowing one of its known members to enter the extermination camps. [22]

They are but a few words which do not seem to have much consequence—except to make us ask ourselves: how did the psycho-analytic institution go about preventing the deaths of its "known members" from Central Europe, all Jewish? This question can only return us to the history of the analytic movement and to the dealings of the directors of the I.P.A. between 1933 and 1935, Ernest Jones in particular, with the Nazis, represented by Dr. Goering, nephew of the sinister Nazi official.[19] An agreement was struck. Freud, then much weakened, denounced it, but only in private. The terms are well-known. In exchange for the "maintenance of psychoanalysis" (although it was to change its name), the Berlin Institute of Psycho-analysis founded by Max Eitingon would be purified of its Jewish members, including its founder.

On the surface it seems to have been a deal where both sides were duped. What is this sinister joke, the "maintenance of psychoanalysis" in the shadow of the camp watchtowers and then of the crematory

18. Lacan, *The Four Fundamental Concepts of Psychoanalysis*, ed. Jacques-Alain Miller, trans. Alan Sheridan (London: Hogarth, 1977), 274–75.

19. Cf., particularly the anthology of texts compiled by Jean-Luc Evard, *Les Années brunes: La Psychanalyse sous le Troisième Reich* (Paris: Confrontations, 1984). In particular see p. 191 of E. Branin and I. Kamener's article, "Psychanalyse et national-socialisme" in that volume.

chimneys? Either the directors of the I.P.A. were imbeciles, or they had obtained another advantage about which they are, to this day, discreet: "to save the lives of its known members." In 1967 this affair was known only to a very restricted circle which practiced a strict policy of silence. Of course, the great biographies of Freud discuss it,[20] but only in the diminished sense of an event tragic, but past. This apparently was not Lacan's opinion.

One must reread through this coded perspective the 1957 seminar on *L'Ethique de la psychanalyse*.[21] Why has Antigone—a woman who preferred to give up her life and to share the fate of her dead brother left unburied, rather than accept the order of a tyrant no matter what his name is—entered the field of psychoanalysis here? Let us go even further: if we are to interpret things in this way, where is the relationship between the conduct of the directors of the I.P.A.—who refused the only true fate worthy of a psychoanalyst, that of Antigone—and the synagogal structure of the I.P.A., denounced in Seminar XI? Precisely in the status of extra-territoriality—this will not to share a common destiny—which characterizes (alas!) the common orientation of the synagogue. The history of the Jewish people is filled with episodes of leaders—and among them the illustrious Maimonides and numerous other Jewish thinkers of the Spanish Golden Age—who attempted to turn in a different direction, that of inscribing the Jewish people *and its difference* into the community of peoples. But this direction never succeeded in supplanting the one which is still in place and which consists of remaining apart from the affairs of the world. The psychoanalysts of the I.P.A. conducted themselves with respect to the community of their Jewish brothers in the same way that the synagogue conducts itself with respect to the community of men. Such is the veiled accusation which seems to arise from this analysis.

Lacan showed a great deal of courage regarding this affair, which probably resulted in his expulsion from the I.P.A. The years which followed would more than prove him right. The silence which surrounds this shameful affair to this day weighs heavily on the whole field of psychoanalysis. To convince ourselves of this fact we need only remind ourselves of the scandal whose name we derive from the players at both ends of the chain, the "Kemper-Lobo" scandal.

20. Marthe Robert, *La Révolution psychanalytique* (Paris: Payot, 1964), 248 ff. See also Ernest Jones's *The Life and Work of Sigmund Freud* (New York: Basic Books, 1957), vol. 3.

21. Lacan, Seminar VII, *L'Ethique de la psychanalyse* (Paris: Seuil, 1986).

During the war, Kemper was, at Dr. Goering's side, the director of the ex-Psychoanalytic Institute of Berlin, now *judenrein*, disinfected of its Jews. Once the war was over, Ernest Jones advised him to lose his identity in South America where he founded, in 1946, the Psychoanalytic Institute of Brazil. In the 1980s, the scandal of Dr. Lobo, a psychoanalyst and member of the I.P.A., exploded. Lobo acknowledged, after having been recognized by one of his victims, that he had served as an assistant to the torturers of Videla's dictatorial regime. He had been in charge of medical surveillance during the torture sessions. Lobo at first had fiercely denied the accusation, *with the support of his analyst and the authorities of the I.P.A.*, in particular French Jewish analysts who rejected as pure slander the testimonials collected against him. When he lost his nerve, he decided to tell all, that he had, for example, confided his "moonlighting" to his analyst, who withdrew behind the famous "analytic neutrality." It happens that this analyst himself had undergone analysis with Dr. Kemper, who was able to analyze in the shadow of the Nazi's torture victims. What a horrible return of the repressed! Frightening repetition! But it has hardly aroused any emotion in circles of analysts, either in the I.P.A. or among Lacanians. It appears, then, that these circles no longer think, that they do not reflect and are moved only by their own internal institutional quarrels.[22]

When they learned of this affair, Lacan's own students decided it was without great importance. Likewise, confronted with the passages from the "Proposition du 9 octobre 1967" on which I have commented here, they merely shrug their shoulders. How weighty could these few pamphlets be, from which one cites only a page or two, compared with the thousands of pages of seminars and articles by Lacan? Or rather, what weight do these students have, Jews included, who were repudiated by their master at the moment of dissolution?

Lacan dared what no Jewish analyst had ever dared: he went against the current of strict—but superficial—secularism of the Jewish psychoanalysts who directed the I.P.A., and he seriously contemplated and questioned Judaism. For these I.P.A. analysts, to show an interest in Judaism, of which they conserved within themselves a mummified memory, seemed at once dangerous and sacrilegious, as if one were

22. Public conference at the Maison de l'Amérique Latine (217, boulevard Saint-Germain, Paris), Monday, 16 January 1989 by Dr. Elena Besserman-Visanna, a psychoanalyst affiliated with the I.P.A. and the ex-director of the Psychoanalytic Institute of Rio de Janeiro.

raising a hand against a senile ancestor to whom one owes respect for services rendered. For Lacan, however, the Jewish question, in its theoretical aspects as well as its practical and historical ones, was one of the essential questions of Western culture.

Beyond this interest, what was Lacan's emotional and intellectual link to Judaism? It is a difficult question to answer. Obviously he shows no trace of anti-Semitism. But one detects in his writings expressions of antipathy, of a "negative transference" which he claimed to experience with respect to Freud, but doubtless just as much regarding Judaism. One must therefore appreciate that Lacan—who had been formed by Christianity, that is, in a necessarily deep-set tradition of hatred of Judaism—had confronted this feeling instead of turning away from it. He recognized the importance of Judaism at a time when nothing would have pointed him in this direction, allowing himself to be drawn into the whirlwind. Lending support through his interest in the Talmud, the Midrash, and the Kabbalah, he contributed to the ferment of Jewish studies in France indirectly, at a distance, reaching beyond his own circle of students.

But why then have the Jews, for better or for worse, marked this century as they have? Perhaps we can answer this question with the hypothesis which the Israeli philosopher Yeshayahu Leibowitz dared to formulate, that beyond appearances this period was the swan song of a prodigious and ancient culture which today is in the throes of death. The Holocaust doubtless brought the final blow.[23]

In the same way, Lacan, the greatest analyst since Freud, by the brilliance which he brought to the discipline throughout his lifetime, dared to suggest that psychoanalysis, as a living practice, also lay dying. The Academy, the Lyceum of ancient Greece, ceased to exist all the while leaving for our contemplation several of the most prodigious texts in human history. Human groups are visited by the same death drive as human beings.

—Translated by Noah Guynn

23. Yeshayahu Leibowitz, *Al olam u-m'loho* (Jerusalem: Keter, 1987). A French version exists, translated and with a preface by Gérard Haddad: *Israël et judaïsme: Ma part de vérité* (Paris: Desclée de Brouwer, 1993). See part 3, "Judaïsme."

ÉLISABETH DE FONTENAY

On the *Quant-à-soi**

Below is the translation of a contribution to a colloquium of French-speaking Jewish intellectuals, held in Paris in December, 1989. The author elaborates at length her understanding of the quant-à-soi, *an expression that means "keeping to oneself," as well as "dignity, reserve." Many French consider the* quant-à-soi *to be a national characteristic. The term takes on several variant forms in this piece, even though in contemporary French only* quant-à-soi *is commonly used. Depending on the particular juncture in the discussion* quant-à-soi *and its variants have been translated into English or left in the original French.*

The idea of *quant-à-soi* or "keeping to oneself " both unites and divides us. There are three elements I shall attempt to connect here and offer up for debate: the need for reason and universality, for a common world; the deep sense of belonging and community found among Jews; and our grounding in the French language. It must be recognized from the outset that such a debate not only pits us against one another, but even divides some of us within ourselves.

I have evoked our grounding in the French language. Consider our language in its history, but mainly in its present form: how much leeway does French allow the formula *quant-à-soi*? One must first note that use of this expression is exclusively restrictive, or, if you will, defensive and reactive. In French, one may *rester* or *se tenir sur son quant-à-soi*, or one may *garder son quant-à-soi*. These all describe postures of "keeping," "guarding," "preserving" one's primarily defensive position. One may even have *un certain quant-à-soi*, "a certain self-sufficiency" of manner or outlook. One thing is obvious from the consistency in its usage: the expression *quant-à-soi* has very limited versatility. If one were to adhere to strictly correct grammatical usage, the *quant-à-soi* might not even legitimately rise to the status of a concept.

*Elisabeth de Fontenay, "Intervention," in Jean Halpérin and Georges Lévitte, ed., *Le "quant à soi": Données et débats: Actes du XXXe Colloque des intellectuels juifs de langue française* (Paris: Denoël, 1991), 184–89.

YFS 85, *Discourses of Jewish Identity in Twentieth-Century France*, ed. Alan Astro,

The history of French further teaches us that *quant-à-moi* [keeping to *myself*] was the first to appear, around 1485. The grammarian Vaugelas would later sanction a *quant-à-nous* [keeping to *ourselves*] and even a *quant-à-vous* [keeping to *yourselves*]. Finally, one must note that the standard references, lexicographers Littré, Bloch and Wartburg, and Furetière, or grammarians Vaugelas and Grévisse, all agree on a certain reserve as a defining characteristic of the *quant-à-soi*. It evokes a form of reticence, a distancing or independence, pride, and even a kind of authority. Here is a paradox indeed, as Claude Riveline observed last evening:[1] the persistent affirmation of one's own being, of one's distinct and perhaps even separate identity, coexists with an extreme degree of discretion, almost a right of withdrawal, the right to retreat, to silence.

Insofar as Vaugelas and Grévisse recognize the expression *quant-à-nous* [keeping to ourselves], it is that particular variant which interests us now, for it seems the most relevant to the issue of Jewish identity. Indeed, no matter how alienated I may be from my community or even my family, I can never be a Jew all alone. If I claim to be Jewish, I must necessarily refer to some genealogy, to some past, present, or even future history. There are memories and premonitions of a destiny both individual and collective; these inform the most self-absorbed consciousness as soon as the words "I am a Jew" are spoken, even if only inwardly.

This *quant-à-nous* may take on diverse and perhaps contradictory forms. I will evoke three, and my categories are by no means scientifically rigorous. This is merely an attempt to do some empirical clearing of a semantic field. The *quant-à-nous* is first and foremost that of the practicing Jew, and therefore pertains to tradition. Can strict adherence to Judaism be reconciled with our definition of *quant-à-soi* and its inherent reserve? Is not the separation from others implicit in that way of life necessarily noticeable and even ostentatious? I am simply asking the question. And to be absolutely clear, I am not criticizing that which is at the very root of the perseverance of the Jews; but I must point out that French usage most probably prevents us from including this traditional way of life in the *quant-à-soi*, from defining it with an expression denoting extreme discretion.

1. Claude Riveline, "Le quant-à-soi aujourd'hui," in Halpérin and Lévitte, 13–24. [All notes to this article are by the special editor of this issue of *Yale French Studies*.]

Secondly, a Jewish *quant-à-nous* may have more to do with our cultural than with our religious status. This is secular Judaism if you will, or rather cultural Judaism. One can be a Jew freely versed in Hebrew and a nonbeliever as well. One may read Elias Canetti and Primo Levi while knowing nothing of the Kabbalah; one may be a Jew whose philosophical taste runs to Spinoza rather than Maimonides; one might also, like Moses Mendelssohn, acknowledge the possibility of reconciling tradition and the Enlightenment. It is here we find the people commonly referred to as Jews of the *Haskalah*.[2] In this group there are as many ways of being Jewish as there are Jews. This Jewish spirit of the Enlightenment, as it is lived and understood, has evolved in such a manner that a Jew cannot remain merely Voltairian without encountering a certain Jewish opacity, a network of mysterious quasi-prereflexive connections. These concern gestures, musical intervals and harmonies, linguistic idioms, cooking, and storytelling, all sprinkled with a little presence of God that need not be taken too literally. Whether or not there exists a formal institutionalized community, there will always be a milieu or a context, a family, close friends, and relatives. You can be with them, be yourself in the shadow of others, relax without being branded as a Jewish ethnocentrist. In other words, there will always be a *mishpokhe*, either one that was inherited or one that is being built.[3]

Thirdly, there exists another *quant-à-soi*, another form of keeping to oneself, which does not belong anymore to the *quant-à-nous*. It consists merely in holding on to a Jewish name, in agreeing to be perceived as a Jew; one reacts to historical events with a sensibility born of and shaped by the teachings of the Prophets and the memory of persecution. This Jewish *je ne sais quoi*, this "almost nothing" is at the root of the work of the philosopher Vladimir Jankélévitch, for example.[4]

It follows that the *quant-à-nous* or keeping to ourselves, in its literal meaning, pertains only to the second group, or Jews by culture. The completeness and self-sufficiency inherent in the first group, and the shortcomings of the third, place them outside of our categories and beyond our realm of inquiry. Let us therefore focus on the second group, for whom the concept of *quant-à-nous* is indeed a relevant issue: it is Jewish identity poised between religion and culture, and takes on as many levels and shapes as there are Jews. A quick aside is needed here.

2. Hebrew: *Haskalah*, "the Enlightenment."
3. Hebrew and Yiddish: *mishpokhe*, "family."
4. Vladimir Jankélévitch, *Le Je-ne-sais-quoi et le presque-rien* (Paris: Seuil, 1980).

It is useful to ask indefinitely, "What does it mean to be a Jew?" That question remains a fundamental and seminal source of debate, precisely because there is no answer or because there are too many answers. It is, however, extremely harmful to ask, "*Who* is a Jew?" The answer to that question is a matter of counting. And we must ceaselessly ask the census-takers *who* authorized them to decide who is and who is not a Jew. There is a law of logic well known to philosophers, the inverse ratio between extension and inclusion. The more a concept is extended to cover a larger number of individuals, the less it entails and the less specific become its defining criteria. If you include more criteria in the concept of Jewish identity, if you define Judaism in an extremely precise manner with more and ever more specific standards, then fewer and fewer Jews can be embraced by Judaism. If on the other hand you wish to make room in Judaism for as many Jews as possible, as well as half-Jews, quarter-Jews and relatives of Jews, then, without a doubt, the concept of Jewish identity bears a diminishingly precise definition, and Judaism becomes ever more abstract. Can anything be done about this law of logic? Should we acknowledge it as a principle of mutual destitution? Or should we not, rather, serenely accept both this law of inverse ratio and the productive tension inherent in it? We shall then have to preserve both the integrity of tradition and its capacity for integration; we shall then welcome all who consider themselves Jews, no matter how tenuous or even non-existent their link to tradition.

Having made this aside, let us consider those who tend more to culture than to religion, yet are not completely divorced from religious practice. What exactly does the *quant-à-nous* mean for them? Language, once more, identifies only reserve and a certain distancing. The most semantically restrictive model of *quant-à-nous*—and I do mean semantically speaking—is Marranism. Without privileging this extreme model, we must nevertheless recognize in the *quant-à-nous* a need to differentiate ourselves from others who are not Jewish or are not Jewish as we are. More to the point, the *quant-à-nous* requires us to distinguish between public and private spheres, professional and confessional concerns, civic duty and civil rights, the secular and the sacred or holy, the demands of general education and the needs of the community. Once we recognize this crucial separation, we may claim the lesser distinction between the *quant-à-nous* [keeping to ourselves] of the Jews and the *quant-à-vous* [keeping to yourselves] of the seventy nations, including the one to which we as Frenchmen and Frenchwomen belong.[5]

Otherwise we are no longer referring to the *quant-à-soi*. Indeed one may wonder whether these categories and divisions are not deeply alien to Judaism, as they probably are to Islam as well. They seem to be inherently Catholic distinctions. It is easy for a Roman Catholic to render unto Caesar what belongs to Caesar, and to God what belongs to God, not to mention to the Pope what belongs to the Pope! This division between the temporal and the spiritual is typical of Catholicism. It is very difficult for a Jew, or a Muslim, to achieve this separation between spiritual and temporal. And yet, if we fail to make that distinction, our *quant-à-nous*, our separateness or distinctiveness, could degenerate immediately into the tendency towards secession of a group that could no longer be integrated. It would also cause us to misunderstand radically the nature of our ties within the political system.

The Jewish supporters of the French Third Republic, whom we now view with such contempt, had resolved the issue by defining themselves as Frenchmen of the Israelitic faith. Nazism changed the parameters but the problem remains. I will quote as proof André Neher's 1950 work entitled "Laïcité profane et laïcité sacrée":

> In a singularly capricious turn of history, the etymological source of the word *lay* is found in a Jewish text. Indeed, the word first appears in its Greek form *laikos* in a version of the Bible produced by the proselyte Aquila. He uses it in several passages to translate the Hebrew word *khol*. Now *khol* means "profane." It is the antonym of *kadosh*, "holy" or "sacred." Thus the opposition between secular and religious is etymologically rooted in the conflict between the profane and the sacred.[6]

And Neher goes on to recall that it was the Jewish Prophetic tradition that led the charge against the autonomy of the monarchy and of military and economic powers. Thus the Prophetic tradition seeks to integrate the secular and the religious, and struggles against the autonomy of the political.

5. Seventy was traditionally considered to be the number of Gentile nations or *goyim*.

6. André Neher, "Laïcité profane et laïcité sacrée," *Revue de la pensée juive* 2 (January 1950): 91.

That it is precisely the Prophetic tradition—often held as a lowest common denominator by those who consider themselves Jews— which should have called for the integration of politics into religion, can only heighten our perplexity; one might even say that some consciences are obsessively unhappy over this fact. For what our secular leaders denounce as the intermingling of politics and religion turns out to be, in its essence and in our history, the challenge posed by the Prophetic tradition to the realm of politics.

Yet, at the same time, one cannot reconcile this fusion of politics and religion with the separation of the fundamental spheres of power in a state of law. Neither can it be reconciled, then, with the ethical subtleties of a *quant-à-nous* defined as a singular and separate unit while retaining its reserve, its discretion and even its secretiveness. This *quant-à-nous*, in its quasi-aristocratic way, relies on its own modesty to remain unaffected by ostentation or exhibitionism, by expansionism, and all other forms of pressure. Let it not be said here that minorities in the United States do not face these particular dilemmas! Any observations on the *quant-à-soi* in the United States would be thoroughly irrelevant. Indeed, it is as if our *quant-à-soi* or *quant-à-nous* referred only, and by choice, to the republican facet of French democracy.

We come here to an additional problem, a paroxysm of paradox. It arises from the existence of the State of Israel. What can we make of the *quant-à-nous* and its inherent discretion, when dealing with a loyalty so very fundamental and a love that demands proof? The transparent elegance in the articulation between French republican principles and the Jewish *quant-à-soi* or *quant-à-nous* becomes muddled the instant we are torn between our primordial concern for the safety and existence of the Jewish state and our preoccupation on those occasions when Israeli governments transgress the law. At that point, we must affirm the Jewish state's historical right to exist, and affirm it openly rather than discreetly, just as we must openly disavow policies contrary to the teachings of the Prophets. For politics does not bear the secretiveness, the discretion, and the reserve inherent in the *quant-à-nous*. There can be no Zionist *quant-à-soi*, no Jewish pro-Israeli *quant-à-soi*. We must act at both appropriate and seemingly inappropriate moments, here and over there. We must write, speak up, take action. We must take a stand, effectively and publicly.

Thus we return to an earlier question: what does it mean to be Jews, and how should we behave? How far we have wandered from the concept of *quant-à-soi*, of keeping to oneself! Or perhaps we need to invent a new mode of behavior: we must now keep in mind the existence of the Jewish state, and the necessarily public stand we shall have to take because this state exists and is threatened. Our new posture will be republican, to be sure, but also Jewish, rooted in 1945 and 1948. We must follow a political agenda heretofore unimagined. I, along with like-minded people, have tried to do so; it does not necessarily follow that we have been successful.

Nevertheless, and this will be my final point, even the most extreme form of *quant-à-nous*, of keeping to ourselves, must recognize that the legal foundation of the Republic, and the resulting state of law, is what protects, liberates, and emancipates the Jews. This includes those Jews whose particularities or tribalism alienate them from the concept of emancipation. They decry emancipation and exclude themselves from the social contract. Their thoughtlessness threatens us all. It even threatens the *quant-à-nous*, and the *quant-à-soi*.

I would like to end with a reference to *ahavat yisrael*.[7] Unlike Hannah Arendt, I read substantial meaning into that expression.[8] I might even say, for my part, that *ahavat yisrael* works nicely to delineate between those who belong to my *quant-à-nous* and those who do not. Yet I must add something taken from Montesquieu, which makes us French even as we remain Jewish. He too speaks of love, a love "at the very root of the republic." I will now end with this quotation from *L'Esprit des lois*:

> It is in a republican government that the whole power of education is required. . . . Political virtue entails self-renunciation which is ever arduous and painful. This virtue may be defined as the love of our laws and of our country. As such love requires a constant preference of public good over private interest, it is the source of all private virtues; for they are nothing more than this preference itself. [IV, 5][9]

—Translated by Françoise Rosset

7. Hebrew: *ahavat yisrael*, "love for the Jewish people, for Israel."

8. See the criticism of Hannah Arendt's alleged lack of *ahavat yisrael* in Gershom Scholem, *On Jews and Judaism in Crisis*, ed. Werner J. Dannhauser (New York: Schocken, 1976), 302–03.

9. Charles de Secondat, Baron de Montesquieu, *The Spirit of Laws*, trans. Thomas Nugent (Chicago: Encyclopaedia Britannica, 1952), 15 (translation modified).

RACHEL ERTEL

A Minority Literature*

To speak of a "Jewish literature in the French language" not only goes against custom but violates taboos proclaimed by the dominant ideology—the "centralizing" ideology, I shall say, somewhat summarily. Such custom and taboos have been internalized by the very authors whose work could be subsumed under that label. Moreover, the idea of "Jewish literature" written in the language of a majority group raises exceedingly complex political and theoretical questions.

Politically, the observation of certain particularities, which is an integral part of Jewish literature written in non-Jewish languages, has often been exploited to racist ends. However, the abuse of a concept does not invalidate it and must not force us into self-censorship.

As far as theoretical questions are concerned, their complexity is such that we can only outline some directions for thought. The first question is general, bearing upon literary creation itself and the relationship between artist and society. Though I fully recognize that a work proceeds from a uniquely individual consciousness, I am also aware that it is—like language itself—the product of a collectivity. Therefore, it is necessary to consider the nature of the collectivity. The existence of national literatures—French, English, American, Israeli—is taken for granted. Authors who belong to these national entities create works that partake wholly of those entities. But why should nationality—specifically, the fact of belonging to a particular nation-state—be accorded greater relevance than other criteria? More importantly, why should it be considered to the exclusion of all other criteria? After all, an

*Rachel Ertel, "Une littérature minoritaire," Traces 3 (1981): 88–91.

YFS 85, Discourses of Jewish Identity in Twentieth-Century France, ed. Alan Astro, © 1994 by Yale University.

author participates in different collectivities, in various cultural systems. It would certainly not be too strange to suggest that Jewish writers are at least as involved in Jewish culture (or in one of several Jewish cultures) as in the cultures of the countries where they live.

One of the main arguments against the existence of certain Jewish literatures is their use of non-Jewish languages—a position untenable in the face of Jewish history. In writings intended for their coreligionists as well as in those meant for a wider public, Jews have traditionally employed not only their own languages—Hebrew, Aramaic and fusion languages[1]—but also the major languages of culture and the tongues of the countries in which they have resided.

The second obstacle to the recognition of a Jewish literature written in the language of a nation-state is a certain conception—to my mind erroneous—of universalism and particularism. The two are not antithetical: the universal is at the heart of the particular and any particularity reflects the human condition in its entirety. Moreover, why would a French, English, or American work necessarily be more universal than a Jewish one, in whatever language it may be composed?

The Jewish identity of those writing in non-Jewish languages may take diverse forms: historical, religious, national, or simply residual—consisting of real or imagined memories, other people's memories assumed as one's own—fragmented, broken, scattered memories. The literary work, which Henri Meschonnic has called "the product of the homogeneity of language and life,"[2] bears the imprint of Jewish identity ineluctably and perhaps all the more strongly the more unspoken that identity is. The alchemy involved in creation makes isolation of diverse components of a work difficult, but that is a general problem. Any text poses a challenge to analytical tools, resistant as it is in its core to all forms of analysis.

Nonetheless, certain criteria may be proposed, despite the gap that remains between the analytical tools and the work to be studied. The simplest criterion for whether a work is Jewish bears upon the presence of themes and characters drawn from the Jewish world. An obvious instance is the American Jewish literature of Bellow, Malamud, Roth,

1. The term "fusion languages," as used here, refers to Yiddish, Judezmo (Judeo-Spanish), Judeo-Arabic and other languages, which merge elements of Hebrew and Aramaic into the tongues of countries where Jews have lived. [*All notes in this piece are by the translator.*]

2. Henri Meschonnic, poet and linguist, is the author of the five-volume *Pour la poétique* (Paris: Gallimard, 1970–1978), among several other works.

Wallant; in French, Albert Cohen, the author of *Mangeclous* (1938) and *Les Valeureux* (1969), constitutes another example, as do certain young Sephardic writers who have recently emerged on the literary scene.[3]

The self-reflective condition of the Jews, their particular situation in both time and place, their movement inside and outside the social classes to which they belong: such are identifiable elements of a Jewish work. The ambivalence towards oneself and others entailed in these traits tends to find expression in a certain humor or self-irony, which may well be a compensatory attitude as far as psychology is concerned. It is also, in this case, a source of creativity.

Finally, what is hardest to identify is the Jewish writer's relationship to language, firstly because every language has its own idiom, but also because language is at the very heart of writing. In this regard, one aspect of Jewish literature may well be the "deterritorialization of language" pointed to by Deleuze and Guattari.[4] The Jewish writer's language may be laden with elements from forgotten tongues, foreign to the land in which he lives. Such is the case of the North African authors in France and of the American Jewish writers. Or else, his language may be at once near to him and far, familiar and strange, as German was to Kafka.

It goes without saying that to identify a literary work as Jewish in no way exhausts its relevance or significance, which are infinite. But to deny the existence of a Jewish literature seems to me to proceed from a positivistic methodology and an excessive fondness for definitions and simple categories. Indeed, because of its complexity (but life itself is complex!), Jewish literature is atypical and cannot be contained within a one-dimensional definition.

To my mind, speculating on the existence of a Jewish literature in a non-Jewish language is tantamount to reflecting upon the existence of the Jewish people itself. If the Jewish people—geographically and linguistically dispersed, partaking of various national, social and cultural groupings—exists, so does its literature exist. It is created in the image of the Jewish people: it is diverse.

—Translated by Alan Astro

3. Ertel is speaking here of such authors as Gil Ben Aych and Paula Jacques (translations of whose writings appear in this volume) as well as Claude Kayat (author of *Mohammed Cohen* [Paris: Seuil, 1981]), Katia Rubinstein (née Banon, author of *Mémoire illettrée d'une fillette d'Afrique du Nord à l'époque coloniale* [Paris: Stock, 1979]), and Gilles Zenou (author of *Mektoub* [Paris: Blandin, 1987]).

4. Gilles Deleuze and Félix Guattari, *Kafka: Towards a Minor Literature*, trans. Dana Polan (Minneapolis: University of Minnesota Press, 1986), 18.

ORA AVNI

Patrick Modiano: A French Jew?

"Who am I?" is more than just a fashionable question. For roughly two centuries, it has been the crux of our run-of-the-mill modern notion of subjectivity. "Who am I?" inquires into one's specificity, tries to delineate the ways in which one may be unique, or at least, perceive oneself as unique. It does not ask what I have in common with others, but what I alone have, what distinguishes me from the rest of my community, what singles me out and eventually justifies the intimate feeling I have of my unconditioned singularity.

We may trace the prevalence of this self-absorbed line of inquiry to Romanticism. In France, a new poetics was loudly proclaimed at the beginning of the nineteenth century, as language, meter, and images became individualized and were called upon to reflect the genius of the poet, rather than to conform to poetic norms and rules. This is the gist of *La Préface de Cromwell* and "la bataille d'*Hernani*," two landmarks of French literary history. Novels like *Oberman, Adolphe, Les Confessions d'un enfant du siècle*, and later, the realist novel (in particular the *Bildungsroman*), all follow one character as he/she either searches for his/her inner truth or attempts to adapt that inner truth to the demands of the time.

Since then, "Who am I?" has been a foundation of our modern imaginary: it behooves something of the order of "myself," "my singularity," "my identity," etc. to appease our modern angst. Some hold that this identity exists prior to the quest itself (the realist's view), others, that it comes into being as the result of the quest. Although the former approach ends up with quasi-essentialist definitions of immu-

YFS 85, *Discourses of Jewish Identity in Twentieth-Century France,* ed. Alan Astro, © 1994 by Yale University.

227

table selves, and the latter with the construction of the same selves through the very process of attempting to discover them, they are similar in that the subject remains at the heart of their poetics. We should also mention later attempts to shake the yoke of Romanticism and to renew literature by targeting the oneness of the subject itself (especially the poetic subject), be it "Je est un autre" (Rimbaud), "la poésie doit être faite par tous" (Lautréamont), "la disparition élocutoire du poète" (Mallarmé), and even the more recent displacement and explosion of the subject extolled by the *nouveau roman* and the theorists of the sixties. These attempts did little to shake the centrality of the subject, however, since, following the basic paradox of negation (every negation necessarily presupposes an affirmation of the very proposition it negates), the question of the subject has remained in the foreground. All in all, what matters here is not how we *answer* or even go about answering the question "Who am I?" but the very fact that it has prevailed throughout our modern (Romantic and post-Romantic) era, and that in so doing, it has continuously renewed our notions of both subjectivity and literature. Even more importantly, what matters is that the subject of the question, "I," has consistently been construed *differentially*, as an "I" that is not "you," "she," or "they," but remains, for the most part, resolutely and consciously an egotistic subject. Our Romantic legacy demands that narratives probe into the subject to expose his or her uniqueness, so that Jean-Jacques, Adolphe, Emma, or Marcel will be singular and distinct individuals. The better characterized, the more singular a fictional subject, the closer the readers come to believe that they know him or her (the way we feel that we "know" Jean-Jacques, Adolphe, Emma, or Marcel), and the more pleasure they find in reading.

To clarify this point further we may contrast "Who am I?" with inquiries into generic attributes, that is, into characteristics I may *share* with others. The question "What am I?" is a case in point. Possible answers include a human being, an American, a truck driver, a parent, a woman, a university professor, a working-class person, a Democrat, an African-American, a Catholic, etc. We normally object to being identified with these classifications, however. We find them reductive, limiting, and—at least politically—downright irrelevant. We say of someone that she is a "character," to express our (perhaps mixed) admiration for her uniqueness. We tout our equal opportunity programs precisely because they disregard these generic classifications and address instead the intrinsic properties and achievements of each individual, that which accounts for his or her specificity. In literature and films, we shun allegories and stereotypes and prefer strong characterization and individuation. For sure, we readily concede that to some extent, generalizations are unavoidable, but we also generally expect them to act as a foil for proper characterization.[1]

Today, however, this picture is no longer completely true. In American academia, for example, we have witnessed the explosion of new programs and areas of study, all defined by some new generic and hotly debated classifications: gender, African-American, and ethnic studies, and even the new vogue of cultural studies, all point to an attempt to regroup characteristics and redefine collective boundaries. Similarly, we are witnessing an awakening of aggressive religious consciousness and loud religious adherences (the various forms of fundamentalisms are only the most extreme manifestation of this tendency). Ethnicity is in. Nationalism is on the rise. Clearly, the well-trodden, narrowly differential Romantic "Who am I?" is shifting. While its sense of urgency may have increased, the object of the quest, the notion of "I," is changing. No longer an atomist differential "I," this subject is becoming increasingly inclusive. It is an "I" *and* "you," a selective "we" ("I" and "you," but not "I" and "they"). In short, it is a new subject that seeks self-definition through its adherence to a well-defined group. The contemporary subject is relinquishing a large part of its individual specificity for the benefit of such groups. Bookstores teem with autobiographies of African-Americans, women, or numerous first-person attempts to sort out the legacy of colonialization and its undoing. These works underscore the shift from the egocentric individualism of the Romantics to a new social self defined by its positioning in the conflict that opposes "us" and "them" (women/men, African-American/Caucasian-American, indigenous/colonizer, etc). These current anti-assimilationist political and intellectual movements answer to the same two principles: a) "I" belongs to a community, b) this community is distinct from other communities. These premises

---

1. I am clearly simplifying here, but I believe that in its simplicity, my description sketches truthfully the most basic assumptions of our age. The counterexamples each reader will undoubtedly readily cite were mostly confined to scholarly journals, and have not largely affected our contemporary imaginary: in the sixties and seventies, the period of the most extreme literary theories and experiments, the prevailing social slogans were nonetheless "searching for myself," "finding myself," "being myself," "speaking for myself." Similarly, we may note that the heyday of deconstruction, in which the subject was radically put into question, was also the decade commonly referred to as the "Me Generation."

entail in turn social and political action of the kind "this difference is worth preserving," "this community should have special privileges," or "history owes us."[2] Only through such a sharp and complex sense of inclusions and exclusions can the new subject reach fulfillment. In short, today we no longer ask what makes each of us different from any other subject, but, on the contrary, what intimate and fundamental beliefs and characteristics we share with a select group (these characteristics may be physical, religious, historical, political, social, etc.), and, more importantly, what degree of personal and political *engagement* results from our perception of these similarities.[3]

In this respect, the work of Patrick Modiano is of exemplary interest: not because major French literary awards were lavished on his work;[4] not because each of his books is a media event;[5] not even because his novels invariably focus on the question of identity; but because his literary début masterfully tackled one of the thorniest collective identities of our times: Jewish identity. What I find perhaps most exemplary about him is, paradoxically, that he deviates radically from the picture I have just sketched: his personal journey takes him upstream, from an early agonizing and frenetic search for a suitable collective identity to a resigned and sober egotistic quest, seasoned with just the right touch of romantic melancholia. This countercurrent is, I think, a testimony to the intrinsic specificity of conflicts felt by the Jews in France today as well as a somber prediction for the resolution of these conflicts.

La Place de l'étoile (1968), Modiano's first and best novel, opens with the question of intergenerational integration. "It was the time

2. Dogmatism and even some forms of institutional terrorism set in when this acute state of societal pluralism leads to special claims on behalf of one privileged group, either because it is inherently "right" (as is the case of racism, fundamentalism, and extreme nationalism) or because, historically, this group has been oppressed (as some practitioners of gender, class, and race studies would have it).

3. No judgment of this change is intended here, although I find major differences in the social, intellectual, and ethical values of the various manifestations of the new principle of inclusion.

4. Prix Nimier and Prix Fénéon for *La Place de l'étoile*; Prix de la Plume de Diamant for *La Ronde de nuit*; Prix du Roman de l'Académie française for *Les Boulevards de ceinture*; Oscar anglais for his film with Louis Malle, *Lacombe Lucien*; Prix des Libraires for *Villa triste*; Prix Goncourt for *La Rue des boutiques obscures*.

5. Interviews with Patrick Modiano have appeared in *Le Magazine littéraire, Le Point, Libération, Le Débat, Le Monde, La Croix, Les Nouvelles littéraires, Paris-Match*, to name just a few French publications, and in *Playboy*.

when I dissipated my Venezuelan heritage"[6] says the narrator, Raphaël
Schlemilovitch. "Héritage," in French, can mean a fortune or a cultural heritage; in this case, it is both. But why would one choose to
dissipate it? Furthermore how does Schlemilovitch's opening declaration lead to the public uproar described in the novel's next sentence?
After all, dissipating one's heritage is a rather private activity that need
not be of any concern to the media or give cause to popular French
journalists' vociferous criticism of Schlemilovitch's "neurosis and epi-
lepsies," "mixed race," "Jewish scum," "awfully stinking ghetto rot,"
"kike of international palaces," "Yiddish gigolo," and so on and so on
for a page and a half (13–15). But then we may notice that Schlemilovitch's first critic is Léon Rabatête, whose name combines Léon
Rebatet's, a virulent French anti-Semitic journalist in the thirties and
forties, and the expression *rabattre les oreilles* (to rehash incessantly)
in which *tête* (as in *casse-tête*) replaces *oreilles*, and that his second
critic is "le docteur Bardamu," one of Céline's best-known characters,
and that the whole section is a pastiche of Céline's invective style.
Schlemilovitch's endeavor thus resonates across French cultural life,
as language (wordplays), low culture (journalists and newspaper head-
lines) and high culture (Céline) rise to defend their patrimony against
dissipation by the Jew. Throughout *LPDLE* a hallucinatory memory
conjures up France's hatred of the Jew as a foreign, corroding, and
corrupting agent of "real" France: French history and French literary
history alike clamor against Jewish foreignness. Can it come as a surprise that under the circumstances a Jew, and a "schlemiel" at that,
might wish to do away with his heritage?

Anti-Semitism is hardly new, however. What is new here is Modiano's treatment of Jewish identity as a foray into time and memory.
Like *A la recherche du temps perdu*, *LPDLE* opens with a temporal
expression ("*Longtemps*" vs. "*C'était le temps*"). Unlike Proust, however, Modiano does not set out to recover time but to liquidate it, to
dissipate its legacy. His disregard for the socio-economical retentive
principle inherent in the notion of patrimony amounts to a repudia-
tion of both linear temporality and a vision of self-definition that rests
on contemporaneity. Linear, because we normally expect that, from
one generation to the next, riches be preserved and bequeathed within

6. Patrick Modiano, *La Place de l'étoile* (Paris: Gallimard, 1968). Hereafter, *LPDLE*.
All translations from Modiano's novels are mine.

a closely knit group.[7] Contemporaneous, because the linear unfolding of time as well as the linear transmission of goods this unfolding entails are subordinated to the idea that at any given time, the whole of a heritage is nonetheless available, at hand, to be used by the last in line, the current heir. In dissipating his heritage Schlemilovitch thus refuses to capitalize on the past, at least, on his Jewish past. True to the topos of the upside-down world that governs *LPDLE*, he does everything backwards: either he squanders the gifts of the past, or, reversing the normal course of time, he bequeaths the remainders of his fortune to his father and mother. In short, thanks, but no thanks: Jewish time and Jewish heritage are to be neither cherished by this generation, nor passed on to the next.

A past is not an abstraction, however, as Modiano's quarrel with Proust in *LPDLE* illustrates. Hardly a page goes by without a Proustian reference, allusion, pastiche, or rewriting. I take the main relationship of *LPDLE* and *La Recherche* to hinge on the construction of the self, through a recovery of one's personal past for the former, and the recourse to a group to which the subject can adhere and whose past he can claim as his own for the latter. In Marcel's case, for example, the *madeleine* opens up the door to Combray, that is, to a protected childhood complete with good village folk, little dwellings, a pretty parish church, flowers aplenty, and above all, a caring and comfortably established family. Marcel has every reason to celebrate, for, by integrating the taste of a pastry or the feel of an uneven pavement experienced in childhood into the fabric of later life, not only can he recapture time, that is, remedy the discontinuity of time and consciousness, but he can also recover an undisturbed sense of his integral self—an immensely rewarding experience. In *The Past Recaptured*, musing on the peal that used to signal the end of Swann's visits, Marcel observes that it

> had always been there inside me, . . . for me to still be able to hear that peal, there must have been *no break in continuity, no single second at which I had ceased or rested from existing, from thinking, from being conscious of myself.* [271][8]

7. We should note the inordinately high number of names with a *de* in Modiano's work, at once a sign of French pedigree and of a tie to an inherited land that defines the family.

8. Marcel Proust, *The Past Recaptured*, trans. Andreas Mayor, (New York: Vintage Books, 1971). All emphasis mine unless otherwise noted.

This newly found happiness comes at a price, however: in order to recover his past and achieve this sense of continuity within himself, Marcel must first block away any commerce with others and withdraw into the sanctuary of his private inner self:

> *I was obliged to block my ears to the conversations* which were proceeding between the masked figures all round me, for in order to get nearer to the sound of the bell and to hear it better *it was into my own depths that I had to redescend.* [271]

In other words, to reclaim fully the bits and pieces that constitute his inner self and to reach a sense of completeness and coherence within himself, Marcel must exercise a form of solipsism.

To this romantically egotistic conception of the self, Modiano wistfully opposes Mauriac's deep rootedness in his native Bordeaux:

> This town where we were born, where we were a child [*où nous fûmes un enfant*], an adolescent, is the only one we should not allow ourselves to judge. It is one with our selves, it is ourselves; we carry it within us. Bordeaux's history-story [*l'histoire de Bordeaux*] is the history-story of my body and my soul. [57]

Note that the contrast between Proust and Mauriac does not hang so much on their treatment of the past—both preserve and carry it within themselves—as it does on the object of the preservation, the past itself: while Marcel's past encompasses only private incidents of little significance to anyone but himself (a pastry's taste, a bell's peal, an uneven pavement), Mauriac appropriates the stories-history of a group of which he is a member and with which he fully identifies (his town).[9] In other words, while Modiano's Proust illustrates a Romantic vision of the self, his Mauriac suggests a fusion between the self and its social environment.

While generally espousing the view that the self is a construct mediated by contextual forces, *LPDLE* is however also quick to point out that this view is subject to abuse by extremists whose claims of adhesion and, most regretfully, of exclusion may bring about radical cultural and political segregation, intolerance, and even violence. Thus Schlemilovitch reminds us that "Charles Maurras wrote that one cannot understand Mme de La Fayette or Champfort if one has not

9. This section is not intended as a reading of either Mauriac or Proust but as an analysis of the *use* Modiano makes of them to map his concept of memory and selfhood.

plowed France's soil for a thousand years" (88). Hence, for Maurras and his nationalist and anti-Semitic followers, Jews cannot grasp French or Catholic values and culture ("French" and "Catholic" are interchangeable in Maurras's inflammatory writings) and should therefore be excluded from all public functions (media, legislative, executive, and educational). Jews, on the other hand, may claim a radical collective specificity that renders their cultural productions inaccessible to non-Jews. Schlemilovitch, forever a champion of absurd appropriations and *reductio ad absurdum*, says, for example, to a Communist classmate:

> Let me say this to you in return, my little Saint Thibault. A
> thousand years of pogroms, autodafés, and ghettos are needed to
> understand the shortest paragraph of Marx and Bronstein . . .
> BRONSTEIN, my little Saint Thibault, and not Trotsky as you so
> elegantly say. [88][10]

This sort of *reductio ad absurdum* is one of the most consistent narrative strategies in *LPDLE*. What is a Jew? In a perfect enactment of Sartre's theories in *Réflexions sur la question juive* (another of Modiano's *bêtes noires* in *LPDLE*), Schlemilovitch appropriates, as if to try them out, the various definitions of the "Jew" hatefully thrown at him by French anti-Semitism in the opening pages of the novel:

> The fashionable journals and the tabloids insist on lavishing me with
> praise. I am a charming and original young heir. Jewish? Like Jesus
> Christ and Albert Einstein. And next? Out of desperation I buy a
> yacht, the Sanhedrin, which I transform into a luxury brothel. I
> anchor at Monte-Carlo, Cannes, La Baule, Deauville. Three
> loudspeakers attached to each mast broadcast the texts of Dr.
> Bardamu and Rabatête, my favorite public relations men: Yea, I
> direct a worldwide Jewish conspiracy with orgies and millions. Yea, I
> am a kind of Bluebeard, a cannibal who eats little Aryan girls after
> having raped them. Yea, I dream of bankrupting the entire French
> peasantry and of jewifying the Cantal region. [48–9]

> I felt like telling the headmaster that, unfortunately, I was Jewish.
> Consequently, I always ranked first in my class. . . . Didn't he know
> about the Jewish spirit and intelligence? Had he forgotten that we had
> given France very great writers: Montaigne, Racine, Saint-Simon, Sartre, Henry Bordeaux, René Bazin, Proust, Louis-Ferdinand Céline. [69][11]

10. Trotsky's original name was Bronstein.
11. For this aspect of *LPDLE*, see my "Narrative Subject, Historic Subject: *Shoah* and *La Place de l'étoile*," *Poetics Today*, 12/3 (Fall 1991): 495–516.

His is a thorny appropriation, however, since a French Jew has at least two identities and therefore, at least two memories and two histories. He may be or wish to be French, but he is also a Jew, and if his family has recently immigrated to France, he may also have an East European or Mediterranean heritage. Thus, commenting on Mauriac's comfortable identification with Bordeaux, Schlemilovitch ponders:

> What adolescence could I refer to, I, Raphaël Schlemilovitch, except for the adolescence of a wretched little stateless Jew? I shall be neither Gérard de Nerval, nor François Mauriac, nor even Marcel Proust. There is no Valois to warm up my soul; no Guyenne, no Combray. No Aunt Léonie. [57]

At other times, he wished he had had Maurras, Pujo, or Maxime Real del Sarte as doting grandfathers (sic) instead of his own, "an obscure Jew from Odessa who did not speak French" (36). There is of course a logical solution; Schlemilovitch could "forget" Odessa, and with time, establish his French pedigree (as so many other French Jews thought they could do).

Schlemilovitch soon finds out that dissipating a heritage is more easily said than done, however, as he trips over the law of the excluded middle. France would welcome him if only he could become exclusively French and completely shed his Jewish heritage.[12] Similarly, Israel would reclaim him if only he could renounce his French or his Jewish (that is, European Jewish) heritage. Schlemilovitch is perfectly welcome as a Frenchman in Israel, until he declares to the Israeli authorities, "I am not completely French, Admiral, I am a French JEW, a French JEW" (175). He is jailed and abused on the spot. In the superlogical world set up in *LPDLE*, no community that owes its self-definition to its coherent vision of its past (its history) can accept the multiple and contradictory pasts inherent in the modern Jewish heritage. "We wished Raphaël Schlemilovitch would be satisfied with being a Jew, *tout court*" (119). But being Jewish is anything but *tout court*.[13] A Jew

---

12. Such was indeed the reason for the profound dislike of French Enlightenment luminaries by the Jews who clung to their "unenlightened" traditions. Jews who refused to dissipate their heritage were accused of racism. This argument has often been used by French anti-Semitism; it also found its way to Céline's pamphlets.

13. It is for not having understood the constitutive pluralism of modern Jewish historical consciousness (contradictions and all) that Israel, in *LPDLE*, bears an uncanny resemblance to Nazi Germany and occupied France. In *LPDLE* there are two alternatives only: multiculturalism or totalitarianism (and totalitarianism wears an SS uniform). Jewish identity fits neither.

can no more be a Jew *tout court* than he can be a Frenchman *tout court*. He is both. When he tries to immerse himself in French history (that is, in French patriotism) and to teach in grammar school, he fails:

> I soon realized that I lacked the *furia francese*. The blond knights left me behind and the banners bearing the fleur-de-lis fell off my hands. The lament of a Yiddish singer spoke to me of a death that did not wear spurs, *casoar*, or white gloves [118].

In *LPDLE*, Jewishness consists therefore of a little bit of this and a little bit of that, but the coexistence of this and that is grueling. Schlemilovitch's father's showy attire, for example, which could easily bring him to the top of the ten worst-dressed men list, is made up of a ridiculously inappropriate mixture of styles, fabrics, and colors reminiscent of Charles Bovary's cap (55, 62, 68, 74). In his outlandish outfits the father is, like Charles, an outcast and a freak. The Jewish this and that do not add up to a stylish, harmonious, and coherent whole. In a powerful vignette Modiano illustrates the unforgiving cacophony that resonates throughout the Jewish memory:

> I got two record players. To compose my *Judeo-Nazi Requiem*, I played simultaneously the *Horst-Wessel Lied* and the *Einheitsfront* of the international brigades. Then I mixed the *Hitlerleute* with the hymn of the Thaelmann Kolonne, which was the last cry of the Jewish and German communists. Finally, at the very end of the *Requiem*, Wagner's *Twilight of the Gods* evoked Berlin in flames and the tragic destiny of the German people, while the litany for the dead of Auschwitz brought to mind the pounds to which six million dogs had been taken. [162][14]

We can rephrase this cacophonic French Jewish consciousness as follows: in light of the particularities of recent French history (France's anti-Semitism between the two wars and its enthusiastic collaboration with the Nazis to rid the country of its foreign Jews in World War II), if to be a Frenchman is to adhere to an anti-Semitic state program, how can a Jew be French?[15] On the other hand, how can he not be

14. The only instance of disparate elements that yield a somewhat coherent and contemporaneous whole is the image of the kaleidoscope (Schlemilovitch's father owns a kaleidoscope factory in the U.S.). But precisely, the "kaleidoscope market falls a little more every day. . . . Dreams do not sell anymore . . ." (55). The kaleidoscope is a better metaphor for the composition of the novel than for the Jewish condition.

15. Although in other European countries anti-Semitism may have caused infinitely more spontaneous violence towards Jews than it did in France, no other country in

French, if his cultural memory teems with French heroes from Clovis to Joan of Arc to Pétain, and with French letters from Montaigne to Céline?[16] To further complicate matters, what is a French Jewish patriot to do when his French memory, the *same* memory, can also recount violence against Jews from France's inception (Clovis and the *vase de Soissons*, 118), through the massacres of French Jews by French crusaders (125, 127), all the way to the Dreyfus affair and finally to the Vel' d'Hiv[17] (16, 24–27, 52, 89)? Dissipating a heritage therefore becomes imperative for one who aspires to identify fully with the French national project—at least, dissipating the Diasporic part of a Jewish heritage, the part that consists of persecution, victimization, and Yiddish laments, but also of lofty literary and artistic achievements that include Proust, Kafka, the Marx Brothers and, yes, even Trotsky. But then, can a sacrificial dissipation be extended to all the Jewish past and its memory? Can all fathers be eradicated to free the last heirs from the awesome burden of their Jewish heritage? Can a collective future be built upon a collective murder, real or symbolic (Freud's Moses notwithstanding)? And mostly, would that hecatomb not simply validate, nay, *complete* the unfinished task of the Nazi final solution?[18]

The most painful conflict of today's French Jews is therefore *within* the Jewish community, between fathers who wish to perpetuate their heritage the way their fathers and their fathers' fathers had done before them, and their heirs who see a historic opportunity to turn Jewish history from persecution to normalcy, and who would therefore rather be free of the violent contradictions to which their heritage subjects them—who would rather obliterate the memory of the fathers. Ironically, since cultural and biological generations are not identical, the conflict between past and future can also occur in reversed terms: between those fathers who thought they had already dissipated enough of their heritage to be comfortably "French" and their sons who realize

---

Europe went back two generations to define what a Jew is in order to institutionalize anti-Semitism as state policy (*antisémitisme d'état*)—except, of course, for Nazi Germany.

16. It should be noted that *LPDLE* is a patchwork of literary allusions, quotations and pastiches, all of which underscore the immersion of French Jews in French cultural past—its literary history.

17. In 1942, the French police conducted a mass arrest of Parisian Jews. They were herded into the Vel' d'Hiv and eventually deported to Auschwitz.

18. This last aspect of the question may explain why, in *LPDLE*, young Jews who opt for "forgetting" their Jewish past in order to iron out their conflicts are consistently dressed in Nazi uniforms.

that heritages are here to stay and who find it more comfortable to reclaim their Jewish heritage openly than either have it thrown at their face as happened in World War II or simply live with less (less culture, less memory, less Jewish tradition . . . less heritage). One way or the other, it remains a conflict between fathers and sons.[19] It is therefore not a coincidence that fathers figure most prominently in Modiano's early, Jewish novels, while they are practically absent from the later novels in which the character conducts his search for memory and identity egotistically, through personal recollections.[20] But it is in *LPDLE* that the ambivalence between father and son is the most telling and poignant, whether the novel deals with Schlemilovitch's absurd fantasies or his relationship with his pathetic father. Predictably, the father-son relationship follows the desperately agonist model inspired by the uncompromising excluded middle: there is no room for fathers (persecuted and non-French Jews) in the sons' project of assimilation with the winners. At the same time, however, if to be Jewish means to participate in and identify with Jewish memory and Jewish history, there is also no escape from fathers. The father lives on in his son. Patricide is therefore a form of self-immolation. The conflict between fathers and sons is thus a dirty trick played on Jewish consciousness by a history that has cast Jews in a part they cannot play. It is the Jewish version of being-in-the-world: at once being-in-history and being-at-war-with-history.

This impasse is relentlessly explored in *LPDLE*. The closer Modiano/Schlemilovitch comes to realizing that history leaves him no way out, the more frantic and violent, the more incoherent *his* tone and fantasies turn. Having written and produced a play about fathers and sons, for example, he raves about the finale, a scene in the unbearable burlesque vein of the cacophonic composition quoted above:

> In a white-walled room, the father and his son confront each other:
> the son wears a patched up SS uniform and an old Gestapo raincoat,
> the father side-curls and a rabbi's beard. They parody an
> interrogation with the son as the torturer, the father as the victim.
> The mother barges in, arms stretched forward, with a hallucinated
> look in her eyes. She howls the ballad of the Jewish whore Marie
> Sanders. The son clutches his father's throat and strikes up the

19. "Father" here is not to be taken biologically, but as a marker for the solutions that past generations have sought to the question of Jewish identity.

20. Fathers may be mentioned in the late novels, but they do not accede to the status of "characters."

Horst-Wessel Lied, but he does not manage to cover his mother's voice. The half-choked father whines the *Kol Nidre*, the prayer of forgiveness. A door in the back of the room suddenly opens. Four orderlies round up the protagonists and barely bring them under control. Curtain. [51]

Modiano modulates this conflict on all keys, tragic, kitsch, melodrama, and even slapstick. After his father leaves for New York, for instance, Schlemilovitch wonders if they could not have stayed together and put on a show that would have eclipsed the Marx Brothers. A caring filial regret, no doubt. No sooner is it expressed than Schlemilovitch infuses it with ambivalence and hostility. First, he rejects any comparison with his father, "Schlemilovitch *père* is a fat *monsieur* who wears multicolor suits, Schlemilovitch *fils* only looks for ways to ridicule his father. . . . Schlemilovitch *père* and Schlemilovitch *fils* do not look alike: the former carries along a heavy middle-eastern pot-belly, the latter looks great in an SS suit" (75). Then, he plays out the hostility underlying the distinction between them: he sets his father's clothes on fire, pushes the ladder on which he is standing and causes him to fall, or trips him into a bucket of tar. Melodrama may have made way for slapstick, but the confrontational attitude and the filial ambivalence remain unchanged.

In *Les Boulevards de ceinture* (1972), Modiano's third novel, we witness a reverse father/son ambivalence. The son cautiously sets out to find his father, perhaps to save him, perhaps to reclaim him, but also, perhaps to avenge himself, since in this novel, it is the father who had attempted to murder his son. The story takes place during the last days of the Occupation, against a backdrop of anti-Semitism, betrayal, propaganda, racketeering, and easy pleasures, in short, in a confusing and hallucinatory world of immediate gratification and no tomorrow. The Jewish father, a pitiful, contemptible, meek (but typically resourceful) Jew, is the willing whipping boy of a close group of shady collaborators. His worldly and vaguely protective son seems to both love and despise him. If this description seems somewhat tentative, it is because, in Modiano's rendition of the Jewish father/son problem, the boundaries between loyalty and betrayal, love and hatred, memory and forgetting, heritage and dissipation are muddled, just as they are in the domain of Jewish identity and Jewish history, and for just the same reasons. The father, that is, the past, is an unwelcome, discordant, shameful burden that threatens to devour the present, and, more importantly, the future; at the same time, he is also indispensable since the present, that is, the son, has no identity of his own except for the one he draws from his past. At the end of the novel, the son seems to bow to the Jewish fate: when the father is arrested trying to cross the border, the son, who could have crossed the line to the future and left his father to realize his gloomy Jewish destiny, steps forth and reclaims his heritage: "HE IS MY FATHER" (181, capitalized in the text).

Had the novel ended with these words, it would have offered a solution to the fierce and frenzied conflict of *LPDLE*: we would have concluded that Modiano had chosen the past over the future and had renounced the French part of his French Jewish identity—that he had decided to dissipate his French rather than his Jewish heritage. But there are three more pages in which, thrown out the door, ambivalence comes back through the window. Ultimately, the son does not identify with his father. In the police car with his father, the narrator pursues his interior monologue: "Who are you?" he asks of his father. "Although I have followed you for days on end, I know nothing about you" (182). In the concluding page of the novel, presumably years later, he stands in a bar holding a faded photograph of his father with his collaborationist friends. A solicitous bartender informs him that one of them was executed, another may have returned to the colonies, the fat one suddenly disappeared. . . .

> It is impossible to remember all these faces. After all . . . yes, if I want this picture he will give it to me. But I am young, he says, and I should be thinking about the future [*je ferais mieux de penser à l'avenir*]. [181, end of the book]

Which is it then, the past or the future? How does one ensure a better future anyway? Isn't it a task normally assigned to the study of history, that is, to the past (we study history the better to understand our present and manage our future—or so conventional wisdom goes)? These questions are all the more troubling when we notice that this end mirrors the last page of *LPDLE*, where Schlemilovitch, too, is told, this time by Freud, that he is still young and should look to the future rather than to the past. Schlemilovitch, however, vehemently refuses Freud's treatment (only Dr. Bardamu will do as a therapist, he claims), and Freud ends up on all fours on the floor sobbing, whining, and barking pitifully while Schlemilovitch adds rather inconclusively:

> I mused on the future offered to me: a fast cure in the good hands of Dr. Freud, men and women waiting for me at the door of the clinic with warm and fraternal looks in their eyes. The world, full of

amazing building sites, buzzing beehives. The beautiful
Potzleindorfer Park, there, nearby, greenery, sun-washed paths.
    I squeeze furtively behind the psychoanalyst and pat his bald
head.
    —I am very tired, I say to him, very tired. . . . [214, end of the book]

Too hard a choice, Schlemilovitch? too tiring? too painful? Probably. I do not think that *Les Boulevards de ceinture* comes much closer
to resolving the conflict, however. The opportunity to solve it by ending with *"C'EST MON PERE"* is too clearly missed. There is no end in
sight, no closure in history. Will the son take Freud's or the bartender's
advice and look to the future only? I think not. Will he turn to the past?
It is unlikely. My guess is that he is still running, just as at the end of *La
Ronde de nuit* (1969), he is at the wheel of his car, hunted down for
having denounced the head of the Resistance network—himself—that
is, hunted down for having tried to live up to one of his fictional selves,
one of his identities. Running. . . .[21]
    In 1969, a year after *LPDLE*, Modiano published *La Ronde de nuit*,
about a double agent in occupied Paris. Which is his truth, Resistance
hero or informant? Which is his name, Swing Troubadour as his Gestapo friends call him, or La Princesse de Lamballe as he is known to his
resistance network? Which is Paris' truth, the proud city intent on
recovering its freedom and its national dignity or the gang of profiteers
who run the capital for the Nazis? The narrative projects both the city
and the character in a dizzying whirl, out of known categories and
identities, out of right and wrong, out of clear alternatives and moral
imperatives, into a world of double agency—the same world of double
agency we encountered in *LPDLE*, minus the Jewish problem. The
same year Modiano declared in an interview:

> *LPDLE* is the Jewish problem and nothing else. *La Ronde de nuit* is
> not only Vichy France. As I was writing, I used the atmosphere of
> occupied Paris, but at the same time, I did not want to locate my
> narrative in time. In both books, it remains *a quest for an identity*: a
> Jewish identity in the first, and in the second, it is rather *an
> instinctive flight from any identification.* . . .[22]

21. This incident is, once more, a discussion with Sartre: Modiano's is persecuted
not for the identity that is imposed on him by the gaze of the other as Sartre would have
it, but on the contrary, for the fictional identity he creates for himself and of which he
cunningly convinces the other.
22. Patrick Modiano, "Entretien avec Montalbetti," *Le Magazine littéraire* (November 1969): 42.

Modiano's phrasing is awkward and contradictory. How can a "search for an identity" [*la recherche d'une identité*] be a "flight from any identification" [*une fuite instinctive devant toute identification*]? Are the two not diametrically opposed? The inconsistency is, I think, a slip of tongue, sort of "I wanted to flee identification, but still . . . (*mais quand même . . .*)." True, there are no Jews in *La Ronde de nuit*, and therefore no Jewish question, *mais quand même. . . .* Sandwiched between Modiano's two Jewish novels, written in the same convulsive style, and situated in an occupied France so thick and suffocating that instead of being a mere backdrop for the plot it springs to the fore, *La Ronde de nuit* forms a coherent whole with *La Place de l'étoile* and *Les Boulevards de ceinture*.[23] I shall therefore hazard a suggestion: couldn't this flight anywhere out of this world be another of Schlemilovitch's masquerades, another attempt to deal with the Jewish problem, if only by fleeing? In *LPDLE*, we read:

> after having been a collabo Jew, like Joanovic-Sachs, Raphaël Schlemilovitch is playing out a "return to the soil" (*joue la comédie du 'retour à la terre'*), like Barrès/Pétain. When will it be the turn of the filthy comedy of Captain Dreyfus/Stroheim? That of the self-effacing Jew (*Juif honteux*) Simone Weil/Céline? That of the distinguished Jew like Proust/Daniel Halévy/Maurois? [119]

Why not add the comedy of the double agent to this odd list? Isn't it another of those anti-Semitic clichés that Schlemilovitch is keen on acting out? This time, perhaps, by avoiding choice altogether, he may have a chance to please everyone. It is worth a try. To wriggle out of the painful impasse of *LPDLE*, the young writer then immediately goes back to his desk for a fresh start,[24] carefully avoiding the thorny question of identity, carefully avoiding choices, or so at least he thinks. The "flight from any identification" would then be a flight from insoluble Jewish memory and identity. In other words, with the courage and enthusiasm of inexperience and youth the first-time author took the bull by the horns . . . and got hurt. His reaction: if bull, then run.

23. Nettelbek and Hueston also see these novels as a trilogy, although they deem them immature (*écrits de jeunesse*). Young Patrick was learning the tools of his trade through immitation and pastiche. I strongly disagree with this judgment: in my view, the first three novels are by far the most original and best work he has produced so far. Colin W. Nettelbeck and Penelope A. Hueston, *Patrick Modiano, pièces d'identité: Écrire l'entretemps* (Paris: Lettres Modernes, 1986), 8.

24. "I started *La Ronde de nuit* right away," says Modiano in "Entretien avec Montalbetti," 9.

The first trilogy thus carries out a twofold project. On the one hand, Modiano strongly rejects the Romantic egotistic search for a private self and suggests instead that the self is informed by a collective identity, defined in turn by a shared tradition, memory, and history.[25] It is within this framework that we should inscribe his quarrel with Proust and Sartre: with Proust, for his solipsism,[26] and with Sartre, for thinking that a Jew derives his sense of identity qua Jew from the anti-Semitic feelings and "gaze" of the non-Jewish society in which he lives, rather than from his sense of a historical and cultural heritage.[27] On the other hand, within the contemporary project of collective and historical consciousness, Modiano sees a second conflict, this time between past and present, that prevents the Jewish consciousness from reaching the coherence needed for the construction of a self and an identity. Here again, we encounter Proust, this time for his belief, first, in the contemporaneity of experience and memory, and second, in their coalescence into a nonconflictual and harmonious whole.

Modiano's treatment of the Jewish question thus reaches an impasse: either a Jew opts for Romantic egotism and solipsism in the name of a vague notion of Man whose optimistic universality was disclaimed by history—an alternative the novels vehemently reject—or he condemns himself to remain torn between conflicting identities, between his current place in history and generations of culturally segregated and politically persecuted Jews. For the French Jew, Vichy's Jewish statute was the Revocation of the Rights of Man, just as 1685 was the Revocation of the Edict of Nantes. After World War II, assimilation will never be the same (that option has no currency in the first trilogy). At the same time, French Jews can hardly go back, en masse, to *Yiddishkeit*, even if their grandfathers came from Odessa; nor can they try to develop a Jewish life that will not be essentially culturally French (as some Jews do in this country), given the centralized French culture and education system. In other words, in light of France's institutions and

25. Eight years and three novels later, Modiano explains his interest in Emmanuel Berl: "With Berl, I return to my preoccupations: time, the past, memory. He revives these preoccupations. He encourages me in my project: to create for myself a past and a memory made of other people's past and memory." Patrick Modiano, *Interrogatoire . . . Suivi de Il fait beau, allons au cimetière* (Paris: Gallimard, 1976), 9.

26. Proust's ambivalence about his own Jewish heritage, his affectations, his very French brand of snobism, and the hints of anti-Semitism scattered in *La Recherche* are also highly relevant to our discussion.

27. We should note a third quarrel, with Freud, for what I shall call in our context his solipsism, that is, his reduction of trauma to personal (rather than collective and historical) experiences, the treatment of which takes place in the privacy of a doctor's office.

spotty past, *logically*, one should only be *either* French or Jewish; in the less than logical world in which we live, however, a French Jew is in the throes of a violent conflict between mutually exclusive memories—a conflict as unbearable as it is inescapable.

Now, what do you do when you are twenty-three years old and Jewish, when you have just completed your first novel and discovered as you were writing it that the excruciating problem that you had set out to explore, French Jewish identity, *your* identity, is insoluble? When you feel trapped in no-place, somewhere between La Place de l'Etoile and *la place de l'étoile*, between the Arc de Triomphe and the yellow Jewish star? You run.

But then, what do you do when you realize that if you run from identity, it will hunt you down all the same? What do you do when, having given up the search for your own identity, you end up taking up another's, and paying for it, too? You backtrack, you compromise, you make a virtue of necessity and you try to love your past or your father . . . from a distance.

And when this too fails? When even he does not recognize you? When your sacrifice of your future does nothing for him? When at the end you feel so alienated from the alternative he represents that you come to admit to yourself that you do not know him even as you follow in his footsteps? What do you do when you discover that despite your sacrifice you remain an outsider to all worlds, including the only one to which you might have some rightful claim, your father's? You give up. And if *you* do not, Patrick Modiano does.

He gave up the search for a Jewish identity. After *Les Boulevards de ceinture*, Modiano limits his quest to a safer version of the self, one that does not raise the stakes too high. For now on, characters in search of identities meander through their past, collecting *madeleines*, and bells' peals, tucking them neatly between the covers of books. A quick overview of the novels written after the first trilogy (and of the telling blurbs on the back of each volume) suffices to establish the earnestness of his last project.

—1975. *Villa triste*: "A remembrance of things past" (blurb).
—1977. *Livret de famille*: on the occasion of the birth of his daughter whom he registers in his *livret de famille* (official family registration book), the narrator, who knows neither his own parents' names at the time of his birth nor his birthplace, tries to reconstruct his past. Part invention, part memories, "it all adds up little by little to a *livret de famille*" (blurb).

—1978. *La Rue des boutiques obscures*: an amnesiac tries to reconstruct his past and find out who he is by following dubious clues.

—1981. *Une Jeunesse*: a young couple whose life turns "with time, into a beautiful memory of youth (*souvenir de jeunesse*) which they alone share" (blurb).

—1982. *De si braves garçons*: the narrator evokes the memory of *lycée* friends and inquires into their whereabouts; "these memories keep meeting the present along a reality made of dreams and nostalgia" (blurb).

—1984. *Quartier perdu*: a popular writer is back in Paris after an absence of twenty years, determined to "elucidate the mysteries of his past. . . . A whole chunk of lost memory (*tout un quartier perdu de la mémoire*) is thus revisited and gives away the secrets of its charms and spells" (blurb).

—1986. *Dimanches d'août*: after bumping into a long lost acquaintance, the narrator conjures up the memory of a woman he loved and reflects on the unsolved mysteries of that period of his life.

—1988. *Remise de peine*: childhood memories of the narrator and his younger brother hiding in the country during the Occupation and trying to make sense of confused times.

—1989. *Vestiaire de l'enfance*: a French novelist changes his identity and goes into voluntary exile to become a radio announcer and writer, but his past catches up with him.

—1990. *Voyage de noces*: the narrator decides to stage his disappearance and give himself a fresh start on life, only to find out that his friends and memories maintain the continuity he set out to disrupt.

—1991. *Fleurs de ruine*: the narrator remembers his youth: an enigmatic love, an elusive father, a mysterious character with a borrowed name, a mysterious name without a character.

"Nothing disturbed her sleep," says the narrator of his baby daughter in the last sentence of *Livret de famille*. "She did not have a memory yet." Perhaps we do sleep better without a memory, but if the baby has no memory, it is not because she managed to discard it but because she has not lived yet. Furthermore, since in Modiano's universe memory and identity are synonymous, the baby girl has no sense of identity either, no self-consciousness. She lives in an unmediated, prehuman world. "I am nothing" says the amnesiac of *La Rue des boutiques obscures* in the opening sentence of the novel—nothing, or, perhaps, a baby girl. Time catches up with babies, however, and inevitably inscribes a past where there was none. Total amnesia is inconceivable.

The question is therefore not whether one has a memory or not, but what type of memory (*mémoire*) and memories (*souvenirs*) one ends up weaving into the fabric of one's life, and what kind of identity and self-representations these choices entail. In other words, I am what my memory has retained of what I was. Identity is essentially temporal. Reconstructing one's past thus starts out like any other storytelling. Out of the infinite riches of the past, we select the elements we deem significant, expressive, relevant, or consequential and we string them together. The overall narratives by which we represent our past are the wholes of which these privileged elements are the parts. Neither the part nor the whole prevails logically, but each has to reckon with the other. The whole determines the general range from which its parts may be taken, but some parts, less obviously pertinent to the current whole than others, affect and slowly alter this whole until it allows in still more parts, etc. It falls to the subject to negotiate this continuous adjustment.

Storytelling is only the beginning of this process, however, since selecting entails discarding, and this discarding in turn is more attainable in the relative freedom of fictions (the arbitrariness of narratives) than under the pressure of collective memories and self-representations. As French Jews found out in 1940, one may not always have a choice between identities. The discarded past may come back to haunt the Jewish subject. Dissipating a heritage is a privilege best suited to fiction. It is therefore all the more surprising that young Patrick Modiano did not take advantage of the freedom literature afforded him but, on the contrary, used this freedom against itself, first by exploring the self-representation of a collective rather than of a singular identity, and second, by tackling an identity as rife with contradictions as the Jewish French identity after the War and the Occupation. In his three early novels he pitched logic against history: logic, because in identity propositions, the excluded middle requires clear choices; history, because as anti-Semitism and the Occupation have shown, both assimilation and return to Judaism to the exclusion of the French component are not feasible. Memory sees to it that the French Jewish subject does not coincide with his project. For French Jews, say Modiano's first novels, memory is not the blessed mental faculty that grants the subject a peaceful sense of continuity and identity, but on the contrary, the curse that prevents him from ever attaining that haven.

Leaving behind these two equally impossible kinds of collective

identities and memories, Modiano's later work addresses private conflicts over which the characters have more control. The premise remains unchanged: without memory there is no subject, just "nothing," but while the first novels present a subject exposed to the
torrential forces of history, the late novels construct their memories
with prudence and circumspection, sifting out anything that might
disturb the subject's sleep. Perhaps Modiano was ahead of his time. In
1968, reconstructing the subject was an innovative move; reconstructing it along collective historical lines was downright rash, in defiance
of prevailing practices both literary and social; and reconstructing a
Jewish subject at the time when France and its Jews were still living
mostly in denial was simply suicidal.[28] Perhaps Modiano went too far
into Jewish memory, too soon, with too much honesty, lucidity, and
rigor. Like Jacob, he wrestled the angel a whole night—in three rounds.
And then, still carrying the mark of the angel, he went back to business
as usual, to renewed *souvenirs d'égotisme*.[29]

Independently of the intrinsic value and interest of his novels, Modiano's literary itinerary from collective to private identities thus epito-
mizes the difficulty inherent in the Jewish question. Had he only
started with Jewish memory before it became a fashionable subject and
stayed with it, we might have spoken of his foresight. But his turnabout
after the brutal vision of the first novels is more telling than a thousand
novels. It can be read as a parabola. He sketched the Jewish problem in
harsh and bold lines, perhaps too harsh and bold, where some tact, for
lack of a better word, might have been in order. And yet, I doubt that the
solution of the problem posed by precarious French Jewish identity can
be found in tact alone.

28. On Modiano's contribution to the awakening of both the French and the Jewish
French consciousness after a long period of denial, see Henry Rousso, *Le Syndrome de
Vichy de 1944 à nos jours*, (Paris: Seuil, 1990), 152–54, 348.

29. The Occupation remained important in all of Modiano's novels, including the
later ones. And yet, with time, it became one of many facts of life, still part of the sons'
heritage, but not as determining for their identity as their own private past.

MICHEL ABITBOL

The Integration of North African
Jews in France

The uprooting of the North African Jews and their massive departure for Israel and France constitute, beyond any doubt, one of the most dramatic episodes in the decolonization of the southern Mediterranean countries. The Jews of this region had strong links to the former colonial regimes and deep sympathies for the State of Israel. This led them to assume, rightly or wrongly, that they had much to lose in the new political and social order that in the 1950s began replacing the one installed by the French. Their departure put an end to more than two thousand years of Jewish life in the Maghreb, of which they were among the earliest inhabitants, having settled there, like the Berbers, long before the Arabs.

The National Liberation Front of Algeria had issued various appeals inviting Jews to support the Algerian revolution. "You are an integral part of the Algerian people," declared a 1960 communiqué addressed to them by the provisional government of Algeria.[1] "For you, it is not a question of choosing between France and Algeria, but of becoming true citizens of your country." Like their coreligionists in Tunisia and Morocco, few Jews in Algeria heeded such calls.

There had been some Jewish militants in the Algerian national movement, but their numbers decreased significantly in the last years of the war of independence, when terrorists targeted synagogues and other Jewish sites. In fact, these attacks caused some Jews to side with extremists such as the OAS (Organisation Armée Secrète [Secret Armed Organization]), which did not eschew violent means in the

1. *Le Monde*, 19 February 1960, 3.

YFS 85, *Discourses of Jewish Identity in Twentieth-Century France*, ed. Alan Astro, © 1994 by Yale University.

struggle to maintain French control in Algeria.[2] The involvement of a small number in such groups no doubt reflected a more general frustration among Jews over the impossibility of mending relations with Moslems, from whom they had become profoundly alienated after more than one hundred years of French rule.

The alienation was political and not solely cultural. The colonial situation had caused insuperable rifts among various religious and ethnic groups, as they adopted different strategies vis-à-vis the French. This meant that the rate of the North African Jews' departure reflected not only the course of Arab-Israeli relations, but the specific vicissitudes of decolonization in their countries of origin. The Jewish exodus from North Africa was thus hastened by such events as Tunisia's accession to internal autonomy in 1954, Morocco's proclamation of independence in 1955, the Suez campaign of 1956, the 1961 conflict between Tunisia and France over the military base at Bizerte, the March 1962 signing of the Evian agreements that put an end to the Algerian war, and the independence of Algeria in July of the same year.

In fact, the emigration of North African Jewry to France had begun shortly after World War II and grew in amplitude through the 1950s, as large contingents came from Egypt and Morocco. The independence of Algeria then brought 110,000 to 120,000 of its 140,000 Jews to France, causing the population of North African Jews there to reach 250,000 by the early 1960s. At that point they began to emerge as the dynamic community we know today, which has integrated itself into French Jewry and French society in record time and with surprising ease.

I. AN IMMIGRATION UNLIKE ALL OTHERS

Following the Second World War, North Africa was home to some 500,000 Jews, dispersed in hundreds of locations. They represented no more than 3% of the total population of fifteen million, including some two million European settlers, commonly known as *pieds-noirs*.[3]

---

2. See, for example, Régine Goutalier, "Les Juifs et l'OAS en Oranie" in *Les Relations entre Juifs et musulmans en Afrique du Nord, XIXe–XXe siècles* (Paris: Editions du Centre National de la Recherche Scientique, 1980), 188–96; and Daniel Leconte, *Les Pieds-noirs: Histoire et portrait d'une communauté* (Paris: Seuil, 1980), 222–23.

3. The expression *pieds-noirs* (literally, "black feet") designates French settlers in Algeria and includes those of other European origins (mostly Spanish and Italian) who became French after moving to North Africa. The term can be extended—as Abitbol does later—to Algerian Jews, who took on French citizenship and customs. The origin of

The socioeconomic configuration of the Algerian, Tunisian, and Moroccan Jews had changed significantly following the French conquest of their lands in 1830, 1881 and 1912. The Jews had been active as merchants and tradesmen, but their role as intermediaries between local producers and the outside world was seriously undercut by the arrival of settlers, businessmen, and bankers from France and other parts of Europe. Despite the presence of some greatly wealthy individuals, the overwhelming majority of the Jews were of modest means. However, new opportunities for social advancement appeared. A middle class, more numerous in Algeria than in Tunisia and Morocco, emerged among the first generations to graduate from French high schools and universities. Modern education, or more specifically French education, came to be seen as an absolute prerequisite for success. French secular instruction was available to all Jews in Algeria, but to far fewer in Tunisia and especially Morocco. In those countries, outside of the school system set up by the Alliance Israélite Universelle,[4] Jewish children had practically no chance, at least until the mid-1950s, of attending a public institution.

In this domain as in others, differences of development among the Jewries of Algeria, Tunisia, and Morocco were a function, on the one hand, of the length of time of the colonial presence, and on the other, of the particular policy pursued by France with respect to the Jewish populations. Successive French governments favored assimilation in Algeria, reform in Tunisia, and the status quo in Morocco.

French citizenship was granted to Jews in Algeria by the Crémieux decree of 1870, but subsequently withheld from them in the other two countries, which unlike Algeria were not colonies but protectorates. Starting in 1910, French authorities in Tunisia softened their position, easing the naturalization of the young Jewish elite on a selective and individual basis. In Morocco, however, authorities systematically rejected all Jewish applications for naturalization. For the younger generations, immigration to France represented the sole way out of the legal restrictions resulting from the Moroccan citizenship imposed upon them by the 1880 Madrid Convention.

The new Jewish elites of the Maghreb enjoyed a promising eco-

---

the term is supposedly as an appellation for native stokers in boats, whose bare feet became sooty with coal (Institut National de la Langue Française, *Trésor de la langue française* [Paris: Gallimard, 1988], 13: 342).—*Trans.*

4. The Alliance Israélite Universelle, the first modern international Jewish organization, was founded in 1860 and centered in Paris.—*Trans.*

nomic situation and often came from families whose ascent had predated the colonial period. They had much in common, including an attachment to France and a belief in the unshakeable permanence of French rule in North Africa. That faith was shared by all, even militant Zionists whose Jewish idealism went hand in hand with their idealization of French identity. "Remain Jews. That is your best bet for becoming good Frenchmen": such was the advice that the Moroccan Zionist organ, *L'Avenir illustré*, offered its readers in 1930.[5] How great their disappointment must have been a few years later, when Vichy France blithely subjected them to its anti-Semitic laws.[6] After the war, for a time at least, North African Jews stubbornly downplayed that episode. They preferred to see it as but a brief span in their long history, absorbed as they were in the new events that soon challenged their presence, and that of the French, in the Maghreb.

Fated to change French Jewry radically, North African Jewish immigration to France is surely a unique case among contemporary Jewish migrations. It resembles neither earlier arrivals of Jews in France nor the simultaneous arrival of North African Jews in Israel. It has even less in common with the immigration of Eastern European Jews to the New World and elsewhere. What distinguishes North African Jewish immigration to France is the geographical proximity and cultural and political continuity between the countries of origin and arrival. Having lived in lands long under French domination, the North African émigrés arrived with a perfect knowledge of the language, history, climate, and geography of their new home. They did not feel that they were coming to a completely foreign country. Indeed, a great many had already spent long periods of time in France, where they had attended university, vacationed, or served in the military.

With respect to the Algerian Jews in particular, we should not so much speak of immigration to France as of repatriation, as we do when referring to the 800,000 *pieds-noirs* who arrived in July 1962. Touched by the grace of the Crémieux decree, the ancestors of the Algerian Jews had ceased being "Jewish natives" and had become French citizens. Their descendants, like all *pieds-noirs*, were able to benefit from the

5. *L'Avenir illustré*, Casablanca, 9 January 1930.

6. Though severe, these policies in the Maghreb did not lead French officials to hand thousands of Jewish men, women and children over to the Nazis—as did occur in France. For a study of this period, see Michel Abitbol, *The Jews of North Africa during the Second World War*, trans. Catherine Tihanyi Zentelis (Detroit: Wayne State Univ. Press, 1989).

many services provided for repatriated Frenchmen by the government. Unlike the Eastern European Jews who preceded them to France in the 1920s and 1930s, they were not forced to rely almost exclusively on private or Jewish communal organizations, whose resources were hardly up to the task at hand.

Although Frenchmen in their hearts and minds, these new immigrants did not have a totally exalted view of the mother country that had caused them great loss by leaving Algeria. Back in their homeland, *pieds-noirs*, whether Christians or Jews, felt anger and distress as the Evian talks on the future of Algeria progressed. De Gaulle saw the *pieds-noirs* as troublemakers; they considered themselves to be loyal French citizens, so their relationship to the Gaullist government and the entire political class came to be dominated by mistrust. In the history of French Jewry, there had never been immigrants so disrespectful of those in power, so ready to remind them of their failures and broken promises.

Having a less idealized, more critical view of the French state, the Algerian Jews remained long attached to their particularities as *pieds-noirs* even as they quickly adapted to conditions of life in France. "The Algerian Jews," writes Henri Chemouilli, one of their best chroniclers,

> were French for better and for worse. They were sure that the best they had gotten from France was their emancipation, their introduction to modern life, their accession to Western culture. The worst, they felt, was the defeat shared by all Frenchmen in Algeria, who upon arrival in the mother country were greeted by indifference and sometimes even insults. No one seemed to remember that they had made Alger the capital of Free France and that they had fought in the greatest French victories: the battle of Tunisia, the Italian campaign from Cassino to Rome, and the disembarkation in Provence that led troops to the Rhine and the Danube.[7]

The immigration of Algerian Jewry to France was unique in another sense. Never—except for the transplantation of Bulgarian, Yemenite, and Ethiopian Jewries to Israel—has a minority group moved in its near-entirety from one country to another. To use Claude Tapia's expression, this was a "total" immigration, embracing all sectors of the population.[8] Young and old, rich and poor, assimilationists and traditionalists, merchants and farmers, tradespeople and workers, civil

7. Henri Chemouilli, "Les Rapatriés dix ans après," *L'Arche* (May–June 1972): 44.
8. Claude Tapia, *Les Juifs sépharades en France* (Paris: L'Harmattan, 1986), 283.

servants and schoolteachers, doctors, lawyers, engineers, university and high-school students, rabbis and other religious officials—all moved to France.[9] In comparison, earlier Jewish immigrations to France from Eastern Europe and North Africa were "partial," socially and culturally more uniform.

Thus "total" and diversified, the Algerian immigration, whose ranks were swelled by several thousand Tunisian and Moroccan immigrants, constituted a visible community not only numerically—their arrival doubled the French Jewish population overnight—but geographically as well. They spread to all corners of France, including places where Jews had never settled before: Meaux, Angers, Bourges, Annecy, La Rochelle. In older communities, they renewed Jewish life by expanding the existing religious infrastructure and creating new synagogues; kosher butchershops, bakeries and groceries; Jewish day and afternoon schools. In greater Paris, the number of Jewish families grew from 50,000 to 80,000; in Marseilles 16,000 new families arrived. The Jewish population of Toulouse quadrupled, going from 1,000 to 4,000 families; at Nice it sextupled, from 600 to 3,500 families; in Avignon, Montpellier, Toulon, Aix-en-Provence, Clermont-Ferrand and Lyons, it "only" doubled. The number of Jews tripled in Grenoble, Cannes, Lunéville, Rouen, and Perpignan.[10]

II. AN IMMIGRATION REMARKABLE BY ANY STANDARDS

The social advancement of the North African Jews was rapid in absolute terms and in comparison to that of all previous Jewish immigrants to France. This was the result not only of the economic and social environment that greeted the so-called repatriates but also of characteristics specific to them. Because of the political, administrative, and cultural continuity between France and its former North African colonies, a great many repatriates were able to pursue their previous occupations; they were spared the drop in status that often complicated the

9. On the contrary, the Moroccan Jewish immigration to France was much more "selective," largely made up of elements of the community who were bourgeois, Frenchified or in some way skilled. The Tunisian immigration resembled the Algerian one in that it included all social strata.

10. See, in this respect, the data furnished by the Fonds Social Juif Unifié in "L'Intégration communautaire dans l'Hexagone," *L'Arche* (May–June 1972): 53–57.

integration of those choosing destinations other than France.[11] In the case of civil servants working for the French state—schoolteachers, postal workers, policemen, customs officials—the move to France presented the same advantages as any professional relocation.

Since the majority of the Jewish immigrants possessed French citizenship, they were able to benefit from all the housing and employment measures the government had put in place to settle the repatriates. At the beginning of the 1960s, France was on the threshold of a great economic expansion that was to last more than ten years; there could be no better time for the integration of newcomers. What a difference from the situation that greeted Eastern and central European Jews in the 1930s! They had found France in one of the most difficult periods of her history, as the Third Republic, faced with the repercussions of a worldwide depression, was spending much of its energy in an endless battle against openly xenophobic, anti-Semitic, antidemocratic extremists.

That difficult political context does much to explain the lack of courage and generosity shown by the French Jewish religious establishment as it dealt with refugees from the East.[12] This attitude was sharply criticized after the war, so Jewish leaders adopted a completely different position towards their North African coreligionists. Their unfailing solidarity was all the more natural as they were faced not with foreign refugees but with French nationals, for whom the government itself had mobilized great efforts.

A role of the greatest importance was to be played by the FSJU (Fonds Social Juif Unifié [United Jewish Welfare Fund]), which in 1961 took the initiative of creating an information and orientation bureau for the North African immigrants. In the first days of the exodus from Algeria, teams of FSJU volunteers met arrivals around the clock in air- and seaports. Transit centers, canteens and children's shelters were opened in some forty cities by the FSJU, sometimes alone, sometimes in concert with the government or non-Jewish philanthropical organizations such as the Red Cross, the Secours Catholique [Catholic Aid Society], and the Protestant CIMADE [Comité Intermouvement au-

11. A 1970 survey in Paris on this question showed that 50% of heads of households occupied the same positions they had in their homelands and that only 8% had experienced a loss in professional status (Tapia, 278).

12. For an excellent discussion of this question, see Paula Hyman, "The Futile Struggle for Leadership: Jewish Politics in the 1930s" in *From Dreyfus to Vichy: The Remaking of French Jewry, 1906–1939* (New York: Columbia University Press, 1979), 199–232.

près des Evacués [Interdenominational Committee to Aid Evacuees]). The FSJU created a specialized service to put the repatriates in contact with possible employers. Young people received guidance from FSJU counselors who themselves were natives of North Africa, where they had been trained by the Département d'Education de la Jeunesse Juive [Jewish Youth Education Department], whose offices had moved from Morocco to Paris in 1961. While the Central Jewish Consistory opened new synagogues and religious schools, the North African Jews themselves organized compatriots' associations that recalled the *landsmanshaftn* created by prewar Eastern and central European immigrants.[13] There was even born an Association Générale des Juifs d'Algérie [General Association of Jews from Algeria], which in December 1964 organized an impressive convention of delegates from some forty communities. Several months earlier, *L'Information juive*, which had been the principal monthly of Algerian Jewry, began to appear in Paris, but with a significant change: it had become the organ of the French section of the World Jewish Congress.

Such efforts helped the North African Jews settle in and improve their economic and cultural situation so as to become the dominant element in French Jewry. The conclusions of the demographic survey published in 1984 by Doris Bensimon and Sergio Della Pergola are clear: North African Jews now constitute the majority of France's total Jewish population of 550,000 to 600,000, though they have progressively aligned themselves with French Jews of European background in terms of household size, rates of birth, death, marriage, and intermarriage.[14] In that study, more than 23% of Moroccan- and Tunisian-born Jews in greater Paris reported having obtained degrees at universities or other institutions of higher learning; of the remainder, at least 18% said they had finished secondary school. These figures are slightly lower than those for the Jewish population generally (25.4% and 18.3%), but significantly higher than those for Algerian-born Jews (14.2% and 15.6%) and for Jews of Eastern European origin (19.8% and 11.8%). This educational level, incommensurably higher than that attained by North African Jews in their countries of origin or in Israel,

13. *Landsmanshaftn* is the Yiddish term for the mutual aid societies that Jews from a particular town or region of Eastern Europe organized in such centers of immigration as Paris, New York, Buenos Aires and Tel Aviv.—*Trans.*

14. Doris Bensimon and Sergio Della Pergola, *La Population juive de France: Sociodémographie et identité* (Jerusalem: Institute for Contemporary Jewry, 1984). It should be noted that these authors estimate the total Jewish population of France at 530,000, a figure contested by community sources.

reflects their occupational status in France. Thus Bensimon and Della Pergolla found that more than 26% of Jews living in greater Paris but having come from Morocco and Tunisia in the late 1950s were professionals and executives (as opposed to 25.3% for all Jews in Paris and 12.2% for the Parisian population generally); 15.4% were tradesmen or merchants (as opposed to 21.4% and 5.8% respectively); nearly 39% were administrative or clerical workers (as against 24.5% and 25%), and 19.6% were unskilled workers (as opposed to 8.9% and 29.4%).[15] As for Algerian Jews arriving in 1962, some 13% identified themselves at the time of the survey as professionals, 17% as tradesmen or merchants, 60% as administrative or clerical workers, and 9.4% as unskilled workers.[16] To appreciate the strides made by Algerian Jewry, let us consider the census the Vichy government carried out in 1941, the only demographic study available on Jews in Algeria in this century. It reported that only 4.5% were professionals, 33% were tradesmen or merchants, 11% were in administrative, clerical, or civil-service positions and as many as 28% were unskilled workers.[17]

The religious practice of the North African Jews in France has also evolved. It has become far less assiduous than it was in their countries of origin, yet it remains impressive when compared to that of other French Jews. All studies show that among North African Jews religious observance and knowledge of Hebrew, Judeo-Arabic and Judeo-Spanish have lessened with the increase in general education and economic

15. Bensimon and Della Pergola, 184. The figures for immigrants arriving later from these two countries are rather different: professionals and executives, 19.9%; tradesmen and merchants, 8.9%; administrative and clerical workers, 55.1%; unskilled workers, 16.1% (Bensimon and Pergolla, 188).

16. Outside of the Paris area, the socioprofessional configuration for Jews is as follows:

	Moroccans and Tunisians	Algerians	All Jews
Professionals/ executives	12.1	14.1	15.2
Tradesmen/merchants	18.2	21.9	22.2
Lower management/clerical	57.6	48.4	52.7
Unskilled workers	12.1	15.6	9.9

(Bensimon and Pergolla, 199).

17. See Jöelle Allouche-Benayoun and Doris Bensimon, *Juifs d'Algérie hier et aujourd'hui: Mémoires et identité* (Toulouse: Privat, 1989), 53; André Chouraqui, *Histoire des Juifs en Afrique du Nord* (Paris: Hachette, 1985), 397–401; Abitbol, *The Jews of North Africa During the Second World War*, 47–74.

fortune. At present, only 7.8% of Jews from Morocco and Tunisia send their sons to Jewish day schools, as against 10.4% for Jews in France generally and 13.8% for the Algerian-born Jews. The figures for their daughters are even more telling: Jewish day schools receive only 2.3% of the girls of Moroccan and Tunisian origin, as opposed to 5.5% of Jewish girls generally and 6.4% for those of Algerian background (Bensimon and Della Pergolla, 270).

III. A NEW FRENCH JUDAISM?

The rapid assimilation of North African Jewry is not unusual in itself. All previous waves of Jewish immigration underwent a similar process. What is surprising is that while abandoning many of their religious practices, they have developed expressions of Jewish identity that are far removed both from traditionally muted French Judaism and from the more orthodox Judaism of their homelands. For many of them, solidarity with the State of Israel and remembrance of the Holocaust have taken the place of observance of religious law, study of the holy writings, and adherence to the spiritual values that have been the mainstay of Jewish life.

What is no less remarkable about the North African Jews' transformation is that it has affected the rest of French Jewry. It is no doubt exaggerated to suggest, as some have, that the North African Jews' unswerving attachment to the vestiges of their traditions has breathed new life into French Judaism. To make such a claim is to forget that as part of their colonization, these Jews had been brought under the influence of the Consistory—the French Jewish religious establishment—starting in the nineteenth century. Long before arriving in France, the majority of the Jewish *pieds-noirs* had undergone quite a bit of modernization and assimilation. Moreover, we must not neglect that upon coming to France their Jewish cultural background was in general far less extensive, far more indigent, than that of the Eastern European Jews who had preceded them. The earlier immigrants had certainly had a mentality no less "ethnic" or particularistic than that of the North African Jews.

It is clear that the oft-cited "re-Judaization" of French Jewry in the 1970s and 1980s can in no way be attributed exclusively to one or the other segment of the community. It is the result of a series of historical and cultural factors affecting French society generally on the one hand, and Jewish populations throughout the world on the other.

The first of these factors is the waning, as de Gaulle's legacy faded, of the so-called "Jacobin" ideology, the notion (deriving from the Jacobin party of the French Revolution) that the state must level all differences. In the 1970s, minority groups started demanding recognition of their particularities and of their "right to be different." Simultaneously, and no less importantly, universalistic ideologies such as Marxism lost their appeal. In such a climate, it is easy to see how along with regionalist groups seeking various kinds of autonomy, French Jews came to adopt a more "ethnic" posture. They are now less shy about calling themselves French Jews rather than Jewish Frenchmen.[18]

The second factor, more global in nature, concerns the immense interest and anxiety that Israel has inspired throughout the Jewish world starting with the Six-Day War. At the same time, French Jews were finally coming to terms with the fact that their fate had been far crueller than that meted out to other Frenchmen during the Nazi occupation. This admittedly late recognition of the uniqueness of the Holocaust, in conjunction with the threats of extermination made against the State of Israel, led French Jewry to redefine its attitude towards Zionism and to adopt firmly pro-Israel positions, even at the expense of angering their government, whose relations with Israel continued to worsen after May 1967. Thus when de Gaulle described the Jews in November of that year as *"un peuple d'élite, sûr de lui-même et dominateur"* [an elite people, self-assured and domineering], his remark was seen as an affront not only by community leaders and inveterate supporters of Israel.[19] Personalities such as political thinker Raymond Aron, Jewish by birth but far removed from community life, declared their sympathy for Israel in surprisingly clear terms. Aron wrote:

> I have never been a Zionist, firstly and above all because I do not feel myself to be a Jew. . . . But I also know, more clearly than in the past, that in the event of the State of Israel being destroyed . . . I should be wounded in the very depths of my being.[20]

18. "French Jew" and "Jewish Frenchman" may be the best way to render the distinction between the terms *juif* and *israélite* as used here. For a discussion of the two words, see Dominique Schnapper, *Juifs et israélites* (Paris: Gallimard, 1980).—*Trans.*

19. For a recent discussion of this episode, see Maurice Szafran, *Les Juifs dans la politique française* (Paris: Flammarion, 1990), 149–72.

20. Raymond Aron, *De Gaulle, Israel and the Jews*, trans. John Sturrock (London: André Deutsch, 1969), 41.

The contribution of North African Jews to the awakening of French Jewish identity cannot be underestimated.[21] Dispersed as they are through all corners of France, engaged in all walks of life, they have often been at the forefront of new expressions of minority identity as well as the so-called "new philosophies" that have supplanted Marxism and existentialism. Characterized by a fundamental antipathy to the Gaullist régime, the North African Jews were not in danger of idolizing the French state as French Jews had for generations. To the stylish critique of the nation-state they joined a demand for recognition not only of their Jewish heritage but also of their particularities as *pieds-noirs*. This double identification is the fruit of more than a century of a colonial policy of segregation. It had led the Jews, Arabs, and Europeans in North Africa to see their ethnic and religious identities as natural givens that no force in the world could alter or erase.

Moreover, though the North African Jews initially were no more or less Zionist than Jews of French background, the "abandonment" of Israel by de Gaulle had revived their pain over the French "abandonment" of Algeria to the Arabs—those "same" Arabs who now, speaking through Egyptian president Gamal Abdel Nasser and Palestinian representative to the Arab League Ahmad Shukairi, threatened to drive Israel into the sea! Concerned over the fate of the Jewish state as well as of their many family members there, North African Jews in France did not hesitate to proclaim loudly and publicly their disagreement with official Middle Eastern policy. This was hardly the first time that the French republic's handling of foreign affairs went against the wishes of its Jews; we could cite an event as far back as the welcome given to Czar Alexander III at a time when pogroms ravaged Russia.[22] Up to now, however, French Jewry had led their government to expect no more than discreet and contained expressions of displeasure.

The extreme "Zionization" of the North African immigrants reflects the long road they have traveled since 1962 in their relations with Israel. In their homelands, their political options had been limited by the contingencies of the colonial situation. Only in France, where they felt generally at ease as Jews and as Frenchmen, did most of

21. This question is analyzed more fully in my study, "Manifestations of Jewish National Identity in France" (in Hebrew) (Jerusalem: Institute for Contemporary Jewry, 1983).

22. On this episode, see Michael R. Marrus, *The Politics of Assimilation: The French Jewish Community at the Time of the Dreyfus Affair* (Oxford: Clarendon Press, 1971), 154–62.

them "discover" the Zionist ideology to which they had not previously felt very attracted. This was particularly true of the Algerian Jews who had been far more unresponsive to the Zionist message than their coreligionists in Morocco and Tunisia.[23] In fact, the Israeli press had judged them quite severely in the beginning of 1963 when so few of them chose the Promised Land to start their lives anew.

"Israel had slapped a dead man," wrote Henri Chemouilli (44) about the Algerian Jews, "but some dead men revive and some slaps do the job." Feeling themselves ill-represented by the Comité de Coordination des Associations Juives de France [Coordinating Committee of the Jewish Associations of France] that had been set up in May 1967 to furnish aid to Israel, the North African Jews formed, shortly after the Six-Day War, their own assistance organization called the Comité de Liaison des Associations de Juifs Originaires d'Afrique du Nord [Liaison Committee of Associations of Jews from North Africa]. The Liaison Committee soon went beyond its immediate objective and took an interest in the fate of North African Jews in Israel. Redubbed SIONA (for "Sionistes d'Origine Nord-Africaine" [Zionists of North African Origin]), it became a Zionist organization devoted to "political action in favor of Israel." SIONA leaders dreamt of dominating the Mouvement Sioniste de France [Zionist Movement of France], which was to be restructured after elections planned for 1971. At the last minute these were called off, to the great disappointment of the North African militants who had to swallow their anger and search for other areas of action in community life.

Gradually abandoning their separate organizations, dissolving for example the Organisation des Juifs d'Algérie (Organization of Jews from Algeria, as the previously mentioned Association Générale des Juifs d'Algérie had been renamed), Algerian Jews have assumed leading roles in such prominent agencies of French Jewry as the Central Jewish Consistory and the FSJU. The appointment in the last decade of Algerian-born Rabbi René-Samuel Sirat, then of Tunisian-born Rabbi Joseph Sitruk, to the post of Chief Rabbi of France, is a brilliant example of the integration of North African Jewry.

CONCLUSION

Thanks to a series of factors, of which to our mind the most important is the cultural, geographical, and political continuity between France

23. On this subject, see my study, "The Evolution of Zionism in North Africa" (in Hebrew), *Peamim* 2 (1979): 65–91.

and their countries of origin, the North African Jews have made a remarkable and rapid ascent within French Jewry and French society generally. Their prominence has coincided with and no doubt contributed much to the transformation of French Jewry. It is now a community more "ethnic"-minded and orthodox than it has ever been since the emancipation of the Jews at the time of the French Revolution.

Recently, however, some French Jewish intellectuals have criticized what they see as the "sectarian" pronouncements of Jewish leaders and have recalled the great importance attached to universalism and secularism throughout the history of the French republic.[24] So we must wonder how irreversible the new demonstrative trend in French Jewish identity is, especially since some of its components— such as attachment to the State of Israel—are not assured of eternal life.

—Translated by Alan Astro

24. See on this question Frank Eskenazi and Edouard Waintrop, *Le Talmud et la République* (Paris: Grasset, 1991), 203–24.

Contributors

MICHEL ABITBOL is a professor at the Hebrew University of Jerusalem. His books include *The Jews of North Africa during the Second World War*, trans. Catherine Tihanyi Zentelis (Detroit: Wayne State University Press, 1989).

ALAN ASTRO, associate professor of French at Trinity University in San Antonio, Texas, is the author of *Understanding Samuel Beckett* (Columbia, S.C.: University of South Carolina Press, 1990).

ORA AVNI, professor of French at Yale University, has written *The Resistance of Reference: Linguistics, Philosophy, and the Literary Text* (Baltimore: Johns Hopkins University Press, 1990).

GIL BEN AYCH, who teaches philosophy at a lycée near Paris, has published four novels including *Le Livre d'Etoile* (Paris: Seuil, 1986).

MADELEINE DOBIE is a Ph.D. candidate in the French Department at Yale University and is completing a dissertation on figures of Oriental women in eighteenth- and nineteenth-century texts.

RACHEL ERTEL, who teaches Yiddish and English at the University of Paris-VII, is most recently the author of *Dans la langue de personne: La Poésie yiddish de l'anéantissement* (Paris: Seuil, 1993).

CYRILLE FLEISCHMAN, a writer and attorney in Paris, has recently published his second volume of short stories: *Rendez-vous au métro Saint-Paul* (Paris: Le Dilettante, 1992).

ELISABETH DE FONTENAY, who teaches philosophy at the Sorbonne, is the author of *Diderot, Reason and Resonance* (New York: Braziller, 1982).

BERNARD FRANK, well-known for his weekly literary column in *Le Nou-*

YFS 85, *Discourses of Jewish Identity in Twentieth-Century France,* ed. Alan Astro, © 1994 by Yale University.

vel Observateur, is a novelist whose works include *L'Illusion comique* (Paris: Flammarion, 1989).

NOAH GUYNN is a Ph.D. candidate in the French Department at Yale University and the editorial assistant at *Yale French Studies*.

GÉRARD HADDAD, a Parisian psychoanalyst, is the author of *Les Biblioclastes: Le Messie et l'autodafé* (Paris: Grasset, 1990), recently translated into Spanish.

DAVID J. JACOBSON has taught Italian at Hunter College of the City University of New York. His translation of Michel Mazor's *The Vanished City: Recollections of the Warsaw Ghetto* is to be published by Marsilio.

PAULA JACQUES, a literary talk-show host on the France-Inter radio station, has written four novels. The most recent is *Deborah et les anges dissipés* (Paris: Mercure de France, 1991).

MEYER JAÏS was chief rabbi of Paris from 1955 until his retirement in 1980. He was the author of *Un Juif, c'est quoi?* (Paris: Association Consistoriale Israélite de Paris, 1980).

SALIM JAY, a novelist and essayist residing in Paris, has published sixteen books including *Les écrivains sont dans leur assiette* (Paris: Seuil, 1991) and *Du côté de Saint-Germain-des-Prés* (Paris: Jacques Bertoin, 1992).

GUSTAVE KAHN (1859–1936), French symbolist poet, published short stories on Jewish themes towards the end of his life.

ANNA LEHMANN is a Ph.D. candidate in the French Department at Yale University.

SARAH LÉVY is the pseudonym of a novelist and poet active in Paris in the 1920s and 1930s.

ARMAND LUNEL (1892–1977), longtime librettist to composer Darius Milhaud, was a novelist and chronicler of Jewish and non-Jewish life in the Provence region of France.

RYSIA POLONIECKA was born in Warsaw and lives in Paris. One of her texts, "Voyage à Nahariya ou aller-retour à Nahariya," appeared in *Pardès* 15 (1992): 161–66.

HENRI RACZYMOW, Parisian novelist and essayist, has written eleven books published by Gallimard, one of which will soon appear in an English translation by Dori Katz: *A Cry Without a Voice* (New York: Holmes & Meier).

FRANÇOISE ROSSET, assistant professor of Russian at Stonehill College in North Easton, Massachusetts, has done several translations relating to French and Russian literature.

BERNARD SUCHECKY, the director of exterior relations for the Opéra du Rhin in Strasbourg, has translated from the Yiddish Hersh Mendel's *Les Mémoires d'un révolutionnaire juif* (Grenoble: Presse Universitaire de Grenoble, 1982).

GLENN SWIADON has taught French at City College of San Francisco and at the University of Tlaxcala in Mexico.

ARMAND VULLIET, a Parisian postman, is the author of "Réflexions sur *Anarchie et christianisme* de Jacques Ellul" in *IRL: Informations Réflexions Libertaires* 83 (Oct.–Nov. 1989): 21–26.

MICHAEL T. WARD, associate professor of Italian and Spanish at Trinity University in San Antonio, Texas, has published on the history of linguistics in *Italica* and *Hispanic Review*.

OSER WARSZAWSKI, a Yiddish writer in Warsaw and Paris, died at Auschwitz in 1944. His first novel, published in 1920 when he was twenty-one, has been translated into French by Aby Wieviorka and Henri Raczymow as *Les Contrebandiers* (Paris: Seuil, 1989).

ANNETTE WIEVIORKA, research director at the Centre National de la Recherche Scientifique, is the author of five books including *Déportation et génocide: Entre la mémoire et l'oubli* (Paris: Plon, 1992).

WOLF WIEVIORKA, born in Poland in 1898, was a Yiddish writer in Paris, who died at the hands of the Nazis in 1945. A tale of his appears in *"Une maisonnette au bord de la Vistule" et autres nouvelles du monde yiddish*, ed. Rachel Ertel (Paris: Albin Michel, 1989).

SETH L. WOLITZ, holder of the Gale Chair of Jewish Studies at the University of Texas at Austin, has published on Proust, Bernart de Ventadorn, and Yiddish literature.

qui parle

Across and against
the full spectrum of
humanistic disciplines-

Qui Parle publishes
essays and reviews
on philosophy, literature,
history and the arts-

major new works
by notorious personages,
as well as figures and voices
heretofore (but not henceforth)
anonymous...

Contributors include :
Leo Bersani, R. Howard Bloch, Victor Burgin, Hélène Cixous, Jacques Derrida, James Elkins,
Lisa Freinkel, Jean-Joseph Goux, Nasser Hussain, Peggy Kamuf, David Lloyd, Jean Luc-Nancy,
Rainer Nägele, Avital Ronell, Ann Smock, Rochelle Tobias, Samuel Weber, Slavoj Zizek...

Subscriptions

Individual	$10 one year /2 issues	$17 two years /4 issues
Institutional	$20 one year /2 issues	$40 two years /4 issues

Inquiries, Submissions and Subscriptions:

qui parle

**The Doreen B. Townsend
Center for the Humanities
460 Stephens Hall
University of California
Berkeley, CA 94720**

The following issues are available through **Yale University Press,** Customer Service Department, 92A Yale Station, New Haven, CT 06520.

63 The Pedagogical Imperative: Teaching as a Literary Genre (1982) $17.00

64 Montaigne: Essays in Reading (1983) $17.00

65 The Language of Difference: Writing in QUEBEC(ois) (1983) $17.00

66 The Anxiety of Anticipation (1984) $17.00

67 Concepts of Closure (1984) $17.00

68 Sartre after Sartre (1985) $17.00

69 The Lesson of Paul de Man (1985) $17.00

70 Images of Power: Medieval History/Discourse/ Literature (1986) $17.00

71 Men/Women of Letters: Correspondence (1986) $17.00

72 Simone de Beauvoir: Witness to a Century (1987) $17.00

73 Everyday Life (1987) $17.00

74 Phantom Proxies (1988) $17.00

75 The Politics of Tradition: Placing Women in French Literature (1988) $17.00

Special Issue: After the Age of Suspicion: The French Novel Today (1989) $17.00

76 Autour de Racine: Studies in Intertextuality (1989) $17.00

77 Reading the Archive:

On Texts and Institutions (1990) $17.00

78 On Bataille (1990) $17.00

79 Literature and the Ethical Question (1991) $17.00

Special Issue: Contexts: Style and Value in Medieval Art and Literature (1991) $17.00

80 Baroque Topographies: Literature/History/ Philosophy $17.00

81 On Leiris (1992) $17.00

82 Post/Colonial Conditions Vol. 1 (1993)

83 Post/Colonial Conditions Vol. 2 (1993)

84 Boundaries: Writing and Drawing (1994)

Special subscription rates are available on a calendar year basis (2 issues per year):

Individual subscriptions $24.00 Institutional subscriptions $28.00

ORDER FORM **Yale University Press,** 92A Yale Station, New Haven, CT 06520

I would like to purchase the following individual issues:

_____

_____

For individual issue, please add postage and handling:

Single issue, United States $2.75 Each additional issue $.50

Connecticut residents please add sales tax of 6%

Single issue, foreign countries $5.00 Each additional issue $1.00

Payment of $_____ is enclosed (including sales tax if applicable).

Mastercard no. _____

4-digit bank no._____ Expiration date_____

VISA no._____ Expiration date _____

Signature _____

SHIP TO _____

_____

_____

See the next page for ordering other back issues. Yale French Studies is also available through Xerox University Microfilms, 300 North Zeeb Road, Ann Arbor, MI 48106.

The following issues are still available through the **Yale French Studies Office,** 2504A Yale Station, New Haven, CT 06520.

19/20 Contemporary Art $6.00
33 Shakespeare $6.00
35 Sade $6.00
38 The Classical Line $6.00
39 Literature and Revolution $6.00
42 Zola $8.00
43 The Child's Part $8.00
44 Paul Valéry $8.00

45 Language as Action $8.00
46 From Stage to Street $6.00
47 Image & Symbol in the Renaissance $6.00
52 Graphesis $8.00
53 African Literature $6.00
54 Mallarmé $8.00
57 Locus in Modern French Fiction: Space, Landscape, Decor $9.00

58 In Memory of Jacques Ehrmann $9.00
59 Rethinking History $9.00
61 Toward a Theory of Description $9.00
62 Feminist Readings: French Texts/American Contexts $9.00

Add for postage & handling

One-Two Issues, United States $2.90 (Priority Mail)
Single issue, United States $1.75 (Third Class)   Each additional issue $.50
Single issue, foreign countries $2.50   Each additional issue $1.50

YALE FRENCH STUDIES, P.O. Box 20851, New Haven, Connecticut 06520-8251
A check made payable to YFS is enclosed. Please send me the following issue(s):

Issue no.   Title   Price

_____

_____

                                                Postage & handling   _____

                                                            Total   _____

Name_____

Number/Street _____

City_____State _____Zip _____

The following issues are now available through Kraus Reprint Company, Route 100, Millwood, N. Y. 10546.

1 Critical Bibliography of Existentialism
2 Modern Poets
3 Criticism & Creation
4 Literature & Ideas
5 The Modern Theatre
6 France and World Literature
7 André Gide
8 What's Novel in the Novel
9 Symbolism
10 French-American Literature Relationships
11 Eros, Variations...
12 God & the Writer
13 Romanticism Revisited
14 Motley: Today's French Theater
15 Social & Political France
16 Foray through Existentialism

17 The Art of the Cinema
18 Passion & the Intellect, or Malraux
21 Poetry Since the Liberation
22 French Education
24 Midnight Novelists
25 Albert Camus
26 The Myth of Napoleon
27 Women Writers
28 Rousseau
29 The New Dramatists
30 Sartre
31 Surrealism
32 Paris in Literature
34 Proust
48 French Freud
51 Approaches to Medieval Romance

36/37 Structuralism has been reprinted by Doubleday as an Anchor Book.
55/56 Literature and Psychoanalysis has been reprinted by Johns Hopkins University Press, and can be ordered through Customer Service, Johns Hopkins University Press, Baltimore, MD 21218.

Musée Carnavalet

The Past in French History

Robert Gildea

This fascinating book offers a new perspective on French history and political culture by examining how the commemoration of the past pervades French public life. The book surveys the ways that various political communities in France during the past two centuries—proponents of revolution and counterrevolution, church and state, centralism and regionalism, and national identity and nationalism—have used different versions of the past in order to define their identities and legitimate their goals. 24 illus. $40.00

Sisters of the Brush

Women's Artistic Culture in Late Nineteenth-Century Paris

Tamar Garb

The Union of Women Painters and Sculptors was founded in Paris in 1881 to represent the interests of women artists and to facilitate the exhibition of their work. This lively and informative book traces the history of the first fifteen years of the organization and places it in the context of the Paris art world and the development of feminism in the late nineteenth century. 62 illus. $45.00

To order call 1-800-YUP-READ

Yale University Press

P.O. Box 209040, New Haven, CT 06520

Arguing Revolution

The Intellectual Left in Post-War France

Sunil Khilnani

This book examines the rise and fall of the intellectual left in post-war France. Khilnani discusses the forms of political criticism available to intellectuals after 1945, focusing on the arguments of the two most prominent revolutionary thinkers, Jean-Paul Sartre and Louis Althusser.

"A work of unusual intellectual penetration, marked by a rare combination of philosophical sophistication and historical sensitivity."—Tony Judt $30.00

Industrial Madness

Commercial Photography in Paris, 1848-1871

Elizabeth Anne McCauley

"An extraordinary compilation of new information on the rise of photography in Paris. The directory of photographers by itself is essential and the lively narrative demonstrates in fascinating detail how business practices shaped the arena in which the enfant art first fully emerged."—Maria Morris Hambourg 40 illus. $45.00

Yale Publications in the History of Art

New in Paperbound

The Fabrication of Louis XIV

Peter Burke

In this engrossing book, an internationally respected historian gives an account of contemporary representations of Louis XIV—in paintings and engravings, medals and sculptures, plays, ballets, and operas—to show how the making of a royal image illuminates the relationship between art and power.

"A distinguished, lively, and beautifully written book."—Robin Briggs, *Times Literary Supplement*   90 illus. $15.00

Have You Heard the News?

Announcing the second edition of

French in Action: The Capretz Method

For the past six years, Professor Capretz, Mireille, Robert, Marie-Laure, and the rest of *French in Action*'s colorful cast have been leading teachers and students at over 2000 institutions through this innovative approach to learning French.

Now *French in Action*'s second edition includes all of the elements that have made the program so successful, together with many new and updated features:

- authentic documents, more than 200 new to this edition
- great new learning activities for writing and reading
- audio program, digitally remastered and expanded, with realistic sketches, songs, and readings
- comprehensive testing program
- materials graphically redesigned for a fresh look

Major funding for *French in Action* is provided by the Annenberg/CPB Project.

For more information about these and other language learning programs, and to receive examination copies, contact:

Yale University Press

P.O. Box 209040   New Haven, Connecticut 06520-9040
Attn: Special Projects   Phone: (203) 432-0912